9/2018

WITHDRAWN

LIBRARY
LEWIS-CLARK STATE COLLEGE
LEWISTON, IDAHO

D1571557

Lending Power

LENDING POWER

How Self-Help Credit Union Turned Small-Time Loans into Big-Time Change

Howard E. Covington Jr.

FOREWORD BY DARREN WALKER

Duke University Press · Durham and London · 2017

© 2017 Duke University Press
All rights reserved
Printed in the United States of America on acid-free paper ∞
Designed by Heather Hensley
Typeset in Minion Pro by Westchester Publishing Services

Library of Congress Cataloging-in-Publication Data

Names: Covington, Howard E., Jr., [date] author.
Title: Lending power [electronic resource] : how the Self-Help Credit Union
turned small-time loans into big-time change / Howard E. Covington Jr.
Description: Durham : Duke University Press, 2017. | Includes bibliographical
references and index. | Description based on print version record and CIP
data provided by publisher; resource not viewed.
Identifiers: LCCN 2017010997 (print)
LCCN 2017014022 (ebook)
ISBN 9780822372776 (ebook)
ISBN 9780822369691 (hardcover : alk. paper)
Subjects: LCSH: Self-Help Credit Union. | Credit unions—North Carolina. |
Loans, Personal—North Carolina. | Eakes, Martin.
Classification: LCC HG2038.N8 (ebook) | LCC HG2038.N8 C68 2017 (print) |
DDC 334/.2209756563—dc23
LC record available at https://lccn.loc.gov/2017010997

Cover art: Top photo: The Workers' Owned Sewing Company in Windsor, NC.
Photo courtesy of Self-Help. Bottom photo: Walltown development
in Durham, NC. Photo courtesy of the Duke Office of Durham
and Regional Affairs.

Contents

A gallery appears after page 96.

Foreword

•

Darren Walker
President, Ford Foundation

When I was working at the Abyssinian Development Corporation in Harlem, I learned a valuable lesson.

It was the early 1990s, during the height of the crack epidemic. Everywhere you looked, there were boarded-up buildings and broken crack vials under your feet. I had just moved from midtown Manhattan to 120th Street, leaving a career in investment banking for a calling in community development.

I met an incredible community of people up in Harlem. Unfortunately, I also saw how these people, despite their hard work, continued to be disenfranchised and discouraged by systems and structures. As a result, their experience of New York was very different from what mine had been living in Midtown. I saw—not for the first time, or the last—the lived experience of inequality.

Our mission at Abyssinian was to "rebuild Harlem, brick by brick, block by block." As you can imagine, there were plenty of people from outside the neighborhood who thought they understood the best way to rebuild

Harlem—people who proposed projects and initiatives that they believed would work best. It's an approach that, with the benefit of hindsight, feels misguided at best, and patronizing at worst.

At Abyssinian, we realized the people of Harlem understood their neighborhood's challenges far more intimately than we ever could, and because of their experience, they also had tremendous insight into possible solutions. And after listening to the community in Harlem, my colleagues and I discovered that one of the things they wanted—and desperately needed—was something pretty basic: a supermarket.

You see, in those days, when you walked into a bodega in Harlem, the only food you could find was expired or junk. These people wanted a place close by, in their neighborhood, where they could buy essentials for their families without having to travel far or lug their groceries home on the subway. A supermarket would not only provide nutrition for families but also for the whole community in the form of new jobs. And bringing one business back to the community would encourage other businesses to do the same, restarting a cycle of economic growth for the neighborhood that many thought had been extinguished. The potential was profound. So, together we worked to build Harlem's first full-service supermarket.

That supermarket was one of many contributors to what I'd like to think of as a New Harlem Renaissance (you can still see it up on 125th Street). And for me, it also proved the transformational power of listening to local communities and leveraging market tools.

Now, more than two decades later, I've tried to bring these same insights into my work as president of the Ford Foundation. As we strive to address inequality in all of its forms, these principles—listening to communities and building a more inclusive capitalism—inform the basis for what I like to call a New Gospel of Wealth.

At the Ford Foundation, we're committed to putting these ideas into practice as we invest in new ideas, hardworking individuals, and institutions that serve as outposts on the front lines of social change. One such institution is an organization called Self-Help.

Long before I was working in Harlem, or at the Ford Foundation, Martin Eakes was in North Carolina, running Self-Help out of his Volkswagen Beetle. And long before we really talked about "impact investing," Self-Help was finding ways to direct capital toward communities.

Martin and his colleagues understood that access to capital was necessary for communities to thrive, and for too many that access had been largely denied, or was only given by people looking to exploit others, rather than extend opportunity. That's why they've been supporting entrepreneurs and homeowners, developing communities, and defending people from predatory lenders. That's why they've expanded their reach beyond North Carolina to include Chicago, California, and Florida. And through it all, their work has been successful because Self-Help directly engages with the individuals and communities they hope to serve, and enables hardworking people to help themselves and better their own communities.

Today, we see what looks like progress in many of our communities and cities across the country. New development. New residents. New businesses. New investment. But with this progress comes new challenges. Many are being left behind. Many feel like they are getting a raw deal. Too often what looks like progress is just the relocation of prosperity from one place to another. And, in many cases, inequality continues to persist.

Where Self-Help has never faltered is in its firm commitment to the individual—and his or her dignity—as the essential building block of the community and of shared prosperity. They understand that more often than not these individuals—when given an opportunity and the tools to succeed—will do their best to better themselves and those around them. The book you hold in your hand is an incredible testament to this fact.

I often find myself reflecting on the words of Dr. Martin Luther King Jr., who, shortly before his death, wrote: "Philanthropy is commendable, but it must not cause the philanthropist to overlook the circumstances of economic injustice which make philanthropy necessary." Many forget that toward the end of his life Dr. King focused his efforts on economic justice. Knowing this, it seems fitting that another Martin has spent his career, as he has said, "taking the civil rights movement into the economic arena."

Self-Help has found a way to combat the "circumstances of economic injustice" while empowering driven individuals and their ideas. Self-Help is not charity, or even philanthropy in any traditional sense. Rather than being a form of generosity, Self-Help uses inclusive lending as a weapon for justice.

Indeed, at a time when financial institutions have increasingly come under fire, and our very capitalist system has been called into question, Self-Help reminds us that financial services can be a force for good. In this way, the story of Self-Help provides a dynamic model for using economic tools in social justice work and a clarion call for all who aspire to change their communities.

I've had the privilege of working alongside Martin Eakes for many years now. As a member of the Ford Foundation's board of trustees, he has provided me with wisdom and counsel, and lived up to the "genius" grant he was given twenty years ago. I've always been impressed by his intelligence and empathy, and he and his colleagues at Self-Help give more credit than they take and deserve more credit for how much good they have done.

The progress of our communities depends on individual leaders like Martin, institutions like Self-Help, innovative ideas, and countless actions taken, big and small. It's a process of listening, of building, of accretion, and of shared steps forward. I learned that back in Harlem, fighting for that first grocery store; I've learned it at the Ford Foundation, and few documents preach it better than the book you're about to read.

I hope that as you read you draw as much inspiration from Martin and Self-Help as I do.

CHAPTER ONE

Self-Help Who?

A New York surrogate judge wrote in 1866: "No man's life, liberty, or property are safe while the Legislature is in session."[1] That's especially true when the body is charging toward adjournment, as was the case with the North Carolina General Assembly in late spring of 1997. An innocuous bill, embarrassingly devoid of descriptive language, breezed through the senate and landed a comfortable berth in a house committee. There, it was stripped of everything but its title, and language was inserted to allow Blue Cross and Blue Shield of North Carolina to shed its nonprofit status and convert to a for-profit corporation. Similar conversions of Blue Cross and Blue Shield franchises in other states were complete or under way, and the personal fortunes banked by the company's executives were breathtaking.

About the only person paying attention to these legislative shenanigans was a young, newly commissioned public advocate named Adam Searing. He had been on the staff of the nonprofit N.C. Justice Center for about three months when the bill, introduced by two of the state's most powerful legislators, one a Republican and the other a Democrat, caught his eye.

The measure was well down the track to passage in the waning days of the session when Searing rose at a committee meeting, took exception to the bill, and declared the emperor had no clothes. The fix was in, he said, and the bill, which was described as a minor change for N.C. Blue, as the insurer was called, was, in fact, an early Christmas present for company executives. Searing still remembers the bill's senate sponsor, Democrat Tony Rand, growing red in the face and fulminating publicly over the audacity of this "pup." A man still in possession of his youthful appearance, Searing was often mistaken as a legislative intern in 1997. The rant by Rand, a party leader of considerable weight, left him convinced that he was "going to get run over like a bug."[2]

Sitting in on that meeting was Martin Daniel Eakes, the co-founder and chief executive officer of a nonprofit, the Center for Community Self-Help, or Self-Help for short. He had been roused from his office in nearby Durham by Mary Mountcastle, a senior staff member who had read a warning about the bill posted by Searing to his growing list of health care allies. Mountcastle told Eakes that he had to do something. That's when he hopped into his dusty old car (one breakdown away from the salvage yard) and drove the twenty-five miles to the Legislative Building in Raleigh.

At the time, Self-Help was a financial institution, albeit an unusual one. It was a credit union joined at the hip to a charity that was operating as a community development financial institution. It served North Carolina's under- and unbanked population—primarily people of modest means, especially African Americans, single mothers, and rural folks who needed a loan for their first homes or money to start small businesses. Underlying its work was the belief that the civil rights movement was not over until everyone enjoyed the economic benefits of society.

So why was Self-Help getting involved in a legislative fight with a provider of health insurance? In 1997, Self-Help was, and still is today, a nonprofit corporation, just like Blue Cross and Blue Shield of North Carolina. Eakes was outraged that executives at N.C. Blue would use legislative sleight of hand to cash in on six decades of public benefits as a nonprofit, leaving nothing in exchange for the tax-paying public. Such a move, he believed, threatened the integrity and public standing of every nonprofit in the state.

So the battle was on. All of Eakes's years of building coalitions and networking with like-minded people was brought to bear in what would become a tipping point for Self-Help as an institution, and for Eakes personally. Life would not be the same after he launched into this very public fight and Self-Help enlarged its reputation as a public advocacy and civil rights organization that would later include national honors and recognition.

Eakes collared Searing after the meeting, gave him an injection of energy from his own boundless reservoir, and promised unlimited support. Soon, Searing and Eakes were working with a statewide coalition of volunteers encompassing a broad array of public interest and health care groups. Their allies included county health officers, senior citizens' groups, nonprofits of all sizes and descriptions (including board members of influential community foundations), religious and civil rights groups, a few political heavyweights, hospital administrators, and, cheering from the background, corporate clients dissatisfied with N.C. Blue's rates.

Eakes lined up pro bono legal services from one of the top law firms in the state, and, riding a bandwagon of righteousness, this coalition finally stopped N.C. Blue's plans for conversion. Out of it came a compromise that required N.C. Blue—should it ever convert to a for-profit corporation—to put all the assets accumulated since its inception as a nonprofit in the 1930s into an independent foundation. When that happened, if it happened, more than $2 billion could become available to improve the health care of North Carolinians.

It was not a single-handed victory by any means, but it is doubtful if the public campaign and resulting tough, line-by-line negotiations that produced the conversion bill would have been as successful without Self-Help's resources and Eakes's organizing ability and determination not to leave the table until every item had been addressed. Of the forty critical items raised in the negotiations, N.C. Blue's opponents got what they wanted on thirty-nine of them, and Eakes fought to the end for number forty.

N.C. Blue's reputation was dinged and tarnished; Eakes and Self-Help emerged as dragon slayers.

The victory was a long way from the early 1980s, when the Self-Help Credit Union got its first deposit of $77 from a legendary bake sale—most of it from the sale of a $65 pound cake—and began soliciting members among a community of believers eager to organize worker-owned businesses. Eakes promoted this collective approach as the way to save lost jobs as owners closed textile plants and moved production out of the state of North Carolina. If workers controlled their own destiny, then they and their communities would benefit from such empowerment.

Its real muscle and sinew began to develop in the late 1980s after Self-Help began issuing home loans to people on the fringes of the economy whom bankers considered beyond the boundaries of sound risk. Eakes turned such discrimination on its head and later would say that he simply applied old-fashioned banking principles where a borrower's character amounted for as much as a credit profile. His faith was not misplaced. In its first ten years of home lending, the credit union did not lose a single dollar on the mortgages it extended to 1,100 borrowers.

Eakes is a man of missionary zeal and unbending convictions. He is a fierce competitor without a partisan label who believes that democracy's very survival depends on a level playing field for all in the economic marketplace. He is lean and wiry, stands about five-nine, and has a head of gray hair that was once fiery red, a color that he jokes matched the temper of his youth. He has an infectious smile and punctuates his conversation with a mischievous chuckle. Newspaper feature writers have made much of the low-budget cars he drives, and his office is equipped with furniture you might find at a Habitat for Humanity ReStore outlet.

Eakes's range is impressive. His creativity and innovation earned him recognition in 1996 as a MacArthur Fellow, the so-called Genius Grant. In 2011, the Ford Foundation selected him as one of a dozen international "visionaries" for solving social problems and improving the lives of people. He later was elected to the foundation's board of trustees, a rarefied atmosphere, indeed, even for such an innovative social entrepreneur. As he found his footing at Ford, the foundation was shifting its focus to "disrupting the drivers of inequality," a goal Eakes could find easy to live with.

Over the years, Self-Help has attracted a constant stream of bright, young, and talented folk to its work. Most are graduates with impressive academic credentials from elite institutions who want to pursue a social justice agenda and add economic power to the legislative advances of the civil rights era. Some of these disciples stay on to build careers despite Self-Help's notoriously low pay. Others leave for positions in public service around the nation or move to the staffs of foundations and other socially responsible organizations. In time, state and federal agencies writing the rules and regulations under which financial institutions operate in the twenty-first century became populated with former Self-Helpers. One alum moved to the Deep South and created a version of Self-Help serving people in distressed areas of Mississippi, Louisiana, Arkansas, and Tennessee.

A year after the N.C. Blue fight in North Carolina, an issue that was closer to Self-Help's operational core—predatory lending practices in the home mortgage business—came up for review, and the Self-Help crowd was at the table as a full-fledged partner in writing new law. Once again Eakes threw himself into a legislative fight, inspired by the experience of a borrower trapped in a mortgage that stripped the equity from his house while loading him down with thousands of dollars in fees and charges due to the mortgage company. North Carolina's predatory lending bill passed the General Assembly virtually unopposed and became a model for advocates in nearly three dozen other states.

In 2002, the Coalition for Responsible Lending that produced the North Carolina law morphed into the Center for Responsible Lending (CRL) and became Self-Help's national advocacy and policy arm. It moved a staff into a renovated office building that Self-Help bought in downtown Washington, D.C., sending a signal to opponents that it had come to stay. The CRL became the thorn in the side of financial institutions shading the rules and inventing deceptive and, in some cases, downright fraudulent lending practices.

All of a sudden, Eakes and Self-Help were the targets of a national campaign led by mortgage bankers, payday lenders, and the political Right, who were bound to discredit the organization and, according to Eakes, destroy him personally. He says that he was told that $10 million was devoted to the effort to smear him and Self-Help. When Eakes was the victim of a mugging in 2008, some of his friends were convinced that his political opponents were responsible. Eakes and Self-Help were an existential threat to America, according to the writer of a 2013 book titled *Infiltrated,* which concluded that Eakes and company were personally responsible for the crash of the home mortgage industry and the onset of the Great Recession in 2008.[3]

Eakes takes such opposition as a mark of success and with a certain amount of pride. He was not worried about being the sworn enemy of an army of lenders with loan-shark rates using unscrupulous or fraudulent practices to sell home mortgages designed to fail. Most of the bluster over the CRL collapsed after 2008, in the wake of the most devastating economic crisis since the 1930s, when the CRL's early warnings about the approaching disaster in the housing market proved to be correct.

Self-Help's research showing the limits of unsustainable mortgage lending preceded the Great Recession by nearly two years. Eakes offered congressional testimony multiple times about the trouble ahead, but few were listening. As the nation began to dig itself out of the rubble, it was often the CRL research that reporters, columnists, policy makers, and legislators turned to as a balance to the excuses offered by the financial industry. Ultimately, former

Self-Help staff members helped write the home mortgage sections of the Dodd-Frank Wall Street Reform bill and the particulars establishing the Consumer Financial Protection Bureau. Key provisions in the 1999 North Carolina predatory lending bill were imported virtually intact.

Self-Help's balance sheet did not pass undisturbed through the financial storms. Yet, the credit union's loan portfolio of thirty-year, fixed-rate mortgages to low- and moderate-income borrowers, nearly half of them single mothers and people of color, proved to be as sound as institutions that made loans to borrowers with established credit. The success proved to be a re-affirmation of Self-Help's bedrock premise that a home buyer of marginal means was more likely to stand by and do what was necessary to protect an investment in a home, while wealthy borrowers bailed on their mortgages and walked away from their obligations.

When other institutions were contracting during the crisis, Self-Help regrouped and expanded with a new federally chartered credit union that salvaged ailing credit unions in California and later a troubled community bank in Chicago run by and for Latinos on the city's south side. A credit union founded by nuns and serving farm workers in central Florida became part of Self-Help Federal Credit Union in 2016.

Behind it all was Eakes and a belief that the civil rights movement is not over until everyone in society enjoys economic justice as well as the right to eat, travel, and live where they choose, without discrimination, or vote in elections. As long as segments of the society suffer from limited access to the economic benefits of the country, work remains to be done.

Eakes has been driven by that notion since he was arguing religious, ethical, and philosophical points of view with his mates more than four decades ago at Davidson College in North Carolina. It consumes him as much now as it did then: "We felt like the way you prevent violence and poverty is to make a more sensible economic system rather than trying to fix it after it has already broken somebody, broken a person."[4] Somehow, he juggled the competing disciplines of physics and philosophy as a double major, which served him well later. He was able not only to identify a vexing public issue, with all its broad applications, but also to fashion a system to deal with it. It was something he says he learned from his mother, who told him that it was not sufficient to recognize a problem; one also had an obligation to solve it.

Self-Help's story is not simply about a civil rights advocacy organization. It is the story of a creative blending of conservative and liberal fundamentals in business. Eakes is a fierce advocate for the financially marginalized of society, but Self-Help borrowers must repay their loans on time just like customers at any other financial institution. There are no giveaways. At the same time, Self-Help uses the same financial tools perfected by the financial houses on Wall Street to benefit poor people. Over the course of thirty years, a state-chartered credit union begun with embarrassingly modest resources became a financial laboratory that put its stamp on mortgage lending across the nation.

Little ideas expanded into big ones. To help cover expenses in the early days, Self-Help rented unused space in a former toy store Eakes and a few friends owned in downtown Durham to other low-budget nonprofits. Today, Self-Help has reclaimed vacant downtown buildings in a half dozen North Carolina cities and turned them into affordable office space for nonprofit organizations. It was a service that benefited Self-Help's image and coalition-building. It also was smart business. The CRL building in Washington, D.C., was purchased for $23 million in 2003 and was worth more than $30 million a decade later.

Yet, as Eakes himself readily admits, even with its astonishing growth and more than $1.842 billion in assets in 2015, Self-Help is pretty small considering the challenges that remain. All of Self-Help's financial power is equal to what goes on daily in a handful of busy branches of a financial colossus like Bank of America.

No venture quite equaled Self-Help's partnership in 1998 with the Ford Foundation and the Federal National Mortgage Association (Fannie Mae) to create a home-lending program that over sixteen years grew to $4.7 billion and helped 52,000 low- to moderate-income homeowners buy a place of their own. Forty-one percent of the loans went to female-headed households, and 40 percent went to minority households. The borrowers' median income was $30,792, but the fund's cumulative loss rate was less than 3 percent, despite the collapse of the housing market in 2007 and resulting Great Recession.[5]

Self-Help's critics later misinterpreted this kind of risk-taking when everyone was looking for a scapegoat for the financial crisis. The Right jumped on the CRL's advocacy for liberalizing lending standards as the principal reason that America's bankers drove their own train off the cliff. The claim totally disregarded precrash testimony from Eakes and others who warned that it was the type of loan—poorly vetted mortgages with balloon payments and teaser rates that disappeared after two years—and not the type of borrower—low- and moderate-income folk—that was at the heart of the problem.[6]

Indeed, the CRL used the bankers' own data on home lending to produce a report in 2006 warning that as many as 2.2 million home foreclosures lay ahead due to unfettered and dishonest mortgage brokers selling explosive home loans to feverish Wall Street institutions begging for more and more. That number proved to be low. In the end, more than 4.2 million borrowers became victims of unscrupulous practices and found themselves struggling to pay loans on houses worth half or less of their earlier value.[7]

Self-Help is an extraordinary organization, according to researchers who wrote *Forces for Good*.[8] They identified exceptional nonprofits and examined them for the secrets of their success in much the same way that writer Jim Collins did in his book on corporate America, *Good to Great*. The resulting ranking placed Self-Help in a select group of twelve nonprofits in the nation that were singled out for examples of innovation, allegiance to mission, and operational practices.

Yet, even a "visionary" like Eakes could not have imagined what the Center for the Community Self-Help might grow into when, fresh out of Yale Law School, he and a small knot of college friends chartered it in 1980. At the time, he thought he was going to help create a worker democracy where employees would own and operate some of the textile mills and furniture plants that were closing in North Carolina. He jokes that he got his first foundation grant, a blushingly modest one, because his benefactors were afraid he might starve to death.

CHAPTER TWO

A First Step

In the early 1980s, Durham, North Carolina, was just what every mid-sized American city hoped it would not become. The downtown was a retail desert with empty storefronts along Main Street. Long known as a blue-collar, working-class town, the city had seen jobs in the cigarette plants and textile mills disappear from one year to the next. Acres of warehouses, once the pride of the American Tobacco Company, were on their way to becoming huge, empty brick lumps on the landscape. The construction of high-speed, multilane highways connecting downtown to the highly touted Research Triangle Park on Durham's southern doorstep had taken the heart out of the city's storied African American community and replaced it with political turbulence.

One thing Durham had in abundance for a city of 150,000 was its own brand of coalition politics, encouraged by a left-leaning electorate attached by either tuition or payroll to Duke University, whose academic program and medical center made it the biggest game in town. The school attracted well-bred sons and daughters from middle- to upper-class homes, mostly from out of state. A smattering of these individuals stayed behind to improve the woeful condition of North Carolina's impoverished and underemployed. Organizationally inclined, these activists formed groups in the 1970s to help textile workers weakened by an occupational disease called brown lung, battle utility companies over rate increases, save the environment, promote women's rights, and even start a feisty and free-wheeling weekly newspaper called the *N.C. Independent*. It carried ads for funky restaurants and the lesbian alliance, and featured caricatures of U.S. Senator Jesse Helms, the state's contribution to the rising right-wing Republican movement.

Located on the eastern edge of downtown, in a two-story brick building at 413 E. Chapel Hill Street, was the Center for Community Self-Help. The building had once been a toy store, the first stop for kids eager to show parents what they wanted under the tree at Christmas. The Depression-era storefront was outfitted with used furniture and was considered by its new occupants to be a step up from their earlier address two blocks west in a rented room over an aging diner called The Palms.

In its early days, Self-Help was a collection of committed, idealistic, and determined young activists dedicated to the mission of extending the civil rights movement by creating economic equity. Before these crusaders were even out of high school, the civil rights acts of the 1960s had declared de jure racial discrimination a thing of the past, but discrimination still was a fact of life in the 1980s for women and people of color when they looked at their paychecks and modest savings accounts—if they had one.

The solution, according to the founding tenets of Self-Help, was in participatory democracy. If workers owned the businesses for which they toiled, they would be able to acquire a share of the American dream. Self-Help planned to make this dream come true in the hamlets and towns of North Carolina, where the state's vast textile industry was in distress and thousands upon thousands of workers' jobs along with it. It was a tightly focused mission fashioned into an ideological flag that Martin Eakes planned to raise across the state.

Self-Help was a few years in gestation. It was shaped by Eakes's undergraduate studies at Davidson College, where he graduated magna cum laude in 1976 with a double major in physics and philosophy; summer work studying public education and child abuse in Georgia and South Carolina; a postgraduate stint in Botswana; and joint degrees from Princeton University's Woodrow Wilson School of International and Public Affairs and the Yale University School of Law. He and a tight group of friends from

Davidson, including his girlfriend, Bonnie Wright, had settled on helping poor people gain more responsibility and control over their lives. Worker ownership was the movement to which they would devote their talents, their education, and, for Eakes and Wright, their lives. Eakes had just finished law school, and passage of the North Carolina bar examination loomed ahead, when he and Wright co-founded Self-Help on February 4, 1980.

Besides Eakes, the first board of directors included fellow Davidson graduates Roger H. Brown Jr., a Georgian, and David Wiley from Pennsylvania, who had been at the Yale School of Public and Private Management. J. Crawford Crenshaw III from Louisiana had been through Princeton's Woodrow Wilson School of International and Public Affairs, while Andrew Lamas, also from Georgia, was at the University of Pennsylvania Law School by way of the London School of Economics. At Davidson, they had been most intense in their debates about the existence of God and moral action. According to Eakes, "As a group, we were going to go out and change the world, but we were very naive about how to do it."[1]

Any future historical marker for Self-Help, if ever one is erected, really belongs fifty miles west of Durham alongside a suburban road south of Greensboro, North Carolina, near a farmhouse where Martin Eakes first hung out his shingle at the home of his parents, Marion and Mary Eakes. His father was a self-made businessman, a gruff fellow who favored a chew of tobacco and worked with his hands all his life. His business had employed welders and metal fabricators who fashioned ductwork for new industrial and commercial buildings. Martin's mother was the family counselor and had her hands full raising four active and rambunctious boys. Martin was the third from the oldest. When he was born in 1954, he needed an immediate blood transfusion just to survive. In the summer of 1980, he would race his mother to a ringing phone so he could answer it saying, "Center for Community Self-Help," rather than have her give away his modest circumstances.

Eakes was living at home because he was broke. Just as the incorporation papers for Self-Help were being filed, Eakes had polished off a grant request to the Z. Smith Reynolds Foundation in Winston-Salem, North Carolina, where another Davidson graduate, Joe Kilpatrick, was on the staff. At the time, the Reynolds Foundation's resources were second only to those of the Duke Endowment, which was focused primarily on health care. Eakes asked for nearly $50,000 to underwrite his worker-owned business experiment and declared that the final product would be a "successfully operating employee-owned textile mill."

Eakes was not bashful in a declared ambition to reconcile socialism and capitalism. The initiative at hand was different, he confessed, but the benefits to society were worth the effort and expense. He argued that worker-owners could earn higher pay and North Carolina could save an important industry, and, at the same time, enjoy better labor relations. "Self-Help is neither anti-business nor anti-union. In fact, the attraction of employee-ownership is the attraction of combining the best aspects of the so-called 'conservative' and 'liberal' perspectives."[2]

In addition, the foundation could take satisfaction in what Eakes learned along the way to achieving this miracle. He planned to publish a how-to guide for others who might want to follow in his footsteps. The foundation's staff wished him luck but said no. At the time, Self-Help was so new it did not have IRS tax-exempt certification.

Fortunately, Eakes had $2,000 given to him by a friend who had won as an award and had passed it on as seed money. Board chair Crawford Crenshaw was sending Eakes $100 a month. The money helped pay for gas for a white Audi, salvaged from a junkyard, that Eakes drove east to New Bern, North Carolina, in the summer of 1980 after someone saw a simple, photocopied promotional flyer about Self-Help created by Wright. He was asked to come meet with employees of Texfi Industries Inc.

A month earlier, Texfi had closed its New Bern plant without notice at the end of work one Friday. Four hundred people were suddenly and unexpectedly without jobs. This was becoming a familiar story. In just the first half of 1980, thirty-two companies announced closings in North Carolina, displacing 2,773 workers. What Eakes found when he reached a high school gymnasium in New Bern, on a hot, muggy night in August, was a hall packed with hundreds of unemployed workers, their friends, and their family members.

It was trial by fire. Twenty-six-year-old Martin Eakes, still weary from studying for his bar examination, was met at the front door by a seasoned community organizer named Frank Adams. Adams was twenty years his senior, a veteran of the Highlander Folk School in Tennessee, and an old-school community organizer. Eakes followed Adams into the hall where Eakes was introduced to an angry and anxious crowd as the man who was going to save their jobs. Adams maneuvered the largely undisciplined crowd into smaller discussion groups, and out of it came a petition to Texfi management that Eakes promised to deliver to the company's Greensboro head-quarters the very next day.[3]

As he had promised, Eakes showed up at the company's offices and was told that the chief executive officer was not available. He replied that he could go for weeks without eating and would sit and wait for as long as it took to see the top man. Finally, at the end of the workday, Eakes was invited in, and he presented the petition. While there, he learned that the plant had closed because the polyester yarn used in double-knit fabric was not fash-ionable any longer. For the company, the math and reasoning was simple: no sales, no work. Before shutting down the New Bern facility, the company had closed two other plants in Randolph County, just thirty miles south of Eakes's home in Greensboro.

The news Eakes brought back to New Bern did not ease the strain, and the Texfi workers wanted to pursue the notion of finding the $10 to $12 mil-lion they would need to buy the plant and run it themselves. Meanwhile, Wright returned from social work in Ecuador, and in October she and Eakes moved to Durham. They began putting together a meeting for folks interested in worker-owned businesses to be held in Winton, a county-seat town near the Virginia border in northeastern North Carolina.

One of the heroes of the Winton meeting was Tim Bazemore, a bold Afri-can American entrepreneur who had resurrected a failed cut-and-sew opera-tion in nearby Windsor called Workers' Owned Sewing Company. Bazemore was in his late fifties, a World War II veteran, and a pulpwood logger and farmer with extraordinary people skills. He had been something of a trouble-maker for the local political establishment. Whites in the community had tried to run him off more than once since the 1960s, when he pushed for integration of the county's public schools. Frank Adams, then on the payroll of Legal Services of North Carolina, the state's legal aid apparatus, had helped lead Bazemore into the worker-owned camp while Bazemore was scratching around trying to find a way to reopen a bankrupt sewing company.

The Winton meeting attracted a mixture of people. Some of the Texfi work-ers were there, still hopeful of regaining their jobs. A handful of others will-ing to consider worker-owned options showed up, including a female home builder from Carrboro and a young man working with a scrap metal busi-ness in Greensboro. Eakes and Wright had raised enough money to rent the hall of the African American Elks, import some speakers on worker-owned operations, and pay for materials. Two thousand dollars came thanks to

Robert Schall, who was a field man for the state's division of community assistance. A little more financial assistance came from Wes Hare of Chapel Hill. He and his wife were of Adams's vintage and veterans of what Hare called Lyndon Johnson's "skirmish on poverty." They operated a grassroots outfit called Twin Streams Educational Center and had invested $15,000 into Bazemore's worker-owned business. Hare's stake in the business came from an insurance settlement he received after his hand-built log building burned to the ground.[4]

The meeting provided some traction, a network of allies, and a few clients for Eakes, none of whom could pay much for his services. Now a member of the bar, he helped Bazemore negotiate a settlement with the IRS, which did not think much of the sewing plant employees working for no wages until they could share, as worker-owners, in the profits at year's end. Plugged into the legal aid network, Eakes began getting calls from displaced workers needing help in other situations. One such worker was from a group in Lincolnton, North Carolina, which was as far west of Durham as Bazemore's modest shop was to the east. One of Eakes's contacts in the legal aid program thought Eakes could help.

The owners of the Lincoln Spinning Company had run their plant until it was out of money, using the cash due on the last payroll to cover an amount owed to the IRS in withholding taxes, for which they were personally liable. Eakes began meeting with a group of workers interested in reopening the plant. It was New Bern all over again. Workers were angry; they threatened the life of a mill executive, and even blockaded the plant driveway so owners could not remove finished yarn. Lincolnton was a town with a history of impatient men with guns. Some of those who had shot and killed marchers at a Communist Workers' Party rally in 1979 in Greensboro were from Lincoln County. So, when Eakes rented a bus to carry workers to a hearing in bankruptcy court, hoping workers might recover some of their $80,000 in lost pay, he checked those who turned out for the trip for weapons as they climbed aboard.

Eakes worked with a committee of Lincolnton workers to adopt bylaws for worker ownership of the plant, which appeared as hopeless as the situation in New Bern. He also created a business plan and fell back on some accounting methods he had learned one summer when he was a college student and working for Ed Zane, a top-flight Burlington Industries executive and a friend of his father. Years later, he still had the sixteen-hundred-page accountant's handbook that Zane had given him. Over a period of weeks,

Eakes shuttled back and forth from Durham to Lincolnton, a four-hundred-mile round trip. At one meeting, he noticed that Doris, a stalwart in the multiracial group, was absent. He learned she had just lost her daughter, who died because Doris did not have money to pay for medical care.[5]

The news of Doris and her child struck deep. What had begun as an exercise in alternative management, something liberals and activists were talking about in business schools and writers at magazines like *Mother Jones* were extolling as the future of the working class, was very suddenly, and tragically, a situation with real consequences. Eakes now was accumulating names and faces of desperate people to go along with scholarly papers and lofty ambitions that had filled his life to that point.

He would remember Doris and her family for years to come, just as he had the determination of Percy White, another client from those days. White was one of those put out of work in New Bern, before he turned his interest toward opening a commercial bakery. He was an African American who stood well over six feet tall and wore a full beard that was streaked with gray. He had been a baker in the navy and was holding yard sales, borrowing from friends, and going door-to-door selling carpet cleaner to raise money to pay for an oven. After one of the Texfi meetings, White pulled Eakes aside and asked for help to get his business up and running.

Through the cold winter months, Eakes traveled to and from New Bern to meet with White and two other Texfi workers involved with the bakery. When in New Bern, he stayed in White's home, which he found to be terribly hot, but he figured that African Americans just liked to keep their homes warm. Finally, someone who knew White's story told Eakes the family scrimped on heat all week long just to have enough fuel oil to make their guest comfortable when he was in town. A bit embarrassed, Eakes broached the subject with his host. "Oh," White told him, "we thought white folks liked the heat turned up high."

White's bakery opened in December 1981. The last dose of cash White needed to pay for an oven came from Eakes and a couple of others at Self-Help who literally emptied their pockets on White's behalf. The New Bern Bakery was not a textile mill with hundreds of jobs saved, but Self-Help had nursed its first worker-owned business into life and made its first loan.

Eakes had little money when he and Wright moved to Durham. He jokes that it was to save his parents the embarrassment of having their son labeled a communist, or worse. Armed with his law license, he opened an office on the eleventh floor of Durham's tallest building, where Central Carolina

Bank had had its headquarters since the mid-1930s. It was tough going. Eakes was a self-described "academic dilettante" who had, after three years of studying economics and law, said he would have gone on to conquer medicine if he had had the time. However, he knew nothing about earning a living.

For Eakes, law school had given him an academic education in social change. He learned how government, the courts, and the law worked. The courses he enjoyed the most were the most abstract and those on nonprofit organizations. This line of study was of little use to him now. While he could write a treatise on the philosophy of the Fourteenth Amendment to the Constitution, he did not know how to close a home loan.

With the help of another Central Carolina Bank tenant, an older, experienced lawyer, Eakes learned the location of the register of deeds office and how to search real estate titles. He handled a couple of minor criminal matters but quickly decided that was not why he got his law degree. Mostly, he stayed busy preparing the legal underpinnings for developing a worker-owned democracy. From his hand came the papers to organize the Corporation for Cooperative Businesses, a legal entity established to help applicants qualify for Small Business Administration (SBA) loans. He had first called it the Corporation for Democratic Businesses, but SBA bureaucrats thought it sounded too political in the early years of Ronald Reagan's presidency.

Eakes lived lean. He collected a few dollars in legal fees as well as a handful of $25 memberships in Self-Help purchased by his friends. (He asked those he solicited to provide their own postage to avoid postal charges on the business reply mail.) Being short of money was not anything new. He had finished his studies at Davidson College a semester early and had gone to work in Columbia, South Carolina, ahead of his anticipated enrollment in law school in the fall. He survived on subsistence wages—roughly fifty cents a day—while he conducted a study on child abuse for the American Friends Service Committee. Mostly, he fed on shelled peanuts he bought in bulk. He slept on the top of the desk in his office and bathed twice a week in the Saluda River.

For Eakes, food was little more than fuel. Until he was in his late fifties, he maintained the engine of his spare frame on a vegetarian diet supplemented by copious amounts of chocolate and other sweets. One friend called him a "Sugar Pops vegetarian." He dressed simply, usually in brightly colored shirts, khakis, and flip-flops, and he did own a sport coat and a tie. His full head of red hair seldom came in contact with a barber's clippers. His finances were such that he was plagued with repeated late-payment notices at a rental house in a modest postwar Durham neighborhood because he failed to pay bills on time.

Eakes learned some lessons in the year after he was first called to meet with the Texfi crowd in New Bern. Experience showed that it was too late to introduce the worker-owned model after the plant gates had closed. Those workers who had marketable skills and/or management potential quickly left the area for greener pastures after losing their jobs. Moreover, contacts with suppliers and customers evaporated overnight, reducing the value of the business. Both conditions increased the already-difficult task of helping workers get their minds around the unfamiliar concept of managing a workplace. Without abandoning his earlier mission, Eakes took the basic principles he included in the grant request to the Z. Smith Reynolds Foundation and reconfigured it for presentation to a Reynolds cousin organization in Winston-Salem, the Mary Reynolds Babcock Foundation.

Babcock was smaller but had a wider range of interests. It also had a record of approving worker-owned grants. In 1979, the foundation had put up nearly $50,000 to help launch the Industrial Cooperative Association, a worker-owned resource group in Somerville, Massachusetts. It also had made two small grants for "technical assistance" to Tim Bazemore's worker-owned sewing business in Windsor, which Bazemore was subsidizing with the sale of his corn crop.[6]

When Eakes was planning the meeting in Winton, he had asked Babcock for $5,300, but his proposal had been declined. Assistant Director George Penick, the point man for worker-owned projects, urged him to stay in touch, however. Now, Eakes returned with a larger proposition. He asked for $27,120 to underwrite the creation of a strategy to save jobs under the worker-owned model by getting involved with management before a plant closed.

This time, the Babcock board said yes. Eakes would later joke that it was a pity grant: "They thought I was going to starve to death." William L. Bondurant, the foundation's director at the time, said it was far more than that. "The best grants ever made are made to persons—not causes—but to people working within nonprofits. We were looking for people who were enormously persuasive, hard-working, [and] diligent who would go out and make a difference." Bondurant saw Eakes as someone possessed with the same kind of entrepreneurial spirit for a nonprofit as was found in any successful captain in the capitalist system. "Martin walked in the door and showed himself capable of doing that."[7]

The money came through in March 1982, allowing Eakes to hire Self-Help's first employee, Thad Day Moore, who for the past year had been an associate scrambling about in the weeds of worker-owned businesses. Moore had graduated from Wake Forest University and spent a few months at the Baptists' Southern Theological Seminary before deciding that ministry was not his calling. In the late 1970s, he worked for the Brown Lung Association and assisted textile workers suffering from byssinosis (brown lung) in filing workers' compensation claims. He met Eakes and Wright at the Winton conference. At the time, Moore was involved with a Greensboro scrap metal business working toward a worker-owned conversion. The three stayed in touch throughout the following year. Moore was one of those who had chipped in to help Percy White buy the oven for his bakery.

A soft-spoken man with a calming, pleasant disposition, Moore has a compact build and stands about five-eight, just about the same height as Eakes. He liked the appeal of workplace democracy and saw it as a satisfying combination of justice in the workplace and the free enterprise system. It was a way of harnessing the power of capitalism to a social good. "I think a powerful undercurrent [of Self-Help] is the notion that the skills that we are given are not given us to self-empower, to be rich or in power, but to be in service to others," Moore said some thirty years later, sitting at a conference table at Self-Help, where he was still employed. That was the fire he saw in Eakes. "He won't articulate it, but I think it is one of the most important things that drives him and what he is about."[8]

With Wright away at graduate school, Moore moved into Eakes's house in Durham and took up residence on his couch. During the day, he hunkered down in the Duke University law library gathering legal citations and details about the creation and operation of cooperatives in North Carolina. His undergraduate studies had been in anthropology, but he immersed himself in the literature on worker-owned enterprises and was becoming proficient in the legal and tax issues of business conversions. One thing he discovered was that North Carolina permitted cooperatives for agriculture but not for industry.

At the time, Self-Help had a post office box, an office above a downtown diner, and a lot of ambition. Eakes and Moore were in a steep learning curve. Community organizers such as Frank Adams and Wes Hare were good at gathering people together and converting energy into action, but that was only so much talk if there wasn't someone who knew the ins and outs of forming corporations, preparing a financial plan, creating legal documents, and, most importantly, finding money to make it happen. "The core activity at that point was responding, looking for opportunities, [and] plant closings," said Moore.

Over the coming months, Eakes and Moore talked to bankers, business brokers, economic developers, community leaders, and others. There was modest interest in worker-owned businesses, particularly among some legal and financial advisors dealing with family-owned enterprises where the principals were ready to retire. Often, these were companies with long-standing relations with their workers; selling the business to them seemed more humane than dumping them into the hands of a corporate conglomerate. What Self-Help needed was a bona fide demonstration project. That's when they settled on working with the employees of Service Printing Company in Durham.

Service Printing was a fixture in the business district of Durham's Hayti district, a once-thriving African American community whose shops and businesses had been devastated in the 1960s by urban renewal and highway construction. Remnants remained, and that included Service Printing. The company had begun as part of the *Carolina Times*, an African American newspaper with a fifty-year history. It had printed the flyers and posters during the civil rights demonstrations in the 1960s and the weekly bulletins of White Rock Baptist Church, a spiritual bastion in the community. When Dr. Martin Luther King Jr. came to Durham in the early 1960s, he spoke from the White Rock pulpit.

Now, Service Printing's owners were ready to retire. They talked to Eakes and Moore about this worker-ownership idea. It looked like a good fit. Nathaniel White said he and the current owners had bought the business in 1939. "I guess we were worker-owners then, but we didn't call it that," he said later.[9] For Eakes and Moore, the business offered two main advantages: it was close at hand, not two hundred miles away, and the work there would connect Self-Help with the most politically engaged and influential African American community in the state. Moore turned to what he was learning in the accounting courses he was taking at night and began a financial analysis of the business.

Meanwhile, Eakes and Wright were working with Hare and his wife to organize another worker-ownership conference with the support of a grant from the Babcock Foundation. They hired a hall at Guilford College, a Quaker institution on the edge of Greensboro. It was a small liberal arts school that practiced its heritage; service to the community was part of its curriculum. When Eakes and Adams called to talk with James Newlin in the college's administration about conducting a summer conference there on worker-owned businesses, Newlin encouraged Guilford's creative new president, William Rogers, to sit in. Rogers was enthusiastic and even open to adding a worker-owned component, teaching democratic management, to the curriculum in Guilford's economics department.

In mid-July 1982, the second worker-owned conference opened on Guilford's campus, as bucolic a setting as one could imagine. While Winton had been a gathering of activists and planners in love with an idea, this session had real worker-owners, around whom many of the sessions were built. Bazemore brought five people with him from the sewing company in Windsor. Susan Fowler of Space Builders, the homebuilder from Carrboro, was there. So were Percy White and others from his bakery, which was limping along. A group of young journalists from Roanoke Rapids, North Carolina, not far from Winton, had plans for a worker-owned newspaper that they wanted to begin publishing in the fall. Those working through the changes at Service Printing also attended. And there was a crowd from a closed zipper plant in eastern North Carolina eager to reopen under their own management. Wright, through Self-Help, was helping them advance their cause.

About seventy people attended the second conference. They came from religious organizations, state government, foundations, and Legal Services of North Carolina. There were people with PhDs and others happy to have a GED. Young women wearing Afros mingled with men in beards and sandals. Most came to learn, some came to teach, others came to make contacts, and still others came to sing a few songs reminiscent of the early days of the civil rights movement. A verse of one song written by Maggie Cherry, one of the sewing company employees, went like this: "We come a long way, on workers' owned / We come a long way, but not on our own / We come a long way, Lord, a mighty long way." Ronald Reagan was in the White House and Dr. Martin Luther King Jr. had been dead for more than a dozen years, but the spirit of the 1960s was fresh and alive.

The weekend featured show-and-tell from White, Bazemore, and Fowler, whose construction company was making money and proving to be successful. They talked about their experiences. Getting coworkers to buy in to sacrificing for the future and the common good was a tough sell, White said. "They want a job, [and] that's it," one worker added. "They don't want any part of organizing." Being a manager with co-owners made for tough days. Bazemore boosted production by posting piece rate scores for workers while notifying all that the slowest workers would be the first laid off if orders declined. Fowler advised that all in the business needed to stay informed about cash flow and the status of slow-pay clients. "They can't afford not to know," she said.[10]

Weaving in and out of the sessions were Eakes, Wright, Moore, and Martin's Davidson classmate and Self-Help founding board member Andrew Lamas. He was down from Philadelphia, where he was engaged in a similar worker-owned initiative. His group, the Philadelphia Association of Cooperative Enterprise, was working with a union local to reopen about one-quarter of more than seventy grocery stores recently closed by the A&P grocery chain.

Lofty ideals came crashing to earth on hard topics. Democratic management was a difficult problem, and so was finding the money necessary to open the doors and quicken a production line. Traditional lenders, such as banks, were not much of an option, certainly not in a day of 18 percent interest rates. There were some government programs aimed at boosting economic development that might work. Bob Schall ran through the prospects for the Corporation for Cooperative Businesses, the Self-Help creation established to assist in landing loans from the SBA. The corporation was still in the formative stages. And then Wright took the floor to talk about another fledgling idea: a credit union.

One of the issues dogging all the efforts of Self-Help was how to get cash into a new enterprise. In a worker-owned company, the workers had to put up money to buy into the business. But, if a prospective worker were unemployed, overdue on personal bills, and struggling to feed his or her family, it would be tough to find $5,000, $500, or even $50 to invest, no matter how good it sounded. Moreover, African Americans found it hard to get business loans. Bazemore once told Eakes that a bank would easily give him a loan for a $20,000 Cadillac, but he could not get $100 to buy an acre of dirt to expand his logging operation. Institutional bias was commonplace in business and residential lending, with banks refusing to invest in certain sections of a community. This was especially true in the state's rural communities, with only one bank around, where economic power was conflated with political power. Old habits were baked into local lending institutions; a segregationist culture still prevailed.

Yet, start-up capital had to come from somewhere other than whatever Self-Help staff members might find under the sofa cushions, as happened with Percy White's oven. Eakes and Wright had talked about organizing a bank, but capital requirements got in the way. A credit union looked much easier, and it was fully compatible with the worker-owner model. It was a long shot, but if Self-Help was going to push the worker-owned model it had to find a source of investment capital. Yes, a credit union looked like a good first step, but it would not be like any other.

CHAPTER THREE

A Financial Institution

The story goes that Bonnie Wright was just starting her freshman year at Davidson College when she came upon Martin Eakes, a Phi Beta Kappa senior, tied to a flagpole wearing only his briefs. Eakes says Davidson's president had stopped by earlier to see that he was unharmed and relatively decent, and then left him to perfect an escape from a predicament arranged by classmates seeking retribution for pranks Eakes had pulled on them.

Wright was a brunette with a broad smile, olive skin, dark eyes, and easygoing manners cultivated by her comfortable upbringing in suburban Atlanta, Georgia. At the urging of a high school counselor, she chose Davidson College and, in 1976, was among the third class of females admitted. Her relationship with Eakes and his friends inspired a political commitment that was probably discomforting to her father, who was a member of the John Birch Society. Before graduation, with a self-designed major in economics and urban studies, she worked one summer as a liaison between health agencies and migrant workers in eastern North Carolina. After her graduation in 1979, she headed off to a stint in Ecuador for her own experience in making the world a better place to live.

Wright was back in the States in the summer of 1980 and helped Eakes design a simple brochure promoting the services of the Center for Community Self-Help. In the beginning, the two worked out of a makeshift office of boxed material in the back of Martin's car. It caught fire on one trip and almost destroyed Self-Help's early archive. In later years, Eakes would be singled out for creating the nation's largest and most successful community development financial institution, but he never failed to say he was only a co-founder. Wright was always an equal partner in the enterprise.

Barbara Marie Wright kept her own name when she and Martin walked over to the office of Durham County's register of deeds and applied for a marriage license. Their marriage was so matter-of-fact that she has a hard time remembering the anniversary. By that time, she had completed studies for a master's degree in economics and public policy at the Yale School of Organization and Management, where she fine-tuned a proposal to create a credit union to support the work of Self-Help. She presented her finished results to her fellow students, who told her it probably would not work. She was not intimidated by their judgment. The guiding dynamic of Self-Help was in the nature of making things change, not in taking the same old paths.

In the summer of 1982, Wright and Eakes began gathering the five hundred signatures necessary to apply for a state-chartered credit union. She had finished her work at Yale by the summer of 1983, in time for the second worker-owned conference to be held on the Guilford College campus. It was even better attended than the year before and drew a broader and more diverse clientele. A lot of the talk and attention was focused on representatives from the successful worker-owned enterprises in Mondragón, Spain. Wright and Eakes had used Mondragón's Caja Laboral Popular, or "Working People's Bank," as their model for the credit union. In fact, in one proposal, Eakes called it a "workers' bank."

A year of hard work had taught a valuable lesson: If Self-Help were to succeed with worker-owned businesses, it would need a ready source of capital, and a credit union was the easiest and quickest route to creating a financial institution. Those who had not already put down as little as $15 to become a member of Self-Help—the common bond required to qualify for membership in a credit union—did so, and the weekend closed with more than one hundred worker-owned evangelists circled and holding hands and singing Maggie Cherry's song.

In September 1983, the Self-Help Credit Union was chartered by the state of North Carolina. The folks in Durham were unlikely up-and-coming financiers—Eakes was not yet thirty years old, and Wright was younger—but North Carolina credit union administrator Roy D. High was impressed with their academic credentials, their diligence, and their interest in doing things right. From time to time, Eakes or Wright would call at High's office with questions that probed the limits of what a credit union could do as well as qualifications for membership. High checked the law, gave a nod in their direction, and they would return with more questions.[1]

High had never seen anything like the application that finally arrived on his desk. Most credit unions served employees of particular businesses, large and small. Duke Power Company employees had one, and so did municipal workers in some cities. There was a credit union for workers at the U.S. Postal Service in Rocky Mount. A handful were associated with religious groups, such as retired Methodist ministers, and fraternal orders.

Self-Help's request was the first High had seen that was organized around common social and economic goals shared by the members of the Center for Community Self-Help. Once Self-Help recruited the required number of members to qualify and satisfied the regulations, High issued a charter. Going forward, all members of the credit union would also have to pay a membership fee ($5 in 2016) and become a member of the Center for Community Self-Help.

Approval from the National Credit Union Administration, which provided insurance on deposits up to $100,000, took a bit longer, but final approval was in hand by December 1983. Wright held on to the first intended deposit for months. It was $77, raised at a sale of baked goods from Percy White's New Bern Bakery, that White donated as seed money.[2] The credit union finally opened for business on March 31, 1984, in the modest building on East Chapel Hill Street where, Eakes would later joke, a previous owner, a printer and counterfeiter, had issued his own money from a press on the top floor. Wright was the general manager. The opening of the nation's first credit union created to assist worker-owned businesses did not rate coverage by the Durham newspapers.

Of course, the credit union had more than the proceeds from the bake sale when it started business. Wright also had a check for $100,000 from the Presbyterian Church, U.S.A. Among the early individual depositor members were outfits that were still learning how to be worker-owned business, as well as the Fund for Southern Communities out of Atlanta, Georgia; a

Durham food co-op; Wes Hare's church in Chapel Hill; and the Sisters of Charity, an investment arm of a Catholic order. Wright said she was expecting a total of $500,000 within the first three months.[3]

Part of that money arrived sixty days later from the Babcock Foundation. The Babcock board doubled down on Self-Help with a grant of $25,000 for administrative support for the credit union, a five-year deposit of $100,000 at no interest, and a $100,000 recoverable grant to be used as a loan-loss reserve. The latter allowed the credit union to begin making loans immediately. In between what Eakes called the "pity" grant he received in 1981 and this latest good news, Babcock had put another $28,000 into underwriting the operations of Self-Help.

After its initial rejection of his plans, the Z. Smith Reynolds Foundation had approved its first grant of $15,000 in 1982, giving Eakes encouragement. He did worry about the impression he left with his funders on the day he received word at their offices in Winston-Salem, however. When he got to his car to return to Durham, he realized that he had locked his keys inside. Should he break a window and incur the expense of repair, he wondered, or acknowledge his ineptitude and ask for help? Operating on survival resources, he chose the latter, borrowed a car from a Reynolds staff member, and met Wright midway with a spare set of keys.

Eakes made sure the confidence of the Babcock and Reynolds boards in his new enterprise was not lost on the Ford Foundation, where he had a proposal moving through the bureaucracy. A substantial $125,000 investment in North Carolina's newest and fastest-growing financial enterprise would arrive just as the credit union was opening.

North Carolina was far from a paradise for worker-owned cooperatives, but you could not tell it by looking in at what was going on at 413 E. Chapel Hill Street. The purchase of the building itself was a venture of like-minded people who had joined Eakes in raising the down payment in April 1983. Eakes had asked his father and his old mentor, Ed Zane, about the deal. They advised against buying the building, but Eakes purchased it anyway under a new corporation called Cooperative Development Associates. The initial tenants were Self-Help and Eakes's law firm, Gulley, Eakes and Volland. The space would later serve as an incubator for assorted nascent nonprofits and cooperative businesses looking for a desk, a phone, and a place to begin work.

Eakes had taken Wilbur "Wib" Gulley as a law partner in the summer of 1981 after Gulley walked into his office in the Central Carolina Bank build-

ing, introduced himself, and suggested they ought to work together. Gulley
was from Little Rock, Arkansas, but had been in North Carolina for much
of the previous decade. He was a Duke graduate who had stayed on in the
1970s to organize the North Carolina chapter of the Public Interest Research
Group (NC-PIRG) before heading off to the Northeastern School of Law in
1978. Thad Moore and some of Eakes's friends at Davidson had been among
NC-PIRG's foot soldiers in campaigns against utility rate increases, inflated
prescription drug prices, and environmental causes. A mutual friend had
suggested to Gulley that he and Eakes shared a similar philosophy about
the law.

"I wanted to practice what I felt like was alternative law and work to use
the law as an instrument for reform of society and to make change," Gulley
said some years later. "Neither one of us saw a typical law practice, and that
is why, that said, it was not an enormously brilliant or successful way to go
after it. Starting your own law practice is a way to guarantee that you make
very little money."

Eakes and Gulley all but insured a life of poverty by settling on an hourly
rate of no more than what their clients earned in their own jobs. Pretty soon,
they had as many clients as their two-room law offices could hold. Most were
blue-collar workers making $8 an hour, and some made as much as $15 an
hour. That's when it dawned on Gulley that they were losing money. Their
egalitarian fees did not cover the $25-an-hour overhead that he and Eakes
were paying to run their business. "We increased our hourly rate a little bit."[4]

Eakes and Gulley became fast friends. Gulley even met his future wife
at a potluck dinner at Eakes's house, which was something of a social hub
as well as the Self-Help headquarters in the early days. Neither Eakes nor
Gulley made much money from the law firm, but they were young and were
not that interested in large bank accounts. Gulley served various types of
clients, while Eakes was proficient in property and small business law, especially for nonprofits. Eakes did the legal work to help Steve Schewel launch
the *N.C. Independent*, an alternative weekly newspaper based in Durham,
and then recruited Schewel as a donor to the credit union's loss reserves.[5]
Gulley did some of the legal work to pull the pieces together to form the
credit union.

Credit unions had been around North Carolina since before World War I.
The first was the work of a Durham banker and first-rank capitalist named
John Sprunt Hill. He had seen the value of credit unions in Europe and
personally financed the establishment of early ones in North Carolina as an

antidote to the pernicious practice of crop liens that burdened farmers with high interest rates. The number of credit unions grew in the 1920s, thanks to Hill's cultivation, but many did not survive the Great Depression. There was a resurgence after World War II. By the 1980s, however, the number of credit unions was declining—there were about 180 in 1985, down from 225 a few years earlier—although membership was increasing as smaller operations merged with neighboring institutions.[6] The largest credit union in North Carolina, and one of the largest in the United States, was the State Employees Credit Union, with more than 200,000 members and assets of more than $1 billion.

Eakes and Wright planned to use the platform of a credit union as a regulated and insured financial institution that would be like the others in organization but unique in most other respects. The legally required "common bond" was membership in Self-Help, which would allow a statewide reach. Further, Self-Help did not plan to have a teller window for retail services, where members could walk in and make deposits or maintain a checking account. Instead, the Self-Help Credit Union would recruit members and their time deposits like the other savings institutions but limit lending to members needing cash to buy shares of a worker-owned business or to capitalize the start-up of worker-owned businesses.

Created at the same time as the credit union was an unregulated entity called the Self-Help Ventures Fund, a nonprofit development corporation whose initial support came from the Reynolds Foundation. The financial resources of the Ventures Fund, which included grants and loans from foundations and others, would allow Self-Help to make larger, higher-risk loans to worker-owned businesses than would have been possible through the credit union.

Deposits by Babcock, Reynolds, and others were critical. Without them, the credit union would have had to limp along for years and build its cash reserves, dollar by dollar, before it could make any meaningful loans. A $100,000 grant for reserves, recoverable by a depositor after ten years, meant that the credit union had up to $500,000 in lending capacity on its first day of business. That was an essential arrow in Self-Help's quiver.

While Wright organized the credit union, Eakes, Thad Moore, and Bill Bynum, a recent graduate of the University of North Carolina at Chapel Hill who joined the Self-Help staff in the summer of 1983, were providing what they called "technical assistance" to struggling worker-owned business. Bynum's principal client was the Durham printing company, while

Moore was devoting much of his time to the newly organized Alamance Workers' Owned Knitting (AWOK) company. It began producing socks just a few weeks after the credit union opened in 1984.

AWOK's story was all too familiar in North Carolina. Traditional knitting operations were shutting down as owners consolidated their operations at more efficient locations or moved production elsewhere. A plant in Burlington, about twenty-five miles west of Durham, had closed in December 1982, when its owner, Genesco Industries, merged operations with a facility in Tennessee. More than a hundred workers lost their jobs. Self-Help was called on for help by the local legal services office, where June Blotnick, who had come to North Carolina with Volunteers in Service to America, was helping workers organize a food cooperative. Blotnick had brought a group of the Burlington workers to the Guilford conference in the summer of 1983.[7]

A full-court press by Self-Help, Wes Hare's Twin Streams, and North State Legal Services produced what had at first looked improbable, if not impossible. Using the proceeds from bake sales and loans from a local bank and the National Rural Development Corporation, along with an interest-free loan from Catholic Charities, AWOK brought together workers and used equipment, and began planning their new business in an old building where the clatter of knitting machines would be heard once again. Moore and Hare conducted classes to prepare workers for what was to come, while an experienced machine operator, who would become the plant manager, handled the installation of the equipment. The organizers formed a board of directors and began making decisions on pay, work hours, vacations, and what do to with the profits, which were not expected immediately. The plant started with eleven workers on three shifts and an order for 18,000 pairs of socks. There were plans to expand to thirty workers.

"I thought it was a little too far out, too good to be true," Betty Lucas told a newspaper reporter at the time. "But the more we met, the more we talked about it, the more we got excited about it. We talked to the bankers, and they were interested in lending us money to get our machines. At that point, there was no turning back."[8]

Meanwhile, Eakes was putting together Self-Help's most ambitious enterprise yet, one that had the potential to be impressive and important. He had heard through his Davidson College connections about members of a family with a large stake in the oldest furniture manufacturing company in the state who were seeking advice on a plan to enable workers to buy the business. White Furniture Company had been part of everyday life for nearly a century in the town of Mebane, just next door to Burlington in Alamance County. The company was in its third generation of family operation, and some of the stockholders were anxious about the future. The company was not on the market, but it probably soon would be—for around $6 million.

It was just the kind of opportunity Eakes was looking for. The plant had not closed, and the business was not in trouble. It was old-style manufacturing, but he saw it as salvaging the kind of business that was disappearing from North Carolina. In this case, White's product line was strong and popular with buyers, and the company was profitable. If Self-Help could structure a deal, five hundred or more workers would have some assurance that they could keep their jobs. In addition, Mebane could retain an industrial anchor that had been part of the community for generations.

Eakes began structuring a deal. He called Crawford Crenshaw, one of Self-Help's founding directors, and asked if he was ready to leave a management-consulting job in Cleveland to come run a business. Crenshaw agreed and came south to look things over. The living room of Eakes's house in Durham became the staging area. There, Eakes, Crenshaw, and Steven A. Zuckerman, a new Self-Help employee, began poring over the company's financials and studying its product line in the summer of 1984. Eakes was in his element. He thrived on working out financial calculations with the same crazy zeal he had used to analyze the physics of oscillating springs in college. Spreadsheets and financial analysis filled his computer.

Zuckerman was the first in what would be a long line of educated and talented idealists who would be willing to invest part—or, in some cases, all—of their working lives in Self-Help. He was a Yale graduate who had spent two years at Bain and Company, the Boston mergers and acquisitions firm. There, he had met Roger Brown, another of Self-Help's founding board members, who suggested that he take a year and spend some time in Durham before heading to business school at Stanford University. Eakes took Zuckerman in and offered him a spare bedroom as temporary quarters—he ended up spending a full year as a house guest.

Zuckerman had not come with the intention of working at Self-Help. He wanted to learn how to run a business, and Eakes delivered his own small enterprise, Eno Computer Company, into Zuckerman's hands. Eakes had created Eno a year or two earlier, just as desktop computers were coming into the market. He was fascinated with this new technology and became an early devotee. More than 20 percent of his first proposal to Babcock had included money for an electric typewriter with a very modest memory capable of rudimentary word processing.

Using one of these early computers, Eakes had marshaled its capacity at the law firm to produce standard forms for property closings, among other routine documents. Eakes had created his own company so he could buy machines at a discount, and then resell them at a below-market price to nonprofits and others. Along with the computers came Eakes-designed routines to produce spreadsheets and other marvels such as mail-merge options, then available with simple software. Attendees at the 1983 worker-owned conference at Guilford found a room full of Eno's computers that they used to learn a new way of doing business that saved time and relieved starving start-ups of some of the expense of support staff.

The industry called these Korean-made Corona computers "portable," but Zuckerman said they were more accurately known as "luggable." One could lug around the twenty-five-pound machines that were roughly the size of a piece of carry-on luggage, but not without effort. The face of the box unhinged and became a keyboard, and images appeared on a screen about five inches on the diagonal. Zuckerman spent about six weeks studying the computer business, decided it was not for him, and returned Eno Computer to its owner. He was much more fascinated with what was going on at night on the living room floor as Eakes and Crenshaw prepared a strategy for White Furniture.

The three men developed an employee stock ownership plan, or ESOP, that would allow employees to buy White Furniture. There were complicated tax issues, but an ESOP had some decided advantages for the workers, something Zuckerman knew about from his work at Bain. It was bold, but new federal tax laws encouraged this sort of thing.

Bold, even audacious, did not bother Eakes, Zuckerman later recalled. He said at one point he, Crenshaw, and Eakes, who ranged in age from twenty-six (Zuckerman) to thirty (Eakes), were meeting with the company officers. "They asked a question, and Martin said, 'Well the way we usually do that is. . . .' Crawford and I are just choking back laughter. This was the first time we had ever tried. It wasn't totally disingenuous. We had researched it and knew that was the way it should be done."[9]

The ESOP failed to clear White's board of directors by one vote. It was dispiriting. Eakes was angry and frustrated, two emotions he had difficulty concealing. "These guys are corporate raiders and pillagers," he declared at one point during the negotiations, quoting a competing bidder's history as reported in a *Fortune* magazine article. A lawyer from the other side cautioned Eakes in his choice of words, saying, "He has plenty of money to wipe you out." Eakes recalled his response some time later. "I was saying, you know, it's not like *Fortune* magazine is some pinko publication that is far left or anything."[10] The winning bidder continued the operations in Mebane for about five years, reducing jobs along the way, and then closed the plant. White Furniture disappeared from Mebane.

The telephone kept ringing at the Self-Help office. Owners of a restaurant called Stone Soup in Asheville, North Carolina, wanted help. So did a legal aid lawyer near Hendersonville working with a group of women to open Busy Needle Inc. and make leotards, sweatshirts, and T-shirts. Wright and others were also working with a family-run casket company in eastern North Carolina and providing assistance, and a small loan, to the *People's Voice*, a worker-owned newspaper in Roanoke Rapids, North Carolina, that wrote about problems confronting African Americans who were trying to make their way in a changing economy. Zuckerman spent his time working with a heating and air-conditioning firm in the northeastern corner of the state. It was slow going. Early on, in one of his first reports to the Babcock Foundation, Thad Moore had reported that their early work at Service Printing Company "has taught us patience!"[11]

Self-Help practiced what it preached, and that, too, produced lessons. In its own workers' democracy, the credit union's board of directors was elected by members and included representatives from companies receiving Self-Help's assistance. With a small staff, the Self-Help organizational structure was flat—one for all, and all for one. Everyone was paid the same. The four or five persons involved in daily operations worked at desks scattered around a large room on the second floor of the East Chapel Hill Street building. They gathered regularly to make collective decisions, when decisions had to be made.

Everyone pitched in to do whatever needed to be done. One day, Nancy Harding Winter, who was part of the group in the early days, confronted Eakes about a policy that required all to share in the typing chores. She was a proficient typist and an experienced office administrator who handled Self-Help's bookkeeping as part of her office services cooperative that operated out of the building. "She sat me down one day and said, 'This just pisses me off,'" Eakes recalled. "'You think that you should be doing typing and you can't type worth a damn and I am really good at it. By you making that scut work that we should all split up, you are demeaning me in my work and I am good at it.' She was dead right. It was in best of intentions . . . young, idealistic . . . but it was disrespectful. I didn't mean it disrespectfully. But it was an interesting on-the-ground learning that all work is noble if you do it well. As a young lawyer who was thinking 'thought work' is the higher order, and clerical work is lower order, she gave me my comeuppance."[12]

Eakes and others were learning real-world business lessons, too. At the top of the list was a growing realization that managers capable of running a business do not always rise from the ranks as they did in Eakes's egalitarian dream. A capable leader such as Tim Bazemore at the Windsor sewing company was not always available in every group of workers. Skills such as Bazemore's desire, ability, and social consciousness were rare.

Self-Help had its hands full tutoring workers in reading, arithmetic, and how to use a calculator. At the same time, staff members were trying to teach relatively unsophisticated folks how to run meetings and manage groups, new challenges that had nothing to do with their jobs on a production line. Management training was not always well received. Some employees did not want to work at this level; they simply wanted a steady paycheck.

"We were trying to facilitate employee groups, and the employee groups didn't have the necessary resolve, leadership, and fortitude to make it happen," said Zuckerman, recalling his experience with the heating and air business. The company got a loan, and it was one of the credit union's first loans to go into default. Self-Help minimized losses with the sale of collateral.

In a summary of the center's first years of work, Eakes told the Babcock Foundation that Self-Help occupied an "anomalous position." On the one hand, it pursued a mandate to bring assistance to the least skilled people with the fewest resources. At the same time, it was engaged in business development that "must address the hard business questions that involve skill, education and resources. Consequently, an important tension exists in every phase of our work. The fundamental social purpose of our vision and organization often wars against business instinct and judgment." That was where Eakes wanted to be, however: in the midst of this "irreconcilable tension."[13]

The greatest success was with the credit union, which had grown steadily. By the end of 1984, it had more than $1 million in deposits. Wright had handed over operations to a new assistant, Katherine Stern, when she left to have a baby, a son whom she and Martin named Justin. Stern had met Wright when Wright spoke to the group about socially responsible investing. Stern was from Greensboro, like Martin, but had been working in California for Democratic Management Services, a company that shared some of the same values as Self-Help. She was familiar with the Santa Cruz Community Credit Union, which had opened in 1977 with the first deposits literally kept in a cigar box. The credit union was dedicated to improving the community it served in much the same ways as Self-Help but without the worker-owned tapestry.

Stern's desk, in the credit union portion of the building, was near the front door, just beyond the old show windows where Eakes had his Eno Computer samples on display. The atmosphere inside was relaxed. When Bonnie and Martin returned from their respective maternity and paternity leaves, Bonnie looked after Justin in the mornings while Martin handled babysitting in the afternoons. Sometimes, the infant ended up in Stern's lap if Martin was called away. It was a great place for talented young people to work if they were willing to work cheap. (Stern's annual pay was $11,000 for a thirty-two-hour workweek.)[14]

Most financial transactions were handled by mail. The emphasis was on raising large-dollar deposits from groups and individuals interested in Self-Help's mission as part of a program of socially responsible investing. It was an old strategy that was gaining popularity in the early 1980s, with mutual fund managers creating sizable investment portfolios for investors who did not want their money supporting defense contractors, tobacco companies, and the like. The growing worldwide rejection of apartheid in South Africa also brought social investing home to U.S. banks and producers of consumer goods such as Coca-Cola, all of which were facing shareholder resolutions demanding divestiture.

Sister Carol Coston, OP, of the Adrian Dominican Sisters, became a national spokesperson on Self-Help's behalf. Her sisters had learned about Self-Help through a mission outpost in Halifax County, where members of her order were helping a casket company convert to a cooperative. She came to Durham to see Self-Help and meet the staff, and was pleased with what she found.

"I really admired their values and lifestyles. The fact that they acted out of their values. I know Martin was very strict about not having huge salaries," Coston recalled years later. She also believed in advancing worker-owned businesses, which she compared to the structure of her religious congregations that shared their money as well as the responsibilities and burdens. "It didn't seem odd to me," she said, although it ran counter to the culture of American individualism. The Adrian Dominican Sisters were among the early supporters of the credit union with a 5 percent loan—well below the prime rate—for $50,000 for five years.[15]

Eakes recruited Coston, with the help of a modest grant, to raise deposits for the credit union, not just with her fellow Catholics but also from other like-minded individuals in the religious community whom she had come to know after nearly a decade of work. This included fellow members of the Interfaith Center for Corporate Responsibility and Catholic orders of all stripes spread across the land. Over time, she raised about $2 million in deposits for the credit union, said Thad Moore. "She would call and say, 'I have another one for you,'" he recalled. "Shortly thereafter, along would come a deposit from The Daughters of the Blessed Blood of Christ, or something like that." "I bet that goes over well down South," she once told him with a laugh.[16]

Lending was on the upswing. At the start of 1985, the credit union had $141,470 out in loans or lines of credit to eleven businesses. It paid for a van and a computerized cash register for a food co-op, helped expand White's bakery in New Bern, gave the Alamance workers a line of credit to buy yarn from which to make their socks, and helped a start-up retailer of outdoor recreational gear purchase inventory. Three thousand dollars covered member shares for workers starting a business in Chapel Hill.

The National Credit Union Administration (NCUA), which was responsible for insuring the credit union's deposits, was not at all pleased. Examiners at the NCUA had never seen a credit union do the kind of commercial lending that was going on in Durham. Credit unions helped members buy a car, refurnish a home, or, in the case of those with the resources, buy a home. At the outset, Roy High, the state credit union administrator, had researched questions about whether Self-Help's credit union could service businesses with commercial loans and determined that the first credit unions, open to members and nonmembers alike as depositors, were established to help farmers buy fertilizer and equipment. He determined that these farmers were a business just like workers running a textile plant.

The NCUA administrator was not persuaded. He called Eakes to a meeting in Atlanta and told him that the Self-Help Credit Union would never have gotten NCUA coverage if he had known what Eakes was going to do with the depositors' money. It's too late now, Eakes told himself; Self-Help was already doing business. He argued that the risk was backstopped by grants from Babcock and others. "The foundation is going to lose its $100,000," Eakes told him, "so it is no sweat off your back. We have got it covered."

Out of the episode came a new phrase in credit union law called "nonvoting equity shares," which North Carolina credit union regulators had helped facilitate and reinforced with a favorable ruling from the N.C. attorney general. What it meant was that money raised from foundations and others was no different than that contributed by depositors and should be counted as part of the credit union's equity. "As far as we knew, there was no other place in the country that had done that," Eakes said years later. In short order, Self-Help was already changing how a new category of lenders, called community development credit unions, would operate in the future.

Eakes had the North Carolina authorities in his corner along with Larry Johnson of the N.C. Credit Union League, an advocacy group, who intervened on Self-Help's behalf. Johnson agreed that commercial loans were indeed novel.

"It was not the thing to do," Johnson later recalled. Johnson said he asked Eakes about auto loans and other types of conventional lending but was told that Self-Help was not any good at that. This was shorthand for "that kind of lending didn't meet Self-Help's mission," a concept that was hard to understand by those unfamiliar with Self-Help's credo. Retail lending made good money, but Self-Help had more important things in mind. The state authorities were comfortable with the equity shares arrangement as well as the clean books of the Self-Help Credit Union that were audited annually by a first-rank firm.

"Not only is Martin Eakes brilliant," Johnson said, but "his vision is brilliant. Brilliance is light. His vision has cast light on a lot of issues that would never have come out of the back room. He thrives on that."[17] For years, federal examiners continued to flag more Self-Help Credit Union loans as problems than did the state examiners reviewing the same files.

CHAPTER FOUR

Turning Point

When the credit union was in its infancy, Martin Eakes carried in his pocket, handy to anyone who asked, a VisiCalc spreadsheet that plotted a ten-year path to sustainability. His reasoning was clear. If Self-Help was to have any meaningful impact, then the organization needed a minimum of $10 million in deposits, eight to nine times the amount of money on the books at the end of its first year. People groaned and rolled their eyes in disbelief when he declared this as a goal for Self-Help's board members.

This was not a pipe dream. Eakes felt confident enough in his analysis to put this goal in at least one foundation grant proposal, where he argued that the $10 million goal produced a very definable result: the credit union would have the capacity to do as much as $200,000 in lending to a borrower under its own conservative risk management policy of putting no more than 2 percent of assets into any one project. Frankly, the $200,000 was not enough to meet the requests for loans. If anything, the goal was not too high; it probably was not high enough.

Self-Help was gaining attention around the nation with its novel approach to enabling worker-owned enterprises. The *San Francisco Examiner* called North Carolina the center of the worker-owned movement in the country. The Canadian government sent a delegation to see what was going on, and inquiries about Self-Help's work in rural development came in regularly to the offices on East Chapel Hill Street from South Carolina, Kentucky, Georgia, and Ohio. Self-Help was invited to participate in an international program on rural development in New Delhi, India.[1] The calls for advice suggested that Self-Help had found the answers, but Eakes was the first to say that the organization was still evolving. Just two years after the credit union opened, it was about to make a shift that would resonate in the decades to come.

Even as Self-Help pressed its appeals to foundations and others for financial support to jump-start lending, it also embarked on an effort to increase the number of individual credit union depositors to secure its base with a self-sustaining source of income. Large depositors could be fickle. Even foundations could change their minds, Eakes reasoned, and should Self-Help's advocacy work become objectionable and provoke reaction, the entire institution could suffer from the withdrawal of one or two large deposits.

Further, the competition for grants was growing, and the pool of funders was limited. One safeguard against the hazard of heavy reliance on a small number of large depositors was a large base of small depositors. Self-sufficiency and sustainability were two of Eakes's abiding, long-term goals. Self-Help would not operate like many nonprofits that kept the tin cup out from year to year, hoping for the best. Eakes did not want outsiders shaping Self-Help's mission, no matter how enticing their resources. He wanted Self-Help's net worth to execute its mission. "That is a fairly simple concept," observed one former Self-Help staff member, "but it is lost on so many nonprofit leaders. Martin saw it early on so clearly."[2]

The credit union was not run out of a cigar box, but it was not far from it at the end of that first year. The modest "back office" operation worked well enough when Katherine Stern had only a couple hundred accounts to manage. If the credit union were to expand as Eakes desired, it would need the capacity to handle thousands of accounts. That's when Eakes paid a call on Jim Blaine, the president of the N.C. State Employees Credit Union (SECU).

Eakes may have dismissed the notion of the credit union opening teller windows and issuing car loans, but he envied SECU's size and network of branches across the state. It had been around since the middle of the Great Depression, when it had begun in equally humble circumstances with seventeen members and $437 in deposits. By the mid-1980s, it had fifty-six branch offices serving more than 200,000 members from the mountains to the sea. Eakes discovered that in the year before Self-Help Credit Union opened its doors, SECU had recruited a thousand new members and increased its deposits by $175 million. Blaine was a savvy administrator with a sly wit, a strong jaw, and a stubborn streak that would serve him well in dealing with Martin Eakes. The personalities of the two were certain to clash, but their common bond was the virtues of credit unions and what they meant to the financial health of their members.

What Eakes wanted was access to SECU's branches. He saw this as an important step toward the creation of what he, as early as 1985, when the credit union was just a year old, was calling "the first significant, privately capitalized statewide development financial organization."[3] He was not out to poach Blaine's customers, but he did want permission for Self-Help members to use SECU branches to make deposits and access money market accounts through SECU's automatic teller machines. It was as close to having a banking network without Self-Help Credit Union erecting buildings and hiring staff of its own.

Blaine's initial reaction was about the same as others in the state's credit union community. When Thad Moore was at a gathering of credit union administrators, he overheard someone say of Self-Help: "They're a bunch of hippies, but they know what they are doing." Someone must have seen Eakes in his tie-dyed shirt and sandals. He once appeared at a business meeting wearing a suit and steel-toed boots with red shoelaces. Blaine endorsed Eakes's ambitions to extend financial services to those who did not have them, but he was also skeptical. "In early discussions, I think they viewed us as unrealistically idealistic," Eakes later told his supporters.[4]

With the first-impression hurdles out of the way, the two organizations decided that the credit union would pay SECU a fee for its services. "The idea," said Blaine, "was that we would provide [services] at a low cost so they did not have to focus on that. It didn't assure that they would succeed, but it assured [that] they would not fail on all those little [regulatory] trip-wire stuff."

Using a grant from the Z. Smith Reynolds Foundation, Eakes launched an advertising and promotion campaign to spread the word about Self-Help, with a particular emphasis on reaching nonprofit organizations across the state. Some of the money paid the salaries of part-time organizers, with Charlotte and Asheville looking like the best prospects for expansion. In addition, a direct-mail effort and newspaper advertising campaign was prepared. It was all part of a grand plan that seemed to have everything going for it. Until it became clear, after a year or so, that the joint venture with SECU really was not a good fit. Self-Help's piggybacking on SECU came to an end.

Blaine managed a large operation designed to compete with commercial banks. He squeezed out every penny of economy. "Rationalizing, standardizing, that is how we make our living," he said. "[SECU members] get greater convenience or equal convenience at [a] lower cost [than banks]." Self-Help's clients were anything but uniform; each loan was tailored to meet the unique conditions of the borrower. Blaine said he began receiving what he called "the idea of the week" from Eakes, which did not suit Blaine's operating strategy. "I loved him, for a very brief time," he recalled with a broad grin many years later. After one explosive meeting, Eakes sent Blaine the book *Getting to Yes*. Blaine responded with a present of his own: a copy of Dale Carnegie's *How to Win Friends and Influence People*. Self-Help and SECU parted ways after a little more than a year of rocky relations. Fortunately, Self-Help was in a position to install its own systems for managing accounts.[5]

Despite its counterculture appearance and alternative vision, the credit union was run with meticulous attention to detail. With regulators looking over their shoulders every quarter in the early days, the books were clean, according to its outside auditors. Beginning with the first year, Eakes built reserves internally and instituted annual tithing of credit union profits, even if it was just a couple hundred dollars. "The credit union was a very educational experience," Eakes said. "It is one thing to debate ideas with a group of friends. It is another thing to have an institution that is regulated and scrutinized carefully and has to be able to make loans to viable businesses that pay them back."

The quality of the work was noticed. The credit union was still in its first year when Roy D. High, the North Carolina credit union administrator, thought enough of Self-Help's operations to ask it to take on an ailing institution set up for Methodist ministers and merge it with Self-Help. Despite the hiccups with the NCUA, Self-Help Credit Union was ready to expand.

Charlotte looked like a good place to start, so Eakes contacted June Blotnick. She had worked with Thad Moore to get the Burlington sock plant up and running and had attended the conference held at Guilford College.

When she told Eakes she was getting married and moving to Charlotte in late 1984, Eakes, ever the opportunist, asked her to establish a Self-Help office there. He suggested that she organize an office services cooperative as a demonstration project of a worker-owned enterprise. Nothing happened for a year, until Blotnick heard from Eakes again when he asked her to lead a fund-raising campaign to build deposits in the Charlotte area. She was stunned. "I don't know anything about people with money," she told him. "I have worked with poor people."[6] Eakes installed one of his luggable computers in a spare room in Blotnick's home. Self-Help was now a multicity operation.

While Blotnick was evangelizing in Charlotte, Eakes got a call in 1987 from Morris I. Karpen, a businessman in Asheville, North Carolina, who offered a grant of $10,000 as seed money to see if there was a need for a western North Carolina office. Karpen's son-in-law, Dana Smith, was a loan officer at a local savings bank. Both were intrigued by the Self-Help mission and the possibility of expanding its reach.

After Eakes talked with Karpen in Asheville, Smith flew to Durham for more conversations. Eakes met him at the airport and drove him to the office in a worn-out Volkswagen. The door latch on the passenger side did not work, and the back seat was jammed full of Self-Help's files. Smith's knees were pressed against the dash. They spent that day and the next talking about possibilities, especially about helping low-income borrowers build wealth through home ownership. Smith stayed overnight where most of Bonnie and Martin's guests stayed—on a futon in their living room at a house they had bought in 1984 on Englewood Avenue. It was a modest bungalow in a working-class neighborhood, just around the corner from the erstwhile staff dormitory the two had lived in on Rosehill Avenue. Rent from a tenant in an upper story of the new place helped pay the mortgage, until he nearly burned the house down by filling a kerosene heater with gasoline.

Smith and Blotnick had the same assignment. They were to spread the word about Self-Help and raise deposits for the credit union, all the while looking for lending opportunities that fit the Self-Help model. The two cities were as different from each other as they were from Durham. Charlotte was a buttoned-up, business town, growing fast and seriously becoming a Big South city. It was a financial center, home to major corporations migrating from the Northeast, and headquarters to the two most competitive banks in the state: North Carolina National Bank and First Union National Bank. Asheville was a schizophrenic mix. In the summer, it was a tourist mecca and was beginning to show the first hints of an eclectic counterculture—from its street musicians and four vegetarian newsletters—that would later become its signature. After Labor Day, Asheville's retailers struggled to survive on customers from the surrounding mountain counties, one of the most economically distressed regions in the state. Few African Americans lived in the mountains, one of Self-Help's primary constituencies, with the heaviest concentration in Asheville. The region was full of poor whites for whom jobs were scarce. Poverty rates were high.

While the worker-owners at Asheville's Stone Soup restaurant knew about Self-Help, Smith was most often greeted with blank looks when he started his educational campaign in 1988. Like Blotnick, he talked to church leaders, those running nonprofits, and business people in an effort to build a coalition of supporters. Asheville's chamber of commerce gave him a cold shoulder; they thought he was pushing some sort of scam.

Smith's goal was $1 million in deposits, $1 million in loans, and $1 million in grants in his first year. "We pretty much pulled [the numbers] out of the hat," he said. (Blotnick's goal was $5 million.) He put ads in the newspaper and posters in public locations, and through word of mouth people began making their way to his second-floor, ten-foot-by-ten-foot office over a shop at 12½ D Wall Street, then little more than a back alley in downtown Asheville. He said no to a lot of visitors who came expecting a handout and were surprised to learn that they actually had to repay their loans.

Smith cultivated contacts, spread the word as best he could, and experimented with a microloan program set up through the YWCA, one of Asheville's most progressive organizations. Called a Working Woman's Fund, it was designed to help women struggling to get a fresh start in new jobs. One of the first borrowers, properly vetted and looking good on paper, needed $500 for car repairs. She got a loan; Smith never saw her again. "The collateral was just too mobile," he said.[7]

There was great hope in Durham over a possible worker-owned venture then being cultivated in the mountains southwest of Asheville. Payson Kennedy was an entrepreneur who had turned outdoor adventures into a thriving business as the Nantahala Outdoor Center (NOC). Kennedy's company offered outings in canoes, kayaks, and rafts on some of the best whitewater streams in the eastern United States. Well into its second decade of business, it was Kennedy's dream to sell the company to his employees, but he was struggling to find anyone who knew how to do that. That was when word finally reached him about Self-Help's efforts on behalf of worker ownership of companies.

The prospect for a successful conversion looked even better to Eakes than White Furniture. This time there were no pesky shareholders eager to cash out. Furthermore, it was a business poised for future growth, and an employee stock option plan was already in place. One of Eakes's new hires in Durham was David McGrady, who was looking for a project like this to sink his teeth into.

McGrady was raised in the Virginia mountains, had graduated from Harvard Law School, and was an attorney at Simpson, Thatcher and Bartlett in New York City when he and his wife, Katharine McKee, left the metropolis behind and moved to Durham with plans to start a family. McKee and Eakes had come to know each other in graduate school. She became a program officer at the Ford Foundation and had helped Eakes get an early Ford investment for the development of businesses in rural areas. McGrady and McKee were vivid testimony to Eakes's style of management. When capable people showed up at his door, he hired them, and then found something for them to do. If they were as bright as he thought they were, they would figure out how to make a difference. At the poverty-level wages being offered, there was not much of a downside to his approach.

McKee and McGrady added some heft to the core program staff, which included Thad Day Moore, Bonnie Wright, Bill Bynum, Linwood Cox, and Robert Schall. Cox was the center's staff accountant and handled the books. Schall had come on in the summer of 1985, just as Steve Zuckerman left for graduate school. Schall was an opportunistic hire, like McGrady. He was finishing up his job at a natural foods distribution company, which included the Self-Help Credit Union among its creditors, when he told Eakes that he would soon be available for something else. Eakes took him out to the usual job interview venue at the bagel shop in downtown Durham, and a week later Schall came to work. His first assignment was to write a foundation proposal that, if successful, would secure his salary for more than a few months.

Schall became president of the Self-Help Ventures Fund, the unregulated, nonprofit, lending component that was established to handle the larger, riskier loans. At the time, it was virtually a shell with little to no money. While all in Durham were awaiting word from New York on the $500,000 grant from Ford that would inject life into the Ventures Fund, Schall began working out a few credit union loans that had gone bad. "It was a heck of a way to learn your job," he said some years later. "You learn from bad experiences first."[8]

The Ford money arrived at about the same time that McGrady and McKee joined the staff in 1986. Since McGrady had been working in the New York law firm's banking section, he brought a satchel full of the legal forms used there in financial transactions. Adjusted to different circumstances, they became the templates for Self-Help's first commercial lending documents.[9]

The Ford money was a program-related investment, or PRI, a form of grant making that Ford had pioneered. A legendary program officer named Paul Ylvisaker had proposed it in the late 1960s. Ford had used PRIs in the 1970s, and Ylvisaker introduced them in North Carolina after he joined the board of the Babcock Foundation in the 1980s. Babcock's first PRI went to Self-Help to create the credit union's loan-loss reserves.

A PRI was essentially a loan with a soft landing. Recipients were obliged to return the money after they had used it for a set period of time, but if they were unable to do so any shortfall was considered a grant. Babcock's PRI had given some confidence to other potential funders who were considering similar requests from Self-Help. When the Babcock money was banked, it became available for economic development through the Ventures Fund.

McGrady was doing his work through a Self-Help subsidiary called the Englewood Investment Corporation, which was similar to the Ventures Fund. Englewood was established to raise capital from private investors and finance conversions for large worker-owned enterprises, such as the outdoors center in the mountains. Since it did not include Self-Help in its name, McGrady hoped Englewood—borrowed from the street where Martin and Bonnie lived in Durham—would blend in as just another of the conventional for-profit investor funds then in the market.

McGrady would later describe Payson Kennedy as the "Martin Eakes of river rafting." Kennedy had taken his passion and turned it into a stimulating, exciting, and productive career. He had surrounded himself with like-minded people who worked at NOC for low pay, compensated in part by the daily pleasure of being in the mountains and running the white water on rivers such as the Nolichucky and French Broad. McGrady's principal contact at NOC was Marc Hunt, the company's chief financial officer. Hunt had created his own outfitter business on the western slopes of the Great Smoky Mountains in Tennessee, and then sold it to NOC. He is a tall, lean, athletic man, easygoing and chatty. His love of the outdoors is apparent at first glance.

Hunt told Eakes and McGrady about Kennedy's plans for the company. Years later, Hunt recalled the energetic response he received. "They really viewed NOC as different," he said. "It was profitable, it seemed to have a viable trajectory for growth, seemed to adapt to the cultural shift in America with the outdoors and the environment, and they wanted to be a part of something that was successful to help build Self-Help's brand a little bit."[10]

Hunt said he and McGrady would talk one day about the particulars of arranging a loan to bridge the completion of the buyout, and on the next day McGrady would transmit a twelve-page fax with spreadsheets showing outcomes under various scenarios. Hunt was convinced that Eakes was not just trying to make a loan; he and McGrady were eager to help Kennedy fulfill a philosophical vision, something he had not found in talks with conventional lenders. With a $400,000 loan from Englewood, NOC went from 35 percent worker owned to majority ownership within a year. In the summer of 1988, NOC became something of a showplace when Self-Help conducted another of its conferences on the grounds of the outdoor center's headquarters on the banks of the French Broad River. The conversion was finally completed in 1990.

Meanwhile, Wright and others were deep into helping Guilford College with a difficult problem. A donor had left the college a controlling interest in an aging hosiery mill, and Guilford's trustees were worried that their "gift" might disappear if the business failed. The hosiery firm was being run by the widow of the company president, who wanted to save the business. To her, worker ownership sounded like a good idea. James Newlin, the college's chief financial officer, had known Eakes since the first worker-owned conference in 1982 and later became a member of the board of directors for the Ventures Fund.

Newlin solicited Self-Help for assistance in arranging worker ownership of the hosiery mill, while the credit union issued a $75,000 loan for use as working capital during the transition. An experienced manager, a man who was a turnaround specialist from Burlington Industries, once the world's largest textile operation, was brought in while Self-Help staff began training workers on the particulars of the new ownership, produced business plans, and prepared financial projections.

The worker training, called "technical assistance," was an expensive service, but Eakes found some foundations and others willing to help pay for it. Nonetheless, it was a serious drain on resources, and after more than five years of promoting the concept of worker-owned businesses Eakes and others were beginning to question whether workplace democracy really was the future of Self-Help. Their doubts were underscored by the continuing struggle of the target businesses to reach profitability, even after heavy investments of time and talent.

The struggle and expense of incubating worker-owned enterprises provoked hours of debate at weekly staff meetings. The reports were not encouraging. Successes were few. Tim Bazemore's sewing company in Windsor was doing well, but it had a rare leader at the helm. Board member Susan Fowler began to think her own worker-owned home-building company was just an aberration. And she knew the downside as well. Some of those who joined her company were not interested in becoming worker-owners, a requirement if they stayed with the company longer than six months. They left to start their own businesses. Alamance Knitting required constant attention, and Thad Moore confessed he just did not know the business well enough to be effective.

"We had everything working against us," remembered Schall, a tall, quiet, and thoughtful guy with an even temper and dry wit. "We had labor forces that were semi- or unskilled, no management experience, industries failing, no investment capital, and no true equity to invest. And we had no idea what the hell we were doing."

Moreover, it seemed like Self-Help was bent on creating demand for a business model that just did not fit the region's culture. The Mondragón model, so admired by Self-Help, had been developed in Spanish provinces where cooperatives had been part of the culture for generations. Americans were more familiar with the bootstraps story of Horatio Alger. "We couldn't keep plowing our own free counseling into a larger and larger group of businesses and we didn't see any demand for that," said Schall. "We were having to create the demand." The Alamance hosiery plant alone consumed $40,000 to $50,000 in staff time and money, and the result was thirteen low-wage jobs.[11]

A 1988 study of Self-Help commissioned by the Ford Foundation found that "the center has learned that worker education is important at a point when the company is profitable. Partly, the company needs to have cash to pay for the assistance, but more importantly, it is difficult for workers to concentrate on governance issues when the company is fighting for survival and cannot implement the workplace changes often desired by the workers."[12]

Years later, Eakes recalled that Self-Help had reached a "crisis of mission" and faced the question of making a difference or remaining pure. "We had pretty substantial conflict inside the organization on whether we should abandon the cooperative, one-person, one-vote structure and move to [supporting] minority-owned businesses as a method of helping, particularly, families of color and communities of color. The more liberal purists among us were saying, 'Why do we want to create black capitalism? What good is that?' We were young and quite certain."

Katharine McKee saw something more. She came from a world of big thinkers with broad visions, and as Self-Help grew it was developing far more resources than could be used effectively with worker-owned businesses. "Here we have all this capacity, great talent, good connections in the state and building a base of financial resources where we were pushing a lot of strings," she said. "Some things were working modestly, but we were or had more organization than that mission needed, and it had some challenges to it."[13]

What they all knew was that African American households had one-tenth of the wealth of white households, and 60 percent had no financial resources and were living from one paycheck to the next or were in debt. Many of the people Self-Help was recruiting to join worker-owned enterprises simply did not have the capacity to start a business. Said Eakes, "We could either be relevant as a civil rights organization that would be relevant in the black neighborhoods where we were working, or we could be true to our cooperative one-person, one-vote philosophy [in worker-owned businesses], but we couldn't easily merge those two together as a sole strategy."

The internal debate produced a realization that worker-owned business was just one strategy, but not the only one, and others might be useful to improving the disadvantaged. "Even now," Eakes said, "I will hear someone in a heated discussion say, 'Well, what are we? Are we a civil rights organization, or are we an economic development, community development organization?' The truth is, we have always been both."

Out of the debate came a resolution: "We said we are not going to choose one thing that is the be all and end all," said Eakes. "We are going to recognize that life is more complicated than that." First, Self-Help would pursue its civil rights mission, whether it made economic sense or not, and pay for it from other operations. Second, it would begin to focus on community development using its financial leverage. Third, it would expand into for-profit ventures as long as these efforts did not negatively affect either of the first two objectives. "So if we are working and it is really making a difference and an impact in the very low-income communities, then that is pretty good. It doesn't have to be a worker co-op and a specific product that will change the world, like LED lighting. It doesn't have to be everything in every single project. That sounds silly now, but it was pretty watershed."

Some years later, Eakes summed it up this way: "I have a need to make a difference that is greater than my need to be pure. When I am on my deathbed, I am going to want to know, Did I make a difference? It is not, Did I stay true to some ideology that I thought was the perfect way? What we were doing wasn't working, but I am so stubborn so I wanted it to work. It took us a while to go through that."[14]

The decision did not sit well with some of those who had been with Eakes from the beginning. Wes Hare and his wife, the activists who had organized Twin Streams and participated in the worker education at the Alamance sock plant, threw themselves into other political issues and moved to Texas. Frank Adams, the community organizer who had asked Eakes to talk to the Texfi workers in New Bern back in 1980, drifted away from the circle, deeply disappointed that worker-owned projects did not occupy a larger share of the program portfolio. A few years later, Adams wrote an article about the success of Tim Bazemore's sewing company as a worker-owned organization. He didn't mention the participation of Eakes or anyone from Self-Help.[15]

The shift in emphasis did not bother Sister Carol Coston. She had put her reputation on the line for Self-Help and had raised hundreds of thousands of dollars in credit union deposits. "It made sense to me," she said years later. At the same time that Self-Help was reconsidering its future, Coston's own belief in worker-owned businesses was growing thin. She had visited Mondragon in Spain, as well as twenty or thirty other hot spots for worker ownership in the United States. The culture was not thriving in this country. "In America, it was very hard to shift to, and appreciate, shared leadership. I know that some women would say I loved worker owned and being our own bosses, but the reality is you had to have people of different skills to hold the whole thing together."[16]

CHAPTER FIVE

Innovation

The Ford Foundation's examination of Self-Help in 1988 found that there was no wavering in its commitment to economic equality to women, people of color, or the low-income folk in the rural reaches of North Carolina. But how was that to be achieved? Few doubted that the outcome would be creative. As one person told the Ford representative, "I don't wake up in the morning and worry about whether the Center for Community Self-Help is doing something innovative."[1]

There had been a "ready, fire, aim" quality to some of the early work, recalled Thad Moore, who had been with Eakes from the start. Projects were often massaged after the fact. Bill Bynum, another early hire, remembered leaving a meeting where he heard Eakes make untested promises. He told his boss, "I don't remember us talking about that. And he would say, 'We'll figure it out.' And inevitably we did. We were smart enough and crazy enough to run through walls and work all hours to make things happen. That confidence and persistence gave us a lot of ability to push forward and build what we were able to build."

With each effort, the staff learned lessons that got folded into the next opportunity. A source of capital was needed, so a regulated financial institution, the credit union, was created. Do not invest in teller windows; borrow them from someone else. Management for worker-owned projects did not naturally rise from the ranks, so outside managers were recruited. Each step forward brought something new to the equation. According to the Ford Foundation study, "The most constant characteristics of the center are growth, adaptation, and change."

There was an adventuresome spirit about Self-Help. Ideas considered impossible were those that were thought to be the most worthwhile. Eakes had read that effective organizations needed outrageous ideas as well as the capacity to know when to discard those that did not work. "I sort of flip-flop between the two," he later explained, illustrating the point with a favorite mechanical metaphor. "I think of a car. You need both a gas pedal and a brake, but you don't want to have both floored at the same time. You rotate between the two."

Said Wright, "There was opportunism in a good way." At the same time, "It would drive some of the staff crazy."[2]

This was not a groping about for renewed purpose within an organization threatened by failure. Self-Help had a track record. By the end of 1987, a little more than three years after it opened, the credit union had accumulated assets of $7.6 million and ranked thirty-first among the 184 credit unions in North Carolina. It had made loans to nearly two dozen cooperatives and worker-owned enterprises around the state. More than three hundred people had jobs that might have otherwise gone to some other country. Three-quarters of these workers were women, of whom half were African Americans. Most of the jobs were in rural areas bypassed by economic development. More recently, about one hundred low-income families were in their own homes and paying regularly on modest mortgages tailored to their situation.

Self-Help's most recent achievement was designation by the N.C. General Assembly in 1987 as the nation's first statewide community development bank, a description rolled into broader legislation on rural development. The handle carried no immediate practical benefits but gave legitimacy to a fledgling community development operation barely known outside of the activist community.

The only thing close to what the crowd on East Chapel Hill Street was trying to do was in Chicago, the home of South Shore Bank (later ShoreBank).

It had been organized about fifteen years earlier by community activists to halt the deterioration of a once-prosperous neighborhood called South Shore. An energized knot of workers, some of whom had banking experience, raised the capital to purchase a commercial bank that had given up on the neighborhood. They refocused the institution and started using its lending power to rehabilitate apartments, energize small businesses, and, according to one of its founders, "restore South Shore's competitiveness by rebuilding the market forces disinvestment had destroyed."[3] The bank's capital came from many of the same sources that Self-Help had tapped—foundations, church groups, and supporters sympathetic to its mission. In ten years, South Shore Bank raised $20 million in "outside" investment and had put it back into the community through commercial and real estate lending.

South Shore's success was all the rage in urban studies classrooms such as the one Wright sat in during graduate school. A few years later, when she and Eakes and their colleagues were beginning to reshuffle the priorities at Self-Help, South Shore was working with a foundation to replicate its success in a twenty-one-county area of southwestern Arkansas, the home of an energetic governor named Bill Clinton. Lawyers were just finishing the organization of the Southern Development Bancorporation when Eakes drafted in 1988 what he titled the "Center for Community Self-Help 'Development Bank' Concept Paper." It outlined Self-Help's intentions.

The development bank—presented only as a concept since a credit union was legally prevented from calling itself a bank—would be organized around three related entities: the nonprofit credit union and its insured deposits; the Self-Help Ventures Fund, which would handle riskier investments; and Englewood Investment Corporation for large worker-owned projects. The three would invest resources in communities all across the state. The paper outlined three major initiatives: strengthening locally owned small businesses "that contribute to the preservation and diversification of a community's economic base"; improving and assisting local community development corporations, including small credit unions; and increasing "access of low- and moderate-income families to affordable rental housing and home-ownership opportunities."[4]

Katharine McKee helped shape this new direction after she and Eakes attended a gathering of community development thinkers in Arkansas that was organized by Governor Clinton. It pivoted around discussions by those from South Shore and brought together the best minds in rural economic development. After attending this gathering, McKee and Eakes returned with new energy for expanding the reach of Self-Help in North Carolina.

Before coming south with her husband, David McGrady, McKee had worked in the Ford Foundation's New York office on a strategy for dealing with rural poverty in America, perhaps even using some of the initiatives Ford had funded elsewhere in the world, such as Africa. Her part was looking for solutions to unemployment and economic justice, which proved a convenient way to reconnect with Bonnie Wright and Martin Eakes.

Ford's funding strategy was to pick bright leaders, and then back them for a long time. McKee guided some Ford money to Self-Help before leaving New York for Durham and jobs at Self-Help. While her husband dove into commercial lending, McKee focused on policies and often huddled with Eakes on new directions.

Fueled by the discussions in Arkansas and nudged forward by the internal debate over moving beyond worker-owned businesses, new ideas flew around the staff meetings at Self-Help like so many disturbed bats. There was talk about finding a small bank to purchase or moving the lending into a savings and loan. The discussion always returned to the member-owned structure of the credit union, although it was the least well equipped to handle commercial lending. Eakes had made some headway with federal examiners and had successfully lobbied against regulations that would have brought Self-Help's commercial lending to an end. Nonetheless, it seemed that each examination turned into a wrestling match with examiners, most of whom had never seen loans like those in Self-Help's portfolio.

In addition to consideration of a broader mission, the staff also talked about changing Self-Help's name. South Shore Bank had started out as the Illinois Neighborhood Development Corporation. The Center for Community Self-Help was now simply Self-Help to most people, even though it sounded a bit strange to those in the financial world. (When the name was chosen in the late 1970s, Self-Help's organizers were more concerned about how they were going to save the world than the name on the door.)

"I think we were pigeonholed," said McGrady. "Because of our name we would always be viewed as a soft, lefty, fuzzy-thinking type. It took a while for the industry to accept the fact that we could be good negotiators, that we could manage risk, that we were really pretty competent and sharp folks." (The creation of Englewood was an attempt at an end run.)

Nevertheless, Eakes had carried this banner for years and was attached to it. This was not just business; it was a cause. "[Kate McKee] wanted us to be more professional," Eakes said, "and I wanted us to be more activist and wear the mission on our sleeve. She was arguing that if we had a more nondescript name we would be able to raise more money. She might have been right."[5]

"We had endless discussions about it," McKee recalled. "What the heck does Center for Community Self-Help mean? The early founders felt very strongly about it, so the rest of us just gave up."

Complicating the discussion regarding the name was the growing disenchantment with worker-owned businesses. "Initially, Self-Help kind of spoke to the worker-ownership ethic," she said. "I think maybe emotionally it was a big shift to give that up, and then go to something that sounded more technocratic at the same time. Self-Help, for the early founders, kind of signaled the specific ideals that this was coming from, the cooperative economy."[6]

After all this, and even more, the staff finally arrived at what Eakes called "a grand compromise." Self-Help's new mission blended the interests of those dedicated to worker-owned businesses and cooperatives with those pushing for the organization to move into a broader field of work.

Recalled Eakes, "We said we were not going to choose one thing that is the be all and end all. We are going to recognize that life is more complicated than that. In these three categories, we are going to have a set of activities that we were willing to cross-subsidize."

Eakes began using the metaphor of a bicycle to explain Self-Help. "An organization like Self-Help is a bicycle where the front wheel is its mission, it is what comes first. It is what changes the direction of the bike. The rear wheel is the financial stability and business activity that give us balance. If we had only one wheel, or looked like circus bicycles that had one huge front wheel and a tiny wheel in the back, we would have fallen off in the ditch."

What Self-Help had succeeded in doing was joining a charity with a market-driven institution. By themselves, each had limited options. Together, they could do much, much more. "We needed to have balance between mission and financial stability so that when we promise a community we can help them, we can actually deliver," Eakes said. "Too much reliance on one or the other would lead to failure."

It happened that the broadening of the Self-Help mission dovetailed with a new state initiative led by Lieutenant Governor Robert B. Jordan III. He came out of the Democratic Party's moderate wing and found himself the head of the party when Republican Jim Martin was elected governor in

1984. Jordan was from the rural hamlet of Mount Gilead, about fifty miles south of Greensboro, where he ran a family-owned lumber company that provided financial stability for much of the surrounding area. He saw economic development blossoming in the state's cities, with new enterprises flocking to urban areas, while rural communities were struggling.

Jordan steered a bill through the 1987 session to create the N.C. Rural Economic Development Center, or the Rural Center as it came to be called, and to fund it with a hefty appropriation. The proposed center had all the earmarks of laying planks in the political platform Jordan was building for the 1988 election, when he planned to oppose Governor Martin, who was expected to run for reelection.

Up to this point, Eakes had mostly left legislative lobbying to others, but the lieutenant governor's interest in helping rural North Carolina attracted his attention. Working with Billy Ray Hall, who would become the Rural Center's director, Eakes arranged for Self-Help to be endorsed as a statewide community development bank in part of the Rural Center's legislation.

The plans for the Rural Center were coming together at about the time that Eakes was being nudged by George H. Esser, Jr., a Self-Help board member, to seek a state appropriation to prime the pump for requests of more multi-million-dollar PRIs from the Ford Foundation and others. Esser knew this game well. He had run the North Carolina Fund, a creative nongovernmental antipoverty effort in the 1960s. Created by Governor Terry Sanford, the fund successfully combined grants from the Ford Foundation and North Carolina foundations to create programs to address poverty, portions of which later became part of Lyndon Johnson's antipoverty program.

With Jordan's initiative gathering momentum, Eakes persuaded state representative H. M. Michaux Jr., of Durham, a leader in the legislature's Black Caucus, to seek a $2 million appropriation as loan-loss reserves for economic development lending in minority communities. In the summer of 1988, just before the state funds were approved, Self-Help submitted a request for a $3 million PRI from the Ford Foundation. A $2.5 million request was already at the MacArthur Foundation. With money from the state and the foundations, Eakes was talking about Self-Help becoming a $50 million development bank almost overnight. It had only been a few years since Eakes's friends swallowed hard when he had announced a $10 million goal.

Eakes later called the appropriation "a random stroke of luck. It was purely being at the right place at the right time. Jordan was running for governor, and he wanted to have an appropriation to mean something to the black establishment."[7]

The legislation passed, but only after it was bundled with a separate measure that extended a million dollars in aid to African American credit unions and $500,000 to support community development corporations. Another $250,000 was approved for support of the N.C. Institute for Minority Economic Development, a relatively new outfit funded by the Z. Smith Reynolds Foundation. It was created to assist minorities and women running small businesses. Some of its clients had commercial loans from the Self-Help Credit Union.

The legislative process reminded Eakes why political waters could be treacherous. Before the final vote on the bills, one legislator, a Democrat, called Eakes into his office and told him the cost of his vote was approval of a Self-Help loan for a constituent. Eakes refused to make a deal and said that he'd rather withdraw from the bill than accept those terms. Eakes added that when he withdrew his support, he would publicly announce why. The legislator dropped his objections, and the bill passed on schedule.

Eakes's negotiating was not over. Next, he had to deal with the Republicans in the governor's office, who refused to release the appropriation. "[Governor Martin's] view was that anything that comes with Mickey Michaux and Bob Jordan sponsoring it has to be our opponents. I said, 'Look, we are just trying to do good,'" Eakes said.

Within a year, that $2 million in reserves was backing loans for thirty businesses, and their accounts were current. The range of opportunities appeared to be endless. Eakes spoke at one meeting of the N.C. Association of Minority Businesses and left with business cards from twenty-five people seeking upward of $10 million in lending. His best guess was that at least $1.5 million of the requests would produce good business deals.

"Despite the stereotype that rural business and businesses owned by women and entrepreneurs of color couldn't make it," Eakes said, "we had made these loans, and they were all doing great. That was the beginning of a new wave of economic development in North Carolina."

Self-Help collaborated with the Rural Center on other dimensions of economic development. The credit union became something of an in-house financial services center for the Rural Center and processed loans for an experiment at microlending. The credit union also serviced loans for farmers under a U.S. Department of Agriculture program. Bill Bynum left Self-Help to manage that program while Eakes did the legal work to organize a support center to assist African American credit unions.

Lenwood Long, a former member of the Self-Help board of directors, worked at the Rural Center. He spent many days on the road with Eakes as they visited African American credit unions building trust, mending fences, and helping credit union managers learn how to make small business loans. "These credit unions could make loans, and then use the deposits of [the] Rural Center as security, so when regulators came in they saw a shared secured loan, not a business loan," Long said.[8]

Some of these African American institutions had been around since before World War II. The first had been organized in the 1920s, but it did not survive the Great Depression. For African Americans living in the segregated South, these community credit unions were usually the only sympathetic lending institutions around. Local banks were not interested in offering home mortgages to African Americans whose neighborhoods were redlined and placed off limits or saddled with low loan amounts. Money meant power, and successful African American businesses and economic independence were considered a threat to the status quo. It was said that at one time, North Carolina had more African American credit unions than any other state, the result of the organizing skill of African American agricultural extension agents who worked with black farmers like Tim Bazemore out in Windsor, where St. Luke Credit Union had been in business since 1944.

By the 1980s, the number of African American credit unions had dwindled to a dozen or so, and almost all of them were struggling. Some suffered from weak management that had made bad lending decisions. Others had systems that were inadequate to meet the demands of regulators, while others were simply underfunded and incapable of providing any meaningful service to their communities. Business lending was virtually unheard of, except for the insider deals that some had made.

At first, the leaders of these credit unions were wary, if not downright hostile, to Eakes and Self-Help. The white establishment had never given them a second thought. In the early 1980s, the N.C. Credit Union League, the state trade association, had turned down federal assistance, available through the U.S. Department of Agriculture, that could have helped these rural credit unions cope with change. Further, there was jealousy over Self-Help's apparent ready access to capital, from the state and from foundations and institutional depositors.

Indeed, the contrast was striking. At the end of 1989, Self-Help Credit Union had assets of nearly $20 million and 1,412 members. St. Luke Credit Union, which was organized a decade before Martin Eakes was born, had assets of about $6 million and 1,688 members. People with graduate degrees ran Self-Help; James Gilliam, who chaired the St. Luke board of directors, operated a funeral home.

As Eakes made the circuit with Lenwood Long from the Rural Center, he began making friends and opening doors, bridging the gap between the African American credit unions and the credit union league where training programs and support were available. Word spread about the staff support from Self-Help that had enabled a troubled institution in Fayetteville to remain in business.

Eakes won over Gilliam at St. Luke after Gilliam discovered that regulators treated him differently when this bright young lawyer with the fiery red hair was seated at his side. Long said some years later he was sympathetic to one beleaguered examiner who was the object of Eakes's wrath over treatment he had visited on a credit union in another North Carolina town. "Martin didn't like what the regulator was saying, and he said, 'One of the problems is that you are just a redneck.' I felt sorry for the guy. Martin would go off. He wasn't scared of them."

Word began to get around that Eakes was "genuine," as Long put it. Andrea Harris, Eakes's ally at the newly organized N.C. Institute for Minority Economic Development, said stories of Eakes's advocacy changed attitudes. "How are you going to be suspect of somebody who is trying to push for change for you in your neighborhood, who clearly does not have to do this?" she said. He was "being there and taking leadership on those issues that were important to them."[9] In time, some of these credit unions began forwarding customers they could not serve to Self-Help.

Collaboration with the Rural Center raised Self-Help's profile elsewhere. Kate McKee was a board member at the Rural Center, where she met and worked with representatives from the top tier of the state's banks and corporations. A crowd that, in its early days, had once purposely kept a low profile out of fear that its worker-ownership focus would be misunderstood as communist or socialist or some such, now had a seat at the table where the state's economic development program was being discussed. "It kind of let Self-Help leverage our institutional presence," recalled McKee. "It gave us a platform from which to pivot from our narrow ownership mission to a broader inclusive economic opportunities mission."

The late 1980s was a heady time of vigorous activity. Internally, the operations continued as they had from the beginning, with decisions made collectively at weekly staff meetings. Wright, now a mother of two (a daughter, Carlyn, was born in 1987), managed the credit union. Eakes signed off on everything else.

"Before anything was done of major strategic importance," recalled McGrady, "it was clearly discussed and vetted at the senior staff level. Having said that, it was absolutely clear that Martin had what at a minimum would be characterized as veto rights, if not a final vote. He is a very open and very democratic individual but at the same time he is . . . I don't know if 'in control' is the way to say it, but he is the dominant figure."

The Ford Foundation study had pointed out some growing pains in Eakes's all-for-one, one-for-all style. After nearly ten years, the organization still had no clearly defined levels of management. June Blotnick, who ran the Charlotte office, was never sure to whom she reported. When she left Self-Help in 1990 to become a full-time mother, she got a warm letter from Eakes and a handmade certificate for the credit union's "Lone Wolf Award."

Eakes commissioned a staff study and learned that out of about two dozen employees, most were what the analysts called "visionaries" and "catalysts"—people who liked to dream big ideas and get them started—but only one or two had the temperament and skills to manage and run what was already in place. Not long after the staff study, personnel matters were added to Eakes's list of annual management goals.

Self-Help's pay structure remained very low. Clerical and support staff were paid at the market rate, but none of the professional staff, including Eakes, was paid more than the prevailing average wage in the state, which in the late 1980s was less than $20,000. Dana Smith, from the Asheville office, said he once got a raise from Eakes, who then convinced him to donate all of it back to the credit union as a deposit. "You didn't walk out saying 'he got me again,'" he said. "You walked out feeling good. None of us were making anything. And he was making the least."[10]

The low pay would become a trademark of the organization. For Eakes, it signaled commitment to the mission, much like his surviving on peanuts that summer he worked for the Quakers in South Carolina. He was adamant, said Crawford Crenshaw, Self-Help's first board chair and Eakes's lifelong friend.

"I kept saying, 'you won't be able to hire the best people,'" Crenshaw recalled. "[And he'd say], 'Well, if people are committed to this, I have got the best game in town. If they want to do this because they are committed, this is plenty to live on. If they want to live higher than that, then that is their problem.'"[11]

At the same time, low pay tended to discourage diversity, one of the things Eakes worked to achieve. Young middle- and upper-middle-class whites could stand a few lean years, but it was tough on those without outside resources. Bill Bynum left Self-Help to run the Rural Center's micro lending program, where he was paid more. He was a first-generation college graduate who was still helping with the finances back home and thinking of starting a family. He could not survive on Self-Help pay. "If you had a nest egg and something to fall back on," he said, "it was easier to work at Self-Help."[12]

Nonetheless, Self-Help continued to attract those drawn to Durham by the prospects of a different style of public sector work. As the staff increased in number, Self-Help acquired a building next door, just across the alley from 413 E. Chapel Hill Street. The branch offices, in Charlotte and Asheville, were also continuing to attract investors, and attention. That was especially true in Asheville in 1988, when Beth Maczka, a Davidson College honors graduate and Dana Smith's successor, got a visit from Julian Price, the wealthy scion of a prominent Greensboro family.

Price had recently relocated to Asheville after living for twenty years on the West Coast growing and selling organic vegetables and creating a market for English seaweed fertilizer. He had planned to resettle in New Bern, a picturesque city near the North Carolina coast, but chose Asheville instead after being taken by the beauty of the classic styles of a host of downtown buildings.

Price had a passing acquaintance with Self-Help, having called on Smith once or twice to sit and chat. One day, he walked across the street from his condominium in a building he was overhauling into residences to pay a call at the Self-Help office. He told Maczka that he wanted to open an account and make a deposit. His check was for $100,000. "So I kind of met my quota that quarter," she said.[13]

Over the next few months, Price gathered additional background on Self-Help before he asked Eakes to meet with him in Asheville. He assured him that he would make it worth his while. The two shared common threads in their lives. Both were vegetarians and Greensboro natives, and Price was a Guilford College graduate, the school that had earlier embraced Self-Help's worker-owned initiatives. Eakes's mother was an Asheville native whose family had once run a small rooming house there. Both men had a disdain for creased trousers and shined shoes. Price showed up wearing frayed blue jeans, old tennis shoes, and socks that Eakes remembered as being "a little ratty." Over breakfast, Price asked Eakes what it would take for Self-Help to establish a real presence in western North Carolina.

The Asheville office had struggled to make a difference, and the experience was not without its troubles. Smith had made some headway, but he had been a handful to manage, often heading off on his own. When he left to pursue other work, Eakes gave him one of his handmade certificates à la Blotnick. This one was the "John Wayne Award." Smith still has it hanging in his office. Maczka arrived with a more cooperative skill set.

Self-Help's western North Carolina office was gaining some footing by 1991, when Price put his question to Eakes. Without hesitating, Eakes said that he needed a reserve fund of $1 million. Price reached into the back pocket of his worn-out jeans, pulled out his checkbook, and wrote a check for a million dollars.

Eakes loves to tell this story, especially to people who ask for money on a regular basis. "I folded up [the check] and put it in my pocket and was riding down the mountain on my way back to Durham, and what do you think I was asking myself? People say you ask if the check is any good. No, the question I was asking the whole way back was why didn't I ask him for $2 million."

With Price's money in the bank, Self-Help became a highly visible presence in the city after the purchase and renovation of an eight-story, Art Deco–style downtown office building that dated to 1929. The Public Service Building had once been the headquarters for a gas utility. The location evolved into general office use, but over the years, as Asheville's downtown declined, the building lost its tenants as the dentists, insurance agents, and the like moved to the suburbs.

The building was clad in dark red brick highlighted by Romanesque and Spanish multicolored terra-cotta designs at the base. Gargoyles perched at the roofline. The windows above the south entrance on Patton Avenue offered an unbroken vista to Mount Pisgah on the far horizon. The north entrance was half a story higher and opened onto Wall Street, just a few doors down from the stairway up to the Self-Help offices.

Years of neglect, shattered windows, and forlorn emptiness had dulled the building's beauty except for admirers like Eakes, who could study its distinctive features from the windows of the Self-Help office. A fellow staffer who accompanied him on trips to Asheville remembered thinking, "That sucker is going to figure out a way to buy that building." He did so as soon as possible and immediately asked Durham architect Eddie Belk to take a look at it. Belk returned to tell Eakes, "I have got to help make this work."

Belk was developing a specialty in historic buildings. He returned to Eakes with documentation for historic tax credits and a remodeling plan that Eakes fiddled with constantly. Classic tile work and interior treatments were salvaged, but interior walls were removed to create larger offices with windows that opened to the mountain air. Belk designed common space that could be shared by the tenants on each floor.

Eakes was recycling a building as well as an idea. The building opened in September 1992 as the western base for Self-Help and a home for nonprofits struggling to make rent payments in the open market, often in less than desirable space. Rent was high enough to cover the mortgage at prices that organizations with limited funds could afford. Workers might not enjoy top salaries, but their offices would have a million-dollar view of the mountains.

The arrangement was not that different from the early days on 413 E. Chapel Hill Street. "We saw the advantages to having space where you could put people near one another who had similar goals, similar businesses," said David McGrady. "There is a lot of synergy to be drawn by proximity, sort of like an early social network."[14]

The NAACP moved its offices to the Self-Help building, as did agencies involved in affordable housing and domestic violence. A small firm that restored paintings favored a dark, windowless space that was literally under the pavement of Wall Street. Belk finally convinced Eakes that struggling young architects qualified as nonprofits and should be admitted.

The partnership with Price came on the cusp of the revival of downtown Asheville, a city with more distinctive aging buildings per block than any other in the state. Price created his own business, Public Interest Projects, and he invested $9 million in the rehabilitation and renovation of dozens of properties. Wall Street became a pedestrian mall lined with shops and restaurants, including a vegetarian eatery, the Laughing Seed, to satisfy the tastes of Price and Eakes.

"This was a critical project in reestablishing downtown Asheville," Eakes said after many years and many more buildings as centers for nonprofits. "That whole area was one of the first to come back. I think we played a real role there. It was just spectacular."

CHAPTER SIX

An "Aha" Moment

After Abdul Rasheed was elected chair of the Self-Help board in 1986, there was no question in his mind that mortgage lending was the best way for Self-Help to accomplish its goal of extending economic equity to those on the margins of society's financial marketplace.

Rasheed came out of the state's Legal Aid network, where he was a community organizer. Before that, he had helped organize a Black Muslim school near Greensboro and even worked for a time with Louis Farrakhan in Chicago before returning to North Carolina to attend graduate school. He would later found and lead for twenty years the N.C. Community Development Initiative, which directed nearly $500 million in development funds into poor communities.[1]

Rasheed believed that Self-Help's best chance at lifting working people out of poverty was to help them become homeowners so they could build equity that could be used for college tuition or starting a business. This was particularly true for African Americans, who had been routinely denied financial services available to others.

"[Banks] were saying poor people can't own a home," Rasheed recalled. "That is ridiculous. Coming out of a poor black family myself, I knew that was one of the aspirations. When those families were able to save up enough money, or create a relationship with the boss that he would agree to sell some raggedy house or land, that was a major goal. They were aspiring to own their own home. The fear was of not having somewhere to live—that was built into me as a child and as a young man."

Mortgage lending also appealed to Andrea Harris, another of Eakes's confidants. A trim and feisty African American woman, she worked on developing minority-owned enterprises in the state commerce department before becoming the first director of the N.C. Institute for Minority Economic Development in 1986. Self-Help needed more meat on the table if it was ever to reach her people, she told Eakes. "If you go in there talking about worker-owned, they are going to call us communist, socialist, everything there is. It takes so much more energy. So let's put some more energy over here on the home ownership side. It's easy to understand."[2]

Staff member Bill Bynum was certainly of that frame of mind, especially after his work with Service Printing Company, a worker-owned project that never recovered from a destructive fire. With more money in the credit union than there were worker-owned projects to finance, Self-Help had to put that money to use somewhere.

"Home ownership was a natural," Bynum said. He had been raised in a mobile home in rural Chatham County, south of Chapel Hill. His family moved from time to time with little hope of permanence. Once the credit union began making home mortgages, his family got a Self-Help mortgage and bought a home of their own. "This was an asset my family could fall back on. Here is an organization trying to put people on more stable footing. Home ownership was an important tool to have at our disposal."[3]

As talk of Self-Help's future was under way in Durham, June Blotnick, in the Charlotte office, announced that Self-Help Credit Union was interested in financing housing cooperatives (one had been organized in Durham with support from Self-Help), rehabilitating substandard housing, and making home mortgages. A few months later, she was in a meeting at the Charlotte Housing Authority when she learned that the agency was having trouble securing bank participation in a program for prospective homebuyers called Turnkey Three. The city had developed two of these federally subsidized neighborhoods that allowed residents to set aside a portion of the rent to be used later as a down payment on the house they occupied. The problem was that banks were not interested in writing mortgages for relatively small amounts—usually $20,000 or less—nor could most prospective borrowers afford the terms they were offered.[4]

Blotnick had attended the worker-owned conference at Guilford College with the workers from the sock plant in Burlington, where one speaker had advised entrepreneurs of all stripes to look for opportunities in the open spaces between the feet of the commercial elephants. For Blotnick, home lending was the space that would allow the credit union to take its first steps in developing a mortgage business and demonstrate that low- and moderate-income borrowers were worth the risk.

Blotnick also saw it as a way to demonstrate to a growing number of Self-Help's depositors in Charlotte—who had put in more than $600,000 in her first year of work—that their money was being used to improve life in the Charlotte community. As soon as she reached her goal of $1 million, she opened a bona fide office. It was a modest space near downtown, and up a flight of stairs, but at least she was no longer working out of the spare room in her home.

The Turnkey Three housing program, designed to assist low-income, first-time homeowners, fit nicely into Self-Help's broader mission of community development and economic outreach. Most program participants were single mothers, of whom a majority were African Americans. They were all employed, albeit at low-wage jobs. As might be expected, commercial banks had little interest in doing business with such marginal customers. The loan applications explained why. In the summer of 1986, thirty-two families had completed applications for home loans. However, many could not meet the federal debt-to-income guidelines. Despite good collateral, steady employment, and good rental payment histories, even a motivated lender like Self-Help could approve only one-third of the applications.[5]

According to Robert Schall, "We didn't bet the farm. We did it very organically. We learned little bits at a time. We made four loans, and we learned from them. And then we learned from the next four."[6]

Self-Help was pushing against more than a half century of institutional bias and racial discrimination as it began its home lending. Federal laws and local ordinances prohibiting discrimination in lending had been on the books for years. Congress passed the Fair Housing Act in 1968, and, in 1977, it followed with the Community Reinvestment Act, which required lenders to be responsive to their entire market, not just those who posed no risk for their business. Nonetheless, racial discrimination remained alive and well within the financial system in the 1980s.

The *Atlanta Journal-Constitution* reported in 1988 that whites in Atlanta, a city that took pride in its progress in race relations, were five times more likely to get a home loan than blacks with the same income. A few years later, research in Boston found that African Americans were two to three times more likely than whites to have loan applications denied. Other newspaper reports of home lending records showed that in New York City, the first in the nation with a fair housing law, entire neighborhoods were placed off limits—redlined by bankers—preventing African Americans from becoming homeowners.[7]

Much of the discrimination was institutional and dated to the 1920s, when housing segregation was the norm and was unabashedly reinforced by real estate agents and banks. One Depression-era program designed to stem the tide of mortgage defaults included a rating system that gave high-income, all-white neighborhoods the highest marks and were shaded in green on local maps. All-black neighborhoods received a D and were highlighted in red. That remained the case in the 1980s.[8]

The Boston study used data newly available under the Home Mortgage Disclosure Act of 1990. In it, the Federal Reserve Bank of Boston reported that minority applicants, on average, had greater debt burdens and weaker credit histories than whites, but even when these differences were taken into account, minorities "are roughly 60 percent more likely to be turned down than whites." Moreover, bank loan officers were more likely to overlook flaws in a credit profile of white applicants. "Whites seem to enjoy a general presumption of creditworthiness that black and Hispanic applicants do not," the report said, and "lenders seem to be more willing to overlook flaws for white applicants than for minority applicants."[9]

The Boston study also confirmed what Self-Help was just beginning to learn from its own lending. The report said a willingness to lend to "imperfect borrowers is justified: historically, residential mortgages have been very safe investments." That appeared to be the case in Atlanta. The newspaper reported that a black-owned bank's lending to its core customers had one of the lowest default rates in the United States for banks its size.

The incremental growth in Self-Help's home lending provided feedback on the process. For example, Self-Help experimented with adjustable rate mortgages, but that did not go well. Borrowers were better able to handle a fixed monthly payment, not one that increased as the market changed without notice. Another important lesson was learning that lenders needed to look beyond the numbers on a credit report. If a prospective borrower had a steady job, good work history, and had been faithful in paying rent, he or she could be just as reliable in making a house payment.

These examples would later become illustrations for Eakes whenever he told Self-Help's story. Once again, he was not just reciting facts pulled from payment records. He knew these customers were the same folk he had known growing up on the outskirts of Greensboro. They were the mothers and fathers of the African American boys who had played in pickup basketball games in the gym in the big barn behind the Eakes home. He came to know the parents of his friends and had pulled his chair up to the dinner table at their homes more than once. They were solid people, and well worth the confidence of a lender, regardless of what the numbers on a loan application said. Deeply etched in his mind was the memory of a childhood mate, an African American friend of his own age with equally brilliant promise who had lost his life in a senseless shooting on a neighborhood playground. Eakes vowed at the time of his friend's death that he would spend his life working for the two of them.

While lending to low- and moderate-income borrowers was not easy, the difference between Self-Help and conventional lenders was that Self-Help looked for ways to overcome challenges. For example, after regulators began flagging the credit union's home loans that were sixty days in arrears, Self-Help created a reserve fund to assist borrowers who missed payments because of some unexpected claim that had upset their finances. Borrowers could tap this fund, for up to ninety days, to cover a missed payment, and then repay it over time. The fund also helped backstop lending to borrowers whose financial profiles did not meet more restrictive home lending requirements that went into effect during the Reagan years.

By the fall of 1988, the credit union had raised $200,000 toward a goal of $1 million for this reserve fund. NCNB (later Bank of America) provided a $50,000 grant. First Union National Bank put $25,000 into the fund along with a $25,000 interest-free deposit in the credit union. Another $100,000 came from the Ford Foundation. In its first year, the credit union made loans to about sixty minority low-income borrowers who had been denied loans elsewhere. Those who took advantage of the reserve fund were able to keep from having their homes, and their credit histories, put in jeopardy. Over time, these borrowers recovered. A few defaulted, and the loans went into foreclosure, but every dollar loaned was recovered after collateral was liquidated.

Though the number of home loans grew with each season, mortgage lending remained a modest affair. The application process was a cobbled-together mix of information compiled in loan application documents borrowed from other lenders, personal interviews, and a review of borrowers measured on the so-called three Cs of lending—capacity to pay, collateral, and credit worthiness. That is what Lori Jones-Gibbs discovered when she came to work at Self-Help to manage the credit union's mortgage lending.

Jones-Gibbs and her husband, an accountant who was working on a law degree, moved to Durham in 1988. Her academic background was in urban planning, but she had some experience with mortgages. After more than one of her friends told her Self-Help was looking for someone to run their lending program, she contacted Eakes. A week later, she was hired. One of the first things she asked for was a copy of the credit union's underwriting guidelines.

"Martin looked at me and said, 'You will have to create them,'" she recalled. "I said, 'You mean we have no guidelines.'"[10] Self-Help was making what the industry called "character loans," where a lending officer's gut instinct could carry as much weight as anything else, particularly if a customer's record showed a history of making good on other bills and obligations. It was not unusual at that time for each lender to have its own lending standards. The automation of loan applications was still years away, and the financial industry's ubiquitous "credit score" had yet to be created.

Schall remembered the early mortgage applications: "We would accept people who didn't meet every one of the criteria, but if they didn't meet them we looked to find out why. If it didn't seem a fairly risky reason, then we would make the loan."[11]

Jones-Gibbs took what she had learned in her training in conventional banking and mortgage underwriting and tailored it to suit Self-Help's mission. Generally speaking, if a client's record of payments for the necessities of life—rent, utilities, or a car loan, for example—were current, without any record of interruptions, and if rental payments were steady and as much or more than the mortgage payment, then that was good enough. Eakes was unshakable in his belief that if given the chance to own homes, poor people would do whatever was required to stay current on their payments.

Under Jones-Gibbs, Self-Help began working with public agencies, church-sponsored groups, and others to prepare people who had been renters to become homeowners. She believed that people needed to know what they were getting into. Eakes told Jones-Gibbs that she was being too "maternalistic," to which she replied: "I am, but I am very conservative when I get to people not wanting to lose their homes. Most people buy one home and that can create generational wealth, or it can create generational nightmare if they don't do it right. I'd rather be on the more conservative side in order for them to own their homes."

The number of Self-Help mortgages doubled to two hundred in 1989, and the credit union expanded to work with housing programs in Durham and Asheville. If there was ever an "aha" moment in the ambition of Self-Help to extend economic justice to women and African Americans, it was the realization in the late 1980s that home ownership was the most effective way for those living on the fringes of the economy to build wealth. Greater resources meant greater access to education, health care, jobs, and even neighborhood stability. Home lending also looked like a way to extend capital into minority communities more efficiently. Commercial loans, especially for worker-owned businesses, had to be tailored for each application. Mortgage lending could be more easily replicated.

If Self-Help could figure out a way to help single mothers, African Americans, and others long shut out of home ownership by commercial banks, that could change the world.

Self-Help's modest record on home lending was strong enough in 1989 that the N.C. General Assembly set aside $2 million for Self-Help and other credit unions in the state to use as reserves for loans to home borrowers with low and moderate incomes. The legislators in Raleigh liked what Self-Help was selling, especially after Self-Help showed how it used the state appropriation, and leveraged it with money from private sources to create a $50 million affordable home ownership loan pool.[12]

"I can see the one-page fact sheets now," said Bill Bynum. "For every $1 in state money, we'd leverage $20 in private funds for communities and generate these kinds of outcomes. That sold it. Ability to leverage sold it to [a] large degree. Self-Help said we could take $2 million and turn it into $50 million."

"Martin Eakes is an entrepreneur," observed Bob Williams, an economics professor who organized the democratic management courses at Guilford College in the 1980s. "In some sense, he doesn't fit, and that is where his genius comes from. If things don't work out, he wants to figure out how to make them work."[13]

Sociologist Melvin L. Oliver would later quantify home ownership as the keystone for asset building among African Americans in his landmark 1995 study titled *Black Wealth/White Wealth*. Martin Eakes had discovered that half a decade earlier making loans to first-time homeowners in Charlotte, Asheville, and Durham.[14]

CHAPTER SEVEN

"We Did Not Have to Be Geniuses"

On the morning of July 15, 1993, President Bill Clinton announced a national initiative for community development lending. Martin Eakes was there, seated among the trees on the north lawn of the White House along with NationsBank CEO Hugh L. McColl, Jr., Ronald Grzywinski from ShoreBank, and a host of others. Under broken clouds in the summer sky, with gusts of wind rippling the notes of the speechmakers, President Clinton praised Self-Help and ShoreBank for leading the way.

Eakes had arrived in Washington, D.C., driving a van full of friends from North Carolina. Riding with him were Tim Bazemore and some of Bazemore's employees at Workers' Owned Sewing Company. Bazemore was one of three entrepreneurs chosen to speak about how nontraditional financial institutions had made loans to enterprises like his that most banks ignored. Bazemore opened the session following his introduction by Vice President Al Gore.

Standing before an array of dignitaries, Bazemore seized the moment. He had been instructed to talk for about two minutes, but he rolled on for eight. In his rough country brogue, he spoke about bankers who had not only turned him down for a loan but had even refused him a checking account. Loans and technical assistance from Self-Help had saved his business. Later that morning, as people mingled on the grounds, Eakes found McColl and Bazemore in conversation and teased McColl about poaching his customer. McColl did not deny it years later. "I wouldn't have been much of a banker if I wasn't," he said.[1]

Ten years before this balmy day, Bazemore, Eakes, and about sixty others were on the grounds of Guilford College singing songs and talking about the virtue of worker-owned business. Now, Self-Help was managing assets valued at about $75 million. It had put nearly six hundred families in homes of their own and had loaned $30 million to some nine hundred small businesses and nonprofits in North Carolina. It was a statewide lending institution with offices in Asheville, Charlotte, Greensboro, Durham, and Greenville, deep in eastern North Carolina. The newest regional office, in Greensboro, was in a ten-story, downtown bank building that Self-Help renovated and reopened as affordable office space for nonprofits, just as it had in Asheville.[2]

Self-Help had become a new kind of antipoverty program, one that leaders of other nonprofits did not fully understand or appreciate, especially after Self-Help's success securing millions of dollars in grants from the state legislature. Critics argued that home lending did not do much to aid the desperately poor. But Self-Help did not propose it was the only solution to relieving poverty. It was but one point of attack on the problem.

Self-Help's approach rested easily on the minds of cautious and conservative legislators in Raleigh who monitored the lending programs it subsidized. Eakes approached each member, regardless of his political affiliation, and presented his case, often armed with examples of how Self-Help had touched the lives of constituents in that legislator's district. It may have been a home loan or support to a small business. This crowd liked Eakes's all-American argument that a family home ownership would produce equity that could later be used to start a business, send a child to college, or ease one into retirement.

Self-Help provided evidence of its work in its periodic reports to legislators. There was a young single mother who arrived with a horrendous credit record, but she completed credit counseling, got a steady job, and began rebuilding her credit rating. "She and her son moved into a modest Durham home of their own, financed by a Self-Help mortgage."

In another example, an elderly couple in eastern North Carolina fell behind on mortgage payments because of medical bills and a misunderstanding with a finance company. "Even though they were scrimping on needed food and medicine to make loan payments, they faced the loss of their home. Self-Help refinanced their loan, allowing them to keep their home and have adequate income for necessities."[3]

Eakes shared Self-Help's good relations in Raleigh and was eager to win state support for other credit unions and grants to boost assistance to minority businesses. His bipartisan approach served him well after 1995, when Republicans gained control of the state house. He was sitting outside a Republican leader's office waiting on the outcome of deliberations on a funding measure when he heard through an open door one legislator complain that the Self-Help crowd was nothing but a bunch of hippies. Another responded, "Yeah, but they are doing all this good work and they don't pay themselves anything."[4]

Self-Help's operation remained lean but growing, with more than thirty employees who Eakes still supervised in a loose, collaborative style that defied modern management techniques. Self-Help remained a worker-run enterprise and enjoyed a reputation as "a home for wayward entrepreneurs who want to do good," said Michael D. Calhoun, a former Legal Aid lawyer who would spend most of his professional career as a senior staff member at Self-Help. "Self-Help has been called at times [a place] for bleeding-heart conservatives. One of the running jokes is that people [here] think beauty is a well-designed spreadsheet."[5]

Calhoun was a 1979 UNC Law graduate whose casework with Legal Aid in the early 1980s often brought him in close contact with the Self-Help crowd. He joined Eakes's law firm in 1985 and collaborated with Eakes on a variety of cases before moving to Self-Help in 1992. "I looked long and hard, but I found a place where I could make even less than at Legal Aid," he said.

Mary Mountcastle also joined the staff in 1992, almost ten years after she had met Bonnie Wright in graduate school, when the credit union was so much theory. She was able and experienced in nonprofits and fundraising, but her hiring was a mixed blessing. A great-granddaughter of R. J. Reynolds, Mountcastle and her family controlled the Z. Smith Reynolds and Mary Reynolds Babcock foundations, which suspended support to Self-Help in order to avoid conflicts of interest. Severing ties with Babcock ended an era. Babcock had shaped and sustained Self-Help during the early, bumpy, experimental years. The foundation "had greater impact on the structure and effectiveness of Self-Help's work than any other investor or grantor," Eakes wrote in 1990.[6]

Mountcastle's office was often a first stop for applicants making inquiries about jobs at Self-Help. "We may not be able to pay you what you can earn elsewhere," she told them, "but the level of responsibility and the freedom to be innovative and put your own stamp on things . . . you are not going to be able to do that by being a junior associate in a law firm or in a regular bank."[7]

In 1995, the top annual salary at Self-Help was $34,000, a number set by Eakes, who calculated it based on the median salary in the state. He suppressed the top end and adjusted up pay for the lowest-wage jobs to reach a three-to-one ratio. It was an improvement over the early days when all employees were paid the same, or a subsequent failed experiment to pay according to need. The underlying principle was that "staff should not be making large salaries while trying to end poverty."[8]

Calhoun and Mountcastle arrived as Wright was leaving her job as manager of the credit union. Wright had thrived during the start-up years and was looking for something new, plus she and Martin had two children, with the youngest just entering kindergarten. She launched a career as a consultant with the National Coalition Building Institute, focusing in areas of diversity and conflict resolution.

Eakes continued to hire the person, not to fill a job. When Bryan Hassell showed up in the summer of 1990, fresh from his studies at Oxford University as a Rhodes scholar, he was one of three highly qualified candidates for a single position. Eakes hired all three. Hassell's first assignment was to enroll community-based service organizations in a statewide computer network. The Ford Foundation provided support with Apple, making its computers available at no cost. "I and a couple of other people were like Johnny Appleseeds going around and meeting with nonprofits and saying there is a whole new way of sharing information that could be helpful. In retrospect, it seems funny, considering the way of things that were to come. We got a lot of blank stares and head scratching at the time."[9]

Laura Benedict had joined the staff as a fund-raiser in 1989 but soon developed a lending program to assist operators of child care programs. After the failure of a state-financed effort to train women on welfare to start their own businesses, she detailed a summer intern to survey licensed child care operators about their wants and desires. The answer: business advice and financing. A subsequent mailing offering technical assistance and financing produced a landslide of mail. "One of the learnings we had," she said, "was that the spark must be there. It is really hard to create entrepreneurs."

Most of those who responded to the survey had been turned down by the bankers who "didn't see it as a legitimate business," Benedict said. The response was different at Self-Help, which placed a premium on assisting small businesses and enabling business opportunities for women while at the same time providing a service to working parents. An operator's manual that Benedict's team developed later was translated into Spanish and became part of the licensure process for the state of North Carolina. "It is such an economic development win, win, win, with few minuses," she later recalled.[10] About nineteen hundred children were in child care centers financed by Self-Help by the end of 1994.

Self-Help's mortgage lending was the hot spot. The business was growing each year, but the pace did not satisfy Eakes. He had never considered Self-Help as an end in itself; he wanted it to be a catalyst for change throughout the market. It had begun as a laboratory to test new economic options for the disadvantaged, and home lending was now part of the package. But, if home ownership were to be made available to low- and moderate-income families, at least in any significant numbers, then Self-Help would need a lot of partners to make it happen.

Speaking at a meeting of like-minded lenders in the fall of 1992, Eakes laid out the path of Self-Help's mission. One institution working alone could do good work, he allowed, but "it would be egotistical self-delusion to think that we will ever finish spooning poverty and disadvantage out of a swamp at that pace. We must take our lending learnings and influence large banks and other institutions to play a role in filling the credit gaps for depressed communities."[11]

Armed with Self-Help's record of success, Eakes believed that if he could convince commercial bankers in North Carolina to change their lending requirements by 0.25 percent and open the door of opportunity a tad wider, then the home lending that would result would dwarf anything that Self-Help could do on its own. He packed up his data on Self-Help's lending history and began calling on the heads of North Carolina's banks, not only to pursue a social cause but to tell them about a market of good business that they were ignoring to their own detriment, as well as the economy of the communities they claimed to serve.

North Carolina had allowed statewide banking since early in the nineteenth century. The largest North Carolina institutions—Wachovia Bank and Trust, First Union, and NationsBank (formerly NCNB)—not only had offices from the mountains to the coast, but they were also doing business all across the Southeast. NationsBank moved first into Florida in 1981 and later into Texas. In addition to a wide reach, these banks also had fat balance sheets and could afford to experiment with the nontraditional loans, the so-called B and C or subprime loans like those that Self-Help was making, in addition to the Class A loans bankers were most comfortable with.

The bankers were curious but skeptical. Eakes's argument challenged virtually everything bankers held dear. He was asking them to take a chance on low-wealth borrowers who had little or no financial history with a standard lending institution. It was a new market that banks knew little about since African Americans, who made up half or more of Self-Help's lending base, were more likely to have a finance company in their neighborhood than the branch office of a commercial bank.[12] Further, these loans did not meet the lending guidelines issued by Fannie Mae, which the banks depended on to buy their loans so they could reinvest in the mortgage business.

Eakes argued that in focusing only on Class A loans, bankers were overlooking a market he estimated to be as large as $6 billion, and that was just in North Carolina. Moreover, low- and moderate-income borrowers were good customers. "Look," Eakes told them, "we have been making these loans to people who have credit blemishes, and it doesn't make any difference. They have performed just as well as people who didn't have blemishes."

One story that always drew a laugh at Self-Help was the response of NationsBank CEO Hugh McColl, whose bank had pioneered interstate banking and was busy acquiring other banks.[13] He listened to Eakes make his pitch, and then turned to an assistant and suggested that the solution was for NationsBank to buy the credit union. One of McColl's lieutenants who had worked in community development for years explained that McColl was not clueless about Self-Help's nonprofit status, and he wasn't overreaching either. Rather, McColl was thinking of a way to get the attention of his loan officers to see that this type of lending was important to NationsBank, even though it did not produce a fat commission.

"Hugh wasn't being megalomaniacal about this," said Dennis Rash, the man who ran NationsBank's community development nonprofit. "He understood that if it had our brand on it, he'd get people to understand that we needed to get it done, and they would salute the flag. For him, they would do that. It was always a good idea for the community."[14]

It was Wachovia, not NationsBank, that became the first bank to experiment with these nontraditional mortgages. CEO Leslie M. "Bud" Baker Jr. agreed to make $5 million available for low- and moderate-income borrowers on a promise from Eakes that he'd leave him alone. Baker told Eakes that he believed the bank would probably lose that money, but, as Eakes recalled the meeting, Baker told him, "'It will be worth it to me just to get you out of my office.' I just shook my head, didn't say a single word, and got up and left the room."[15]

Five million dollars was small—maybe fifty loans in total—but it was a start.

Baker later recalled that Wachovia's margin on such business was thin, largely because its lending program was not run on a shoestring like Self-Help's. "By the time we got through with all the fees and things we had to do, we probably didn't make any money. That is OK. We weren't doing it just to make money, but trying to help somebody, and this time it happened to be Martin, who was an admirable person on this thing." Besides, the program fit into Wachovia's Neighborhood Revitalization Program, an initiative begun in 1989 and designed to enhance the bank's image as a responsible community lender.[16]

Eakes's dogged persistence coincided with a growing appreciation among commercial bankers about the requirements of the Community Reinvestment Act (CRA), a federal law enacted in 1977. Congress adopted further reporting requirements in 1990 to provide more public exposure of the investments that banks were making, or not making, in their total market. Half of a bank's performance rating was based on lending in home mortgages, small business loans, and farm loans.

After the Federal Reserve board rejected merger plans for a Boston bank in 1993, on the grounds it had failed to comply with fair lending laws, bankers became acutely aware that a good CRA score could influence their plans for expansion. Community activists had learned how to read the law, too, and by their calculations most banks were doing a poor job of serving their markets. As a result, an institution's CRA score became an effective ally for Self-Help as Eakes began to tug at the sleeves of men like Baker and McColl.

Self-Help had participated in creating the organization that was calling North Carolina bankers to account. The Community Reinvestment Association of North Carolina, or CRA-NC (called Crank), had been organized in the late 1980s, at a time when Self-Help and Legal Services of North Carolina were closely aligned. Katharine McKee, then the associate director of Self-Help, would leave training classes on mortgage lending conducted by Wachovia that had been opened to help Self-Help staffers and drive across Durham to organizing meetings for CRA-NC.

This close association had been flagged as a potential trouble spot for Self-Help in the Ford Foundation's 1988 study. The report suggested that Self-Help establish itself as a "good cop" with the banks and leave Legal Services and CRA-NC to play the role of "bad cop." Thus, CRA-NC activists held the street rallies and issued the press releases to draw attention to a bank's CRA record, while Self-Help showed the bankers how they could improve their community development lending.

"It was not as calculated as you might think," Eakes said some years later. True, the activists—the "shakers," as Eakes called them—provided the pressure from the outside, while the "bakers" worked on the inside. "I have always said that the bakers owed money and support back to the community organizers because they benefited from that. We were not very good at [street demonstrations]," Eakes said.

Eakes's arrangement with Wachovia appeared to be working well until Self-Help loan officers began getting applications from customers who would normally qualify for service at the bank. He called to find out why Wachovia was no longer accepting loans. "The answer I got was 'you were right, damned right. This is a huge market,'" Eakes recalled. Wachovia's initial $5 million had expanded to $120 million. "The response was 'we can't keep putting nontraditional home loans in our portfolio. So they stopped. They couldn't do anymore.'"[17]

Eakes offered a solution, one that, again, challenged conventional wisdom. He proposed that Self-Help buy $20 million of Wachovia's nontraditional loans, if Wachovia would agree to renew its low-income lending by the same amount. "I think they were sort of tolerating us, not really confident," he later recalled. "They said, 'How are you going to finance this?' I looked at them and smiled and said, 'We are going to do this the way everyone else does their first loan. We're going to do owner-financing.'"

Packaging loans for sale like other financial instruments was not new. By 1993, 60 percent of home mortgages were being sold as securities in the financial markets, either by government-sponsored entities like Fannie Mae or by private mortgage insurance companies.[18] The practice gained popularity in the late 1980s, when lenders were looking for ways to move thirty-year loans that had been issued at unprofitable rates off their books. The situation attracted the attention of Wall Street, where investment houses bought the loans from lenders and packaged them together for sale to investors as mortgage-backed securities.

Wall Street was not interested in the loans that Self-Help was promoting, however, because they did not meet lending standards set by Fannie Mae, which required higher down payments and preferred borrowers with unblemished credit histories. By the time Eakes made his offer, Fannie Mae already had examined the $20 million in loans and declared that only 15 percent qualified for consideration.

Eakes had been trying to find a way to develop a market for nontraditional loans since 1988, when he told the Ford Foundation: "we need a secondary market that can absorb long-term loans on the magnitude of $40 million per year, whether originated by us or by others."[19] The idea had never gone beyond talk, but that did not stop Eakes and David McGrady from poking around the edges looking for an opening.

"Martin came up with the idea of doing a bulk purchase of loans," recalled McGrady. "He was the one who was really pushing it. A lot of us were uncomfortable that it was going to be too big a leap forward."

"We were pretty comfortable with the credit risk within the portfolio," he said, "but it was the scale at which it could become, and did become. That was the scary thing. It is one thing to be an $80 million organization and another to be a $1 billion organization."[20]

Eakes's proposal was certainly novel, but he argued that it was a good deal for the bank. If Self-Help defaulted, the loans would be returned to the bank and would keep Self-Help's $2 million down payment. Going forward, Self-Help would carry the risk of the loans while Wachovia collected an origination fee for new loans and score valuable points under CRA by providing home loans to another four hundred families in North Carolina. Wachovia agreed.

Eakes later said that the Wachovia deal "was like the first boat sailing out into the Atlantic. It was open waters to help families that hadn't been able to get credit at all." Wachovia's participation in this modest secondary market encouraged interest from other banks. Before long, Self-Help was negotiating similar arrangements with five of North Carolina's largest banks that were offering home loans to low- and moderate-income borrowers.

Self-Help worked out lending standards tailored to participating banks that met Self-Help's guidelines on fees, costs, down payment, and terms. There were no surprises in these time-tested thirty-year mortgages. Eakes said banks were told that Self-Help "will find a way to get you new funds so you can keep expanding your program within the guidelines." Self-Help financed its side of the program with loans from banks, insurance companies, and pension funds, as well as foundation grants, state grants, and help from the Federal Home Loan Bank Board of Atlanta.

In the aftermath of the financial crisis in 2008, conservative critics accused banks of lowering their lending standards for political ends, such as achieving a better CRA score. However, a 2000 study by the U.S. Department of the Treasury quoted a report in *Atlanta Banker* that said: "The CRA is not driving the CRA lending, profitability is. . . . Bankers recognized that there were untapped market opportunities in low- and moderate-income lending."[21]

Self-Help's new secondary market would prove to be transformational, but after a little more than two years it appeared to have run its course. "We got to the point where we didn't have room to borrow or to buy any more loans," recalled Eric Stein, who was running it in 1996. He was a Chapel Hill native and a graduate of Williams College and Yale Law. For two years before joining Self-Help, he had helped launch a housing program for the homeless in Raleigh. Stein was a younger version of Eakes, lean and intense, obviously bright and committed, but without the red hair. "We proved the point, but we created the problem that we were trying to solve in other banks in ourselves," he said. "We kind of capped out."[22]

The banks doing business with Self-Help were eager to continue, especially if the program extended beyond the boundaries of North Carolina. Through mergers and acquisitions, First Union and Wachovia were doing business well beyond North Carolina, and NationsBank was on its way to a merger with Bank of America, whose headquarters was in San Francisco. A North Carolina–only option was not that attractive to executives overseeing national markets. Nor was it appealing to Eakes, said Stein. "Martin was like, well, you know what, if our program works for you as a solution in North Carolina, what if we make it larger and make it national?"

Self-Help's success had attracted the attention of Fannie Mae and Freddie Mac, which were under increasing political pressure to expand coverage for loans to low- and moderate-income borrowers. "Where the market had said 85 percent of these loans were nonstandard and shouldn't be made," Eakes said, "we had proven that was wrong. We were convinced these were really great loans and so we were saying Fannie and Freddie weren't doing their job, and they have a mandate to help working families become homeowners."

That's what Wachovia had been doing. A third of the Wachovia loans purchased by Self-Help had been made to African Americans, about half to female-headed households, and more than half to rural residents. Borrowers had incomes that were 55 to 60 percent of the area median income. The loans would prove to be worth the risk. In the years ahead, Self-Help would fore-close on a few of these loans but would suffer no financial loss.

Fannie Mae was in the midst of a major overhaul of its own. In 1995, it had begun to include a limited number of nontraditional loans in packages it prepared and converted into mortgage-backed securities. Fannie Mae's CEO James A. Johnson had used changes in its regulations to negotiate a discounted rate to Countrywide Financial, an aggressive subprime lender, which promised a steady stream of loans, in an effort to generate more money to support its secondary market under its Showing America a New Way Home program.[23]

Self-Help had qualified to do business with Fannie Mae in 1990. Soon after, it had helped test a Fannie Mae program that allowed borrowers to make a down payment of less than 5 percent. In 1997, Self-Help was negoti-ating with Fannie Mae to put $100 million into expanding Self-Help's sec-ondary lending. Talks were going slowly when Eakes learned that the Ford Foundation was interested in doing something *really* big. Rising stock val-ues had boosted the foundation's income, and lots of money was available to put somewhere. At the same time, Melvin Oliver, the co-author of *Black Wealth/White Wealth*, had joined Ford as vice president of a program area devoted to asset building. His book had highlighted the ten-to-one dispar-ity in wealth between African Americans and whites in America, and that was a strong signal to Eakes. Eakes called Frank DiGiovanni, the program officer at Ford who had been working with Eakes since the early 1990s, to find out more.

DiGiovanni admired Eakes and the work at Self-Help. He saw in the fiery southerner a rare combination of a person who thought in terms of broad policy but who also could see that it worked. "Martin Eakes is incredible in terms of figuring out how you get things done on the ground," he said. "But Martin is brilliant at system change and understanding policy."[24]

Those were the same qualities that the MacArthur Foundation had rec-ognized in the late spring of 1996, when it named Eakes one of its ten Mac-Arthur fellows, the so-called Genius Grant it gave annually to a dozen or so unsuspecting recipients. "Eakes is leading the charge to change the face of banking in the United States," the foundation noted, "so that sustainable economic potential can be part of the lives of many more citizens." The first of five annual installments of the $260,000 award was $15,000 more than Eakes's Self-Help salary of $35,200.

DiGiovanni was preparing for an upcoming board meeting at Ford when Eakes called to propose that Ford use Self-Help's lending platform to make a dent in the wealth gap of white America and black America. If Ford, Fannie Mae, and Self-Help worked together to expand homeownership, then the result would build wealth for thousands of African Americans. DiGiovanni told Eakes he wanted to know more.

Stein and Eakes hastily reconfigured the proposal that they were preparing for Fannie Mae and included participation by Ford. They shuffled versions back and forth between their adjacent offices in Self-Help's new home in the former First Union National Bank building at 301 W. Main Street in Durham. Self-Help had purchased the eight-story building in 1996 and moved operations there from East Chapel Hill Street. The credit union occupied the ground floor, with the rest of Self-Help filling three floors above. The balance was rented to existing clients, including law firms and nonprofits.

"In terms of grant dollars per hour, [the Ford proposal] was one of our better investments of time," Stein recalled. Self-Help's request was for $50 million, an unprecedented amount, but "so is the opportunity."

"Over time, the Ford Foundation investment would provide tangible evidence that low-wealth borrowers are 'bankable,' and that Congress should pass a tax credit program to make home ownership available to lower income families. This is Self-Help's ultimate goal."

"Self-Help believes that home equity is the key to wealth accumulation and family stability—a stepping stone out of poverty," the grant proposal said. "Self-Help has the ability to test the risk presented by low-wealth borrowers and, as a result, to demonstrate that many borrowers unable to qualify for traditional financing do, in fact, offer good business opportunities for lenders."[25]

DiGiovanni liked what he saw. "As a national foundation, we were looking for a way to address this problem in scale," he said some years later. "Martin's project gave us a way [of] doing that. If it worked, we could influence underwriting criteria for Fannie Mae, which would then change those criteria nationally. It was a fabulous confluence." With Fannie Mae agreeing to participate by securitizing up to $2 billion in loans from Self-Help's secondary market, the foundation would see its money used over and over again to expand home ownership all across the country.[26]

The challenge was well beyond anything that Self-Help had attempted before. It committed to turn $100 million into a $2 billion investment in lending over five years. That was a huge leap, but Eakes reasoned that if Self-Help could develop $100 million in a secondary market serving only North Carolina, then finding at least ten states out of fifty to buy $40 million in loans over five years was not unreasonable.

Ford announced its grant on July 23, 1998, with Ford President Susan Berresford saying, "This effort has the great potential to start a cycle of investment that will not only benefit homeowners with less savings and income, but also their neighborhoods and communities. It could expand business for banks as well." Johnson noted that the combination of a philanthropy, a community development organization, and a large mortgage investor was "a unique arrangement to benefit American home buyers."[27]

Ford released the money over the next few years as Self-Help expanded its secondary market, eventually serving thirty-five banks and credit unions in forty-eight states. Home lenders far from Durham now had an outlet for the sale of nontraditional loans made at reasonable rates for thirty-year terms. These loans were properly vetted and fully documented, allowed to "season" for six months to a year before they were purchased by Self-Help and converted by mortgage-backed securities that Self-Help held on its books.

"Now we have an asset that everybody would be happy for. So, we could sell it easily to anybody, or we could borrow against it, which is what we did," said Stein. Since Fannie Mae securities were considered a safe investment, Self-Help then borrowed against them to generate more cash to buy more loans.

Before long, Stein and others were negotiating deals with investment banks that went beyond the understanding of most outsiders. One complicated purchase amounted to $265 million that was packaged with various sophisticated credit devices to guard against unexpected shifts in interest rates. "That's not the kind of image you have of a little nonprofit here in North Carolina," he said. "There is no reason why if people in New York could do it that we couldn't do it. It was all a process, but not impossible."

Ford complemented its investment in Self-Help by underwriting a research program at the University of North Carolina's new Center for Community Capital. This investment would produce unexpected and timely benefits. In 2003, researchers began tracking the experience of 46,000 of the 52,000 borrowers who eventually received $4.7 billion in loans through Self-Help's secondary market. Forty-one percent of Self-Help borrowers went to female-headed households, 40 percent were minority households, and the median income was $30,792.[28] The study continued beyond the collapse of the financial markets in 2008 and produced a database that provided a before and after picture of the greatest financial upheaval since the Great Depression.

The numbers proved to be a vindication of Self-Help's mission. Low- to moderate-income borrowers became community builders by establishing roots in a neighborhood and fostering civic life. Owning a home was a solid long-term investment, and children of these borrowers were more likely to become homeowners themselves. Moreover, the thirty-year, fixed-rate mortgages that Self-Help fostered had a delinquency rate one-quarter to one-half that of borrowers of other nonconforming mortgages. In 2012, four years after the 2008 crisis, 95 percent of the borrowers were still in their homes.[29]

"We did not have to be geniuses," Eakes said in 2014. "We just had to have enough faith in simple things." If a person was paying the rent regularly, they would probably make their mortgage payments. "So with little things like that, we were able to break through and open up for tens of thousands of families. Ordinary people, good people who had been working jobs forever, paying rent forever, were able to get their first home loan."[30]

CHAPTER EIGHT

Cy Pres

James Byers was troubled over a transforming wave in banking that had broken over the small town of Forest City, North Carolina, where First Savings Bank was about to merge into Centura Bank Inc. Byers built a strong family business over the past fifty years, and he asked for advice from his son, Tom, who was a member of the Self-Help Credit Union board of directors. The younger Byers did not have an answer, but he was on his way to Durham for a meeting with Martin Eakes. He told his father he'd see what he could find out there.

This was early in the fall of 1993, nearly ninety years after the founding of First Savings Bank's forerunner, First Federal Savings and Loan Association. The thrift had only lately shed its member-owned status to become a stock-owned corporation. It was regarded as one of the strongest and most profitable institutions around. By remaining true to its core mission of providing home mortgages in its community, it had survived the savings and loan industry crisis of the late 1980s, the greatest collapse of financial institutions since the Great Depression.[1] The acquisition was quite a prize for

Centura, one of the emerging regional banks fattening its balance sheet with mergers like this. First Savings was Centura's seventh acquisition in the three short years since it was created in the merger of People's Bank and Planters Bank, both based in Rocky Mount, a tobacco market center in eastern North Carolina.

James Byers did not like the deal, even though it had been approved by three-quarters of First Savings's shareholders. He believed the $8.5 million that Centura was paying was too little for First Savings's $62 million in assets. In addition, he believed that those "in the know" at the bank were enriching themselves in order to make it happen.

As it turned out, he was right. It would later be revealed that rewards to the officers and directors amounted to an estimated $3.5 million, about one-third as much as the purchase price. The payouts included a new car and a whopping pay raise for the president, generous compensation for directors for no-show advisory board meetings, and millions in Centura stock.

When Tom Byers broached the subject with him, Eakes became alarmed. He had long been distressed at the continuing decline of mutually owned, community-based savings and loan institutions. Six years earlier, he had asked the Babcock Foundation for money to help find a way to keep the one-member, one-vote savings-and-loans doing their traditional job of home lending and building communities.[2] The industry had continued its nose-dive as one after the other of these mutual associations had converted to stock ownership, and then disappeared into a bank where future lending decisions were made hundreds of miles away. These so-called conversion-mergers were changing the banking landscape, and Eakes believed that the fundamentals involved in these transactions were wrong. Eakes told Byers that attorney Michael Calhoun would be calling his father soon.[3]

The Forest City bank deal was coming to a close, with ten days left for the final appeal, when Calhoun and Robert B. Glenn Jr., another Durham lawyer, representing James Byers, his son William, and three other First Savings depositors, filed a petition with the state banking regulators seeking to halt the merger.

The legal action came as depositors in other S&Ls around the state were reacting in similar fashion. One member of the state's congressional delegation, Representative Steve Neal of Winston-Salem, co-sponsored legislation calling on regulators to look more closely before approving such mergers. Some banks withdrew from the competition altogether after intense local opposition threatened to dull the shine of their brands. Tempers ran high.

In some communities, neighbors got into fistfights. Sunday school members fell out with one another in Forest City. The uproar prompted directors of some S&Ls to scuttle deals in order to end the controversy. The lawsuit looked to be too late to keep First Savings in Forest City, where the merger was complete. It was not too late to get some relief, however.[4]

For the next three-plus years, the Forest City case wandered in and out of the hands of regulators, and traveled up and down the judicial ladder. Centura's lawyers argued that the defendants were tardy in filing their complaint, and judicial precedent did not justify their claim. The bank cited ten other comparable conversion-mergers during the same time to bolster their argument of equity. The plaintiffs clung to state law that specifically prohibited fiduciaries—bank directors and officers, for example—from unjustly enriching themselves in a business transaction. It was a legal reach, and untested in a case of this nature.

Rulings in court and before regulators were still pending in the early weeks of the summer of 1997 when the same issue—the integrity of mutually owned nonprofits like Self-Help and the S&Ls—was raised again, this time with far broader consequences for millions of North Carolina citizens. One of the state's largest nonprofits, Blue Cross and Blue Shield of North Carolina, looked like it was headed toward conversion to a for-profit entity, just like the Forest City thrift. Once again, Eakes was incensed, and by the conclusion of the fight with N.C. Blue, as the insurance company was called, Eakes and Self-Help would establish a capacity to influence public policy through vigorous, unrelenting advocacy.

Advocacy had long been a part of the Self-Help portfolio, although much had been localized or passed with little public notice. Examiners from the National Credit Union Administration knew something about the lengths that Eakes and others would go to defend minority credit unions struggling to survive. North Carolina's leading bankers knew Eakes as a determined proponent for expanding mortgage lending to low-income home buyers.

From its earliest days, Self-Help had helped build the strength, capacity, and security of nonprofit organizations, lending them money not only to help them fulfill their missions but to improve their systems and accountability. That was why Jane Kendall of Raleigh had asked Eakes to join her in a study when she began thinking about an organization to support nonprofits in North Carolina. Together, they slogged through a months-long series of twenty community meetings as Kendall's group gathered information from one end of North Carolina to the other. When it was over, Eakes signed on as a founding director of an organizational support center called the N.C. Center for Nonprofits. Despite his professed dislike for board meetings and such, he never missed one meeting as the center grew its membership. About a thousand nonprofit organizations were part of the center by 1997.[5]

N.C. Blue was one of the largest nonprofits in the state. It was a product of a 1968 merger of two Blue Cross and Blue Shield systems organized in the 1930s when hospitals and doctors were looking for a way to guarantee payment for medical care. Both had enjoyed tax exemptions available to nonprofits, avoiding millions of dollars in taxes over the years. This favored status had continued after the 1968 merger produced the largest single health insurer in the state. By 1997, N.C. Blue had 1.6 million customers who lived in all of the state's one hundred counties.

The nation's health care providers were anxious about the future in the mid-1990s, particularly in the wake of the failure of President Bill Clinton's initiative to bring about universal health care. Costs were rising, companies were merging, and financial analysts were using a new calculus to configure future obligations. The changes had shaken the leadership of the Blue Cross and Blue Shield franchises around the country, and in 1994 some companies began to convert to for-profit so they could raise money with stock sales and, the management believed, better survive in a competitive market.

This shift had not escaped the attention of North Carolina's Commissioner of Insurance James E. Long. He was an old-style politician with a broad populist streak and a firm hold on his office. His trademark from his days as a young legislator in the early 1970s was a brilliant red necktie. In the run-up to the 1997 session of the General Assembly, Long had asked his department's general counsel, Peter A. Kolbe, to consider the implications of a conversion in North Carolina, because, as Kolbe later recalled, "we knew Blue was going to run some legislation." Kolbe surveyed state law, looked at what was happening elsewhere, and lined up behind a legal doctrine called *cy pres* should N.C. Blue seek to change its status. Loosely defined, this doctrine meant that when a nonprofit changed its corporate structure, the fair market value of the assets should go to the next closest thing, such as a charitable foundation.[6]

This was big. If N.C. Blue's so-called surplus of $500 million were put into a foundation, it would make it one of the largest in the state. If all the assets were spun off, the money available to improve health care in the state could be as much as four times that amount, perhaps equal to the Duke Endowment's $1.9 billion in resources. There was no easy standard to declare just how much money was involved, or even whether N.C. Blue could be required to contribute anything at all. In California, two foundations valued at more than $3 billion had been established, but only after a protracted legal fight. Georgia's Blue had converted with no benefit to taxpayers, and in Virginia the Blue there had put only a token amount into public hands, and only after state officials complained.[7]

Kolbe's opinion was unsettling to N.C. Blue, and the company's lawyer paid him a visit. As the state's largest health insurer, N.C. Blue representatives were often in and out of the insurance department offices, and the appearance of the company's chief counsel, J. Bradley Wilson, at Kolbe's desk was not unusual. "Blue Cross/Blue Shield at that time had a reputation at the department of being tremendously arrogant. Sort of the eight-hundred-pound gorilla," Kolbe said. Kolbe said Wilson handed him a copy of a draft conversion bill that did nothing to benefit the state's citizens. "He informed me that this was going to be the legislation governing how Blue Cross would convert." Kolbe asked Wilson to leave his office. When the commissioner learned of Wilson's visit, Long was furious, said Kolbe.

In late April 1997, as the legislature was starting to wrap up business, the first take on N.C. Blue's enabling legislation breezed through the senate in a bill that contained little more than a title. The language allowing the conversion was finally added when the bill got to a house rules committee, which was not the committee that normally considered legislation dealing with insurance companies. Overall, it looked like a preemptive strike by N.C. Blue. Company officials allowed as much, saying they were responding to intentions of others to hamstring the company, although no bills had been introduced.

Some patches were hastily applied to the original bill after a few house members raised concern, but the new language did not really disturb the essence of N.C. Blue's desires. It passed out of the house and headed back to the senate for concurrence of the amendments. It was there that Adam Searing, a health care analyst with the N.C. Justice Center, a relatively new independent public policy outfit, caught sight of the bill and called it out for what it was, a backroom deal cooked up to benefit N.C. Blue without any fealty to *cy pres*. Searing's declarations infuriated Senator Tony Rand, the bill's influential sponsor. At that point, Searing had been on the job for about four months, and, as Rand put it, "here was a guy who looks like he is sixteen making him go bright red and yell and everything. There were bells going off. [Others now were saying], 'this is really a big deal and we need to take a better look at it.'"[8]

After one particularly contentious committee meeting, Searing was feeling overwhelmed. Some suggested that for his future well-being he might want to make a call at Rand's office and ask for forgiveness. Eakes was not one of them; instead, he pulled Searing aside and offered open-ended support. "What Martin said to me was there are few issues in public policy that are black and white, and this is one of those issues," recalled Searing.

Friends in Raleigh had warned Eakes that opposition was bootless. This was a bill earmarked for passage. Besides, why would he want to alienate Rand, who had seen that millions of state dollars had flowed into Self-Help's home-lending program? Nonetheless, Eakes gave Searing a healthy dose of confidence and let him know he was not alone. More important to Searing, Eakes was the first person who fully understood that this bill was not about health care, or the future of the annual premiums of policyholders, but about appropriation of assets of a nonprofit without any regard to the public's interest.

"When Martin came up to me," Searing said some time later, "he was very intent on saying, 'Let's stop this.' I was so new and feeling out of my depth, and he was saying, 'I know you have been out here busting your ass, but let's go.'"

Virtually overnight, at least when measured by a legislative time clock, Eakes helped organize a groundswell of opposition that included foundation directors and board members; leaders of nonprofits; and the unlikely pairing of spokesmen for the conservative John Locke Foundation, a relatively new crowd that espoused free-market ideology, and the Common Sense Foundation, a group at the other end of the political spectrum. Opponents of the bill rounded up dozens of co-signers to a letter urging the legislature to go slowly on the issue. Among the signatures were those of some of the biggest names in the state, including former governors Terry Sanford, a Democrat, and Jim Holshouser, a Republican.

"Both Jim [Long] and I viewed Martin as the cavalry arriving," recalled Kolbe. "Very quickly we realized that Martin would be a tremendous ally in trying to slow down this legislation and perhaps get it changed so it actually did provide something meaningful, upon conversion, for underserved people in the state and their health needs."

The impressive array of bipartisan political force startled some legislators who were struggling to explain their votes on a bill many really did not understand. Said Searing, "Every time this was in the paper, talked about on the floor of the House, every time it was on TV, the leadership looked like shills for the company. People were really, really angry, and it became a much bigger issue than anybody imagined." He learned a few lessons in politics. "It showed me the strength of the media. It was the best training ever."

The ruckus rattled N.C. Blue, which then miscalculated the effect of a countermeasure of aggravating robocalls that was launched by its public relations firm. The calls were designed to alarm N.C. Blue policyholders and link them directly to the phone in their legislator's office so they could urge favorable passage of the bill. Legislators took exception to the tactic and called on the secretary of state to investigate illegal lobbying. What once looked like a sure thing for N.C. Blue was now hobbled and stalled in a legislative conference committee where the *cy pres* doctrine was finally on the table and gaining appreciation. House and senate leaders began talking about a study commission. The legislative train that Eakes and others had been told had already left the station was now stuck on a siding.[9]

The tough work was just beginning. N.C. Blue remained steadfast in its insistence that while it was a nonprofit, the value of the company belonged to policyholders, not to the state or anyone else beyond the confines of its distinctive headquarters building of slanted glass walls near Chapel Hill. Besides, CEO Kenneth C. Otis II declared that N.C. Blue had no plans to convert. It just wanted to be ready to do so should market conditions require a change.[10] Confidence in its position still reigned as the legislature's regular session closed. But N.C. Blue's reputation for getting what it wanted from the legislature without question was looking a little shaky. Nonetheless, Senator Rand, a wily Democrat who knew how to use the levers of power, would be co-chairing the commission, along with the bill's house sponsor, a ranking Republican named Leo Daughtry.

Throughout the six weeks of the initial wrangling at the Legislative Building, Eakes was dealing with a difficult personal matter. His father was dying of cancer. In addition to minding the store in Durham, where Self-Help's secondary market for home lending was taking shape, and keeping his eye on N.C. Blue, Eakes was shuttling to and from Greensboro to be at his father's side. "He knew this thing was tearing me up," Eakes said some years later. "It was just corrupt. So my father, flat on his back, basically said, 'If you think it is wrong, go get them.' And that did it for me. I was a man possessed at that point. I had permission."[11]

The first round—stopping immediate passage—was akin to firemen rushing into a burning building to rescue the occupants. Eakes and the opposition had responded with whatever they had at hand, which amounted to little more than a hastily compiled list of influential political and business leaders willing to take the word of those they knew that it was an issue deserving deliberate attention, not a legislative end run, regardless of the sterling reputation of N.C. Blue and its professed good intentions. Scorching editorials in the capital city's newspaper, the *News and Observer*, also were changing some people's minds.[12]

Working through months of effort with the study commission, and coming out with a bill that could most likely get the approval of the General Assembly in its 1998 short session, was going to require much, much more. The opposition would need more than a loud voice and some newspaper commentary. It would require the leadership of other nonprofits to move beyond their comfortable seats on the sidelines and hurl themselves into the thick of public advocacy that could have serious and profound political consequences.

Inspired by his father's encouragement, Eakes presented the matter to his own board of directors. The board had long been a friendly and diverse forum that served, in one member's recollection, as a place where Eakes could "run crazy ideas by and say 'what are we missing?'" Members fulfilled their fiduciary responsibilities but generally nodded in agreement to Eakes and his ambitions. It was not a group that said no or tried to restrain its CEO. "We discussed it as a board," recalled board member Jay Silver. He said he and other members were aware that "this was, in fact, staking ourselves out in a political forum in a way that we previously had done only in order to make home loans affordable for a population in North Carolina."[13]

The board members were mindful that the General Assembly had been generous over the previous decade, making millions available to Self-Help. "The conversion legislation was a new thing," said Silver. "We had not focused on health care. It was Martin who said, 'Look at this. This is something we cannot allow to happen, and we can shape and guide something big for the state as a whole.'" Just as home lending was about helping people build wealth and not just compiling a loan portfolio, this public campaign was something much bigger. The board endorsed Eakes's plans to fully engage.

Eakes began making the rounds to talk with likely allies. One of his first stops was the N.C. Center for Nonprofits. Eakes told Jane Kendall's board, where he was well known as a dogged fighter, that this issue was not about health care but about the integrity of nonprofits. Like Self-Help, the center had never touched anything this fraught with political risk. It was not an easy sell. Members were aware that the tax-exempt status of nonprofit organizations was dependent on the legislature. Nonetheless, Kendall said Eakes brought her board members around with a simple argument: "'If we can switch from nonprofit to for-profit and keep the assets, what does that mean about our integrity? Where is our soul?' Based on that principle, he convinced our board to participate," Kendall said.

By summer's end, a base of opposition was coming together under the banner of something called the N.C. Coalition for the Public Trust. Cochairing the group with Eakes was Shannon St. John, the director of the Triangle Community Foundation. St. John's influence reached into every major city in the state where community and regional foundations, like hers, brought together people of wealth and influence, and whose politics was distributed to the Right as well as to the Left. A wavering legislator, not usually inclined to listen to a lefty like Eakes, might find the name of the chair of his campaign finance committee on St. John's list of community foundation directors who were urging the legislature to take a closer look.

It was hard for politicians to oppose the *cy pres* argument, said Kolbe. "That was where Martin was a godsend. The grassroots network that he helped organize and lead really got a lot of light shown on it. It made Blue Cross look even worse to oppose giving their value back to the citizens of the state."

Before long, groups of all kinds signed on. Eakes had spent a decade or more building relationships with minority business organizations, churches, and community groups that had fostered child care programs, credit unions in need of support, and nonprofits looking for lower rents on office space. These connections paid off as he called on his friends to lend a hand. The coalition would later claim upward of eighty nonprofits under its umbrella. Not all rallied to his side. His ally Larry Johnson at the N.C. Credit Union League heard him out, but the League stayed out of the fray. N.C. Blue's credit union was one of its members.

The fire of opposition burned hottest at Self-Help, where Eakes committed not only his own time but that of top aide Eric Stein as well as the labors of two other employees whose job was to keep the coalition organized and fed with information. He plugged holes where he found them. When Eakes discovered that an antiquated computer slowed Searing's work, he sent him a new one. He gave the N.C. Justice Center a hand in getting a $50,000 grant to expand its work. All the communications flowed through the Self-Help computer systems; the coalition's email address was cpt@self-help.org. Altogether, it was a modest contribution when compared to the resources of N.C. Blue and the backing of its national association, which had been down this road before in other states. Yet, despite a relatively modest war chest, Self-Help brought to the fight more firepower than any other group in the coalition could, or would.

While endorsements from supporting organizations were critical and spread the coalition's message across the state, the coalition needed more than political support to get a good bill. It needed legal expertise, especially lawyers familiar with the legislative process, to complete the marathon that it had entered. Eakes and Stein were sharp as tacks, and Adam Searing was becoming an expert in the pitfalls that had arisen in the conversions in other states. For all three, however, this was new territory.

The coalition wanted an attorney experienced in legislation, one whose presence would send a message that the coalition was not some ragtag outfit of Durham liberals but a force with serious intent. N.C. Blue already had the state's top corporate law firm, Robinson and Bradshaw of Charlotte, arguing its case in state superior court, where a separate lawsuit over the company's reserves was under way. The coalition would need comparable help. Eakes called Silver and asked if his law firm, Moore and Van Allen, also one of the best in the state, would take on the coalition's case, pro bono, or at a reduced rate.

Eakes and Kendall rode together to the firm's Charlotte headquarters to make their case to the firm's management. Kendall was in her best suit, and Eakes was dressed more casually. "He wasn't wearing blue jeans, I don't think," she recalled. "They agreed to contribute whatever legal help we needed." The firm offered the help of Silver, a first-rate litigator, and George M. Teague, a registered lobbyist who usually found himself promoting the interests of insurance companies. A measure of Teague's gravitas became apparent about a week later when Teague got a call from N.C. Blue asking if he would work with them. "I am already taken," Teague told them.[14]

In fairly short order, the entire affair evolved into three principal parties: N.C. Blue, the coalition, and the study commission, where the coalition had some of its allies in place, as did N.C. Blue. Attorney General Michael Easley and Insurance Commissioner Long were also eager to take a swing, but their future roles in the conversion process limited what they could do until the issue was officially brought to their attention. Easley had declared in favor of a charitable foundation that Long also supported, but more quietly. For the coalition and for N.C. Blue, it was becoming something of a race against time. All those involved believed that the public would be best served if the coalition and N.C. Blue could work out the main stumbling blocks by the time the commission began its work in January 1998.

After some back and forth in the press that fall, N.C. Blue blinked. The company was ready to agree to a charitable trust, funded at the full market value. "YES, YOU READ THAT RIGHT," Kendall declared in a confidential wrap-up of the meeting to the coalition insiders that was circulated in early December. Negotiations remained delicate, as both sides had little to say publicly.[15]

There remained a host of very knotty details to work out, and suspicion was rampant. In addition, months of study commission work lay ahead before the General Assembly adopted the legislation recommended by the commission early in 1998. It set out a conversion process that N.C. Blue could use when it decided to convert. The final bill was largely to the liking of the coalition's members. Some began planning on what the state could do with a new public foundation with assets of $2 billion or more that would be dedicated to improving the health of the state's citizens. It was a glorious option that only a year before had been little more than a legal doctrine tucked into a lawyer's brief.

Eakes emerged as North Carolina's new dragon slayer, according to some. He had proven to be an unstoppable and irreverent force at times. He was not shy about challenging those who did not see things to be as egregious as he did. Early on, he had browbeat Commissioner Long when he thought Long was not aggressive enough. On another occasion, when he was negotiating particulars of the proposed bill with Kolbe and Alan S. Hirsch, a lawyer from the attorney general's office who did not share Eakes's outrage, Kolbe watched as Eakes berated Hirsch, saying, "I don't need a goddamn facilitator; I need a warrior."

The battle with N.C. Blue happened without warning or planning, but it became a game changer. "The coalition for Blue Cross was a pretty dramatic lesson for us," Eakes said some years later. It had demonstrated the power of digging in and working through difficult negotiations, and the virtue of being nonpartisan. Eakes had lined up with Republicans in the senate when that was agreeable and stood with Democrats in the house when that made sense. "We had to reach out. I had this conversation with [former governor] Jim Hunt one time. I am not politically partisan. I am partisan for poor people. And if that means we fight Democrats, we will fight Democrats.

If that means we will fight Republicans, we will fight Republicans. We are partisan, but it is not based on party."

Eakes said Hunt, a Democrat to the core, shook his head and told him, "I don't understand you. You will fight with anybody."

Eakes did not pull punches, but he kept his affairs balanced. Even as Eakes was backstopping Calhoun in the lawsuit against Centura, Self-Help was buying loans from the bank, working amicably with Joseph A. Smith, Centura's legal counsel, as Self-Help purchased Centura home loans in its modest secondary market.

As for Tom Byers, his father James, and the other depositors at First Savings Bank in Forest City, their case did not save the former savings and loan. Centura settled in October 1997 and agreed to a payment of $3.5 million, with $2.3 million going to former depositors. The court also approved nearly $1.3 million in legal fees and expenses.

The question of N.C. Blue's future lay dormant until 2002, when the company applied to the N.C. Department of Insurance to convert to a for-profit corporation under the provisions of the new law. The foundation created in 1998 to administer the N.C. Blue assets was already in place and anticipating as much as $2 billion that might become available to deal with a broad range of health issues in the state. Liberal and progressive elements in the state, including some of Eakes's closest friends and allies, salivated over the prospects of the good the money could do in improving the public welfare.[16]

It all came to naught. N.C. Blue withdrew its request after more than year of wrangling over the company's value, and how the transaction would be handled, at hearings where Eakes participated. He pushed for the toughest conditions possible and remained stubbornly antagonistic. In the end, the company retained its nonprofit status, much to the chagrin of those who believe Eakes insisted on far too much in the deal.

"I actually disagreed with Martin," said Mary Mountcastle, one of Eakes's top advisors for more than a decade. "I thought that if they had converted, we would have a $2 billion dollar health care foundation right now if Martin hadn't fought that far. And the Blue Cross people would have gotten really rich. His part was, 'This is wrong, and there are so many loopholes in the way that the foundation would get cheated.' And I [thought], 'Hey for a $2 billion foundation, I am willing to live with that.'"[17]

Self-Help's first loan was to Percy Whites's New Bern Bakery, a start-up created by an unemployed factory worker and navy veteran. (PHOTO COURTESY OF SELF-HELP)

The Self-Help Credit Union's initial capital came from members and $77 raised at a bake sale held at a worker-ownership conference on the Guilford College campus in Greensboro in 1983. June Blotnick, who later opened Self-Help's Charlotte, N.C., office, holds one of Percy White's cakes. (PHOTO COURTESY OF SELF-HELP)

The Workers' Owned Sewing Company in Windsor, N.C., was a lone source of inspiration for the future of worker-owned businesses in North Carolina. It operated for nearly a decade after initial legal assistance and lending from Self-Help. (PHOTO COURTESY OF SELF-HELP)

Self-Help's co-founder, Bonnie Wright (left), with Bill Bynum (center), one of Self-Help's first employees, and Wilbur P. "Wib" Gulley (right). Bynum later became the head of Hope Enterprise Corporation, a Self-Help–styled operation in the Mississippi Delta. Gulley was elected mayor of Durham and later to the North Carolina senate. (PHOTO COURTESY OF SELF-HELP)

Business North Carolina featured Self-Help and its co-founders, Martin Eakes and Bonnie Wright, in its December 1993 edition. (IMAGE COURTESY OF *BUSINESS NORTH CAROLINA*)

Eakes opened Self-Help's western North Carolina offices in 1992 on an upper floor of the former Public Service Building, an art deco–style office building that dated to 1929. Self-Help made office space available to nonprofits and charged affordable rents. The restoration helped kick-start a downtown revival. (PHOTO COURTESY OF SELF-HELP)

Asheville's Public Service Building, Self-Help's headquarters in western North Carolina. (PHOTO COURTESY OF SELF-HELP)

Tim Bazemore from Workers' Owned Sewing Company was one of three speakers at the 1993 announcement of President Bill Clinton's community development initiative held on the White House lawn. Vice President Al Gore stands at Bazemore's left with two other small business owners.

The Self-Help staff in the mid-1990s: Front row, left to right, are Joy Rubenstein, Dan Fiscus, Gale Thomas, Joyce Harrison, and Bob Schall. Second row, left to right, are Laura Benedict, Bonnie Wright, Sadie Abdullah, Katharine McKee, Sally Thomas, Jackie Bailey, Thad Moore, Martin Eakes, and David McGrady. Third row, left to right, are Jim Overton, Mike McAllister, Teresa Dickey, Linwood Cox, Beth Maczka, Art Hollander, and Chris Dickey. (PHOTO COURTESY OF SELF-HELP)

When Governor Jim Hunt, seated, signed North Carolina's new mortgage lending law in 1999, one of the pens he used went to Martin Eakes. To Eakes's right are Republican Leo Daughtry, state house minority leader; Democrat Roy Cooper, the bill's sponsor and senate majority leader; and Senator Wib Gulley from Durham. (PHOTO COURTESY OF SELF-HELP)

Martin Eakes testified in 2001 at a U.S. Senate Banking Committee hearing on predatory mortgage lending. Appearing on the panel with Eakes was the board chair of Ameriquest, one of the high-volume lenders that later failed and helped bring on the Great Recession.

Michael Calhoun was president of Self-Help's Center for Responsible Lending when its report *Losing Ground* was published in late 2006. The study's forecast of a looming foreclosure crisis produced by reckless lending practices came months before the collapse of the home lending market and showed its analysis was correct and even worse than predicted.

An early initiative of Self-Help's expansion to California was with the creation of check-cashing outlets where customers were charged fees lower than for-profit competitors and could find options for savings in Self-Help Federal Credit Union. (PHOTO COURTESY OF SELF-HELP FEDERAL CREDIT UNION)

Self-Help Federal's development strategy changed to mergers in order to save California credit unions struggling to recover from the Great Recession. One with a unique history was co-founded by Dolores Huerta and Helen and Cesar Chavez of the United Farmworkers Association in the 1960s. With Huerta at the opening of a new branch (left to right) are Joe Duran, Self-Help Federal Credit Union; Martin Eakes; Huerta; Roberto Hernandez, a credit union member; and state assemblyman Tom Ammiano. (PHOTO COURTESY OF SELF-HELP FEDERAL CREDIT UNION)

Self-Help Federal Credit Union's merger with Second Federal Savings and Loan in Chicago saved a historic community financial institution important to the Little Village community, the largest urban concentration of Latinos in the United States. Flags of Mexico and the United States flew from side-by-side poles over the entrance. (COURTESY OF SELF-HELP FEDERAL CREDIT UNION)

The Self-Help logo was changed after the expansion out of North Carolina to replace an earlier model with stacked chevrons, suggesting a towering building. (COURTESY OF SELF-HELP FEDERAL CREDIT UNION)

The Self-Help Ventures Fund bought Revolution Mill redevelopment in Greensboro, N.C., out of bankruptcy and repurposed the century-old textile mill into apartments, space for small businesses, art studios, and a home for a craft brewery and restaurant. (PHOTO COURTESY OF SELF-HELP)

CHAPTER NINE

"Shit Disturbers"

Martin Eakes had never heard of Herb Sandler when the philanthropist and maverick home lender out in California gave him a call in the summer of 2001. Sandler told Eakes that he and his wife, Marion, were planning a visit near Durham and invited him to dinner at a Chapel Hill restaurant much too pricey for Eakes's taste. Sandler assured Eakes that any time invested would be worth his while. A similar promise, made a decade before by an eccentric Asheville millionaire, came to mind, and he accepted the invitation.

Eakes was just coming off a period of high-profile indignation. He had publicly taken on the likes of Citigroup over its purchase of Associates First Capital Corporation, a subprime lender whose practices had awakened Eakes to the threat such operators posed to the very people that Self-Help Credit Union was working hard to help. Eakes's complaints had made it into the *New York Times* and the *Wall Street Journal,* and he had been asked to testify before a U.S. Senate hearing on predatory lending practices. Sandler had taken notice of this upstart in North Carolina who had dared to challenge the biggest bank in the United States by declaring that Citi was stooping pretty low in acquiring an outfit like Associates First Capital.

Over a long evening at the il Palio restaurant in Chapel Hill, Sandler introduced himself and told his rags-to-riches story that had made his World Savings Bank a leading player in California's booming home-lending marketplace. "I have made a lot of money," Eakes said Sandler told him before pausing a moment for emphasis. "And when I say a lot of money, I mean a *lot* of money. Now, I am a philanthropist, and I am in the business of funding what I call shit disturbers."[1]

Eakes does not shy from salty vocabulary, but Sandler's candor caught him off guard. "I said, 'I don't know what you mean,'" Eakes recalled. "He said, 'Yes, you do. It is somebody who takes a stick and just stirs it up all the time.'" Motioning with his hands, Eakes mimicked Sandler, who continued, telling Eakes, "From what I have been reading in the *New York Times* and the *Wall Street Journal* about Citigroup, you are the best shit disturber that I have ever seen." Eakes usually concludes the telling of this anecdote with a penetrating, cackling laugh.

Indeed, in the years leading up to his introduction to the Sandlers, Eakes had become more of a public advocate than at any time in his previous twenty years of work. During Self-Help's early days, Eakes was seldom the public voice. Bonnie Wright was the one most often quoted by reporters writing about the credit union. When Katharine McKee was his deputy in the early years, as she was busy building alliances among the growing number of community development agencies, many thought she was Self-Help's CEO. McKee was the one who most often attended meetings held outside North Carolina. Eakes had decided early on that his attention would be focused, laserlike, on building Self-Help in North Carolina.

Working in the background did not bother Eakes. He enjoyed the satisfaction of surprising people with what a small operation tucked away in North Carolina had done with $77 raised at a bake sale. The 1997 fight with Blue Cross and Blue Shield of North Carolina had been different, a deviation from the trajectory of the credit union or other initiatives. The resulting victory had gotten his blood pumping. But it was Eakes's next foray into public battle against predatory lenders that had put him and Self-Help in the spotlight of the national media, gained him the attention of the Sandlers, and would lead to another important step in Self-Help's evolution.

It had all begun as the dust settled following the fight with N.C. Blue. Eakes had returned to figuring out ways to make the financial system work for poor people. He and his colleagues were engaged in another battle, one that required careful attention to the money markets, as they recruited banks willing to engage in lending to low- and moderate-income borrowers. Self-Help was just beginning to build working relationships that would eventually expand Self-Help's secondary mortgage market into forty-eight states as it put the Ford Foundation's money to work.

The trajectory began to change in early summer 1998 when Lanier Blum, a Self-Help loan officer, came to Eakes seeking help in getting a potential customer out from under an onerous situation with Associates First Capital. Freddie Rogers was the client, and his case history would become as well known in the lore of Self-Help as the tale of Percy White, the New Bern baker whose bake sale had produced the first deposit for the credit union. Rogers had used a loan from Associates First Capital to fix up a home he had bought for $29,000 with a low-interest Veterans Administration mortgage. Now, he was saddled with a second mortgage and mounting fees totaling $47,476 at an interest rate of 13.7 percent. Eakes did the math. If Rogers had come to Self-Help in the first place, he would own his house free and clear.

Rogers was sinking fast—he had already filed for bankruptcy—and was trying to find a way to keep his house. He had heard about a new lending program Self-Help was experimenting with and thought it might fit his situation. Blum was doing everything she could to close a deal but was getting stonewalled by Associates First Capital, which refused to release the total amount of Rogers's debt. She asked Eakes how to proceed.

It was just the kind of deal that Eakes lived for. Here was a chance to show what the credit union could do to help poor folks build equity and improve their lives. After repeated attempts to secure the details on Rogers's loan from Associates First Capital's headquarters in Texas, Eakes finally got someone on the phone who told him that his inquiry was disingenuous; Eakes was just trying to steal a good customer. Eakes had had enough. He says he just snapped and declared to a faceless agent in Texas that he would make it his business to drive the Associates First Capital out of the state of North Carolina.

Eakes has been known to succumb to severe tunnel vision. His workmates call it the "lighthouse effect." He can sweep the horizon and penetrate dark corners, but he also has a tendency to stop and focus all of his attention entirely on a single problem, or issue, at the expense of everything else. With that phone call, Eakes's focus was now on Associates First Capital.

What Eakes discovered in the case of Freddie Rogers was not an isolated or unknown development in subprime lending. It had been a long-running issue in neighboring Georgia, where a legendary Legal Aid lawyer named Bill Brennan had been fighting lenders like Associates First Capital for years. The show *60 Minutes* had done stories about problems there. ABC News had produced an award-winning documentary on the plight of Brennan's clients. Once Eakes stopped to look, he discovered that in his hubris and anger he had threatened to throw into the sea one of the largest consumer finance companies in the world. But until Rogers showed up at Blum's desk, he had no idea who they were or what they were doing to North Carolina. At the time, Associates First Capital had as many as 6,500 customers in the state.[2]

The lawsuits in Georgia and rumbles of possible trouble from lenders like Associates First Capital in other states had been noticed in Washington, D.C. A task force from the Departments of the Treasury and Housing and Urban Development was about to begin a study of high-cost loans that stripped unsuspecting homeowners of equity they had accumulated over the years. The two agencies had been asked to prepare recommendations to Congress that would curb the most abusive practices.[3]

Eakes was still stewing over Rogers's predicament when Alan Hirsch, one of N.C. Attorney General Mike Easley's chief deputies, invited him to join a group that was looking into mortgage lending fees being charged to borrowers in North Carolina. Hirsch was the head of Easley's consumer protection division and had already met with representatives from the financial industry to talk about possible legislation to curb excessive, and possibly illegal, fees found in mortgage documents that borrowers had brought to the attorney general's attention. One of the first representatives Hirsch had called to discuss the matter was Paul H. Stock, the legal counsel for the N.C. Bankers Association, a group with considerable legislative clout.

Stock had listened to Hirsch and reported the attorney general's interest to the association's legislative committee. Committee members had responded much like Stock did when told about problems in North Carolina: the association's members were not guilty of these abuses. The bankers were about to dismiss Easley's invitation to work on a bill when Stock passed around copies of loan agreements containing provisions that strapped borrowers into bad loans guaranteed to cripple them financially. "When my folks looked at these," Stock recalled, "they shook their heads and said [work with Hirsch] with as little imposition as possible on the people who are doing it right all along. They pretty much gave me carte blanche to work on legislation."[4]

Ernie Ressler, the CEO at Central Carolina Bank, whose office was just across the street from Self-Help's headquarters in Durham, was vice chair of the association's legislative committee, and he aligned himself firmly behind Stock "once he was shown this wasn't squeamishness about paying legitimate fees, but this was people being lied to, taken advantage of, and trapped in inescapable circumstances."

Eakes accepted Hirsch's invitation and joined a working group of a dozen or so lawyers and lobbyists who made themselves at home around a table in a conference room at Stock's office. In addition to Stock and Hirsh and his people, the group included virtually anybody involved in home lending, from homebuilders to the mortgage bankers and mortgage brokers, the salesmen who often were the first and only link between the borrower and the lender. The agenda called for the conversation to focus on "junk fees," but when Eakes arrived, he said that did not go far enough. Eakes then recounted his stories about unsophisticated borrowers like Freddie Rogers who were being steered into high-price loans they could not repay and saddled with prepayment penalties on contracts that were doomed to fail, all the while losing equity in homes they thought were secure.

Eakes was particularly incensed over a dandy moneymaker called single-premium credit life insurance. Inserted into closing documents, it could add as much as $10,000 to the cost of a loan. Buyers paid up front for this service. Lenders did not require it, but many borrowers did not know that and ended up paying for coverage that most would never need or even carry to the end of the term of the loan. Eakes was passionate—a term used by virtually all asked to recall the working sessions—about what he considered outrageous abuses targeted at unsophisticated and unsuspecting borrowers. Eakes said such abuses would lead to a real debacle in the mortgage business in a few years if they were not outlawed.

Stock had never met Eakes and was only vaguely aware of Self-Help, but he knew Eakes was not just another whining consumer advocate who had never seen a balance sheet. Eakes was as much a banker as any of the members in his association. He brought experience from years of providing financial services to people in the marketplace that most bankers never bothered to recruit as customers. Having just given a political thumping to N.C. Blue, Eakes also had demonstrated political muscle, which might prove useful if a bill ever got to the General Assembly. While Eakes agreed with Stock that his member banks probably were not guilty of the abuses he saw, bad actors in the market were still taking advantage of borrowers, and those problems were going to spill over into the legitimate market sooner or later.

Besides Hirsch, Eakes found at least one other familiar face in the room: George Teague, a lawyer-lobbyist representing the mortgage bankers association. A year before, he had been at the table beside Eakes in their contest with N.C. Blue. Teague knew his way around the legislature and, after sitting in on the initial session with Hirsch at the attorney general's office, had told his client that Easley's initiative looked serious and was likely to produce a bill of some sort. He argued that it was better to be at the table putting it together than just walking away and saying no. He liked Eakes and believed he was someone he could work with.[5]

Meeting regularly, sometimes more than once a week, this group began hashing out what would become the first state law designed to curb predatory lending. And the debate was not just about fees. Eakes later joked that he hijacked the bankers' agenda and turned it into something else. That is true in part, but while Eakes often is given credit for the tougher lending regulations that resulted, he readily admits that North Carolina never would have produced early action on predatory lending without the aid and assistance of Stock and the bankers association.

The meetings consumed hundreds of hours; negotiations moved at a slow pace. The challenge was to arrive at legislation that did not impose onerous terms on legitimate commercial and residential lending and that avoided federal preemptions on banking regulations, yet at the same time dealt with the problems at hand. "It was a challenge of finding the right caliber of bullet," said Teague, "rather than adjusting the load for a shotgun."

Stock became the consensus builder, the link between the consumer advocates and the bankers. "He kept people talking when the natural tendency was to come to blows," said Eakes. Stock was herding a room full of natural adversaries. Banks and credit unions seldom agreed on much, if anything at all. Mortgage brokers had the most to lose. They were unregulated at the time and were not wholly trusted by the bankers, and certainly not by Eakes. The vast majority were legitimate, honest businessmen, Eakes said later, but there was the dirty 15 percent who targeted the most vulnerable, particularly the elderly, people of color, and unsophisticated borrowers. They needed to be stopped. Ever one for mechanical metaphors, Eakes said that if one-sixth of U.S. autos were defective, then people would overhaul the auto industry. Why shouldn't that happen for mortgage brokers?

Eakes had a long list of items he wanted to address. When he raised an issue, he often was told that such a thing could not occur in North Carolina, or that it was rare or "anecdotal," a defense that would later become the common refrain for those opposed to further regulations in lending. When Eakes heard that, he returned the following week with more examples. "They would say this is just an anecdote and not an extensive problem," Eakes recalled, "so I would bring in thirty more cases, then thirty more cases, and eventually they said this is a problem." One study would later show that forty thousand loans outstanding in North Carolina had provisions the proposed legislation would disallow.[6]

The sessions were intense. Each word, each mark of punctuation, each tilt one way or the other was studied for its intent and implications. State laws regulating banks had been amended and changed so many times over the years that keeping all the pieces in order was difficult. All in all, it was lawyer heaven, and early on Eakes brought along his own archangel. It was Michael D. Calhoun, and he had an eye for detail and was a veteran of litigation with lenders. Calhoun had a working knowledge of federal regulations and a sensitivity to legal precedent. He also was preparing a lawsuit for Freddie Rogers against Associates First Capital, a case that would eventually morph into a successful class action.

Stock and his boss, the association's president Thad Woodard, kept the sessions on track. They were hopeful that the hard work would actually lead to a bill that all could accept. The implications were obvious to anyone paying attention. "As we represented the bulk of the banking industry, that meant it had a chance," said Stock. "And if consumer advocates were going to support it, everybody else was in a position that if they didn't try to work on it and get it as well crafted as they could for their industry, they might just get run over."

One troubling aspect from the outset was the relative lack of participation by representatives from the state's major banks. The big five—Wachovia, NationsBank (in the process of merging with Bank of America), First Union, Branch Bank and Trust Company, and First Citizens Bank—had left the N.C. Bankers Association about a year earlier and formed their own lobbying group. They called themselves the North Carolina Association of

Financial Institutions and had hired the chief of staff of a former governor as their point man. The attitude among the brass in the suites atop the office towers in Charlotte, where First Union and NationsBank had their head-quarters, was that the advent of interstate banking had all but made state regulations passé. These banks were more concerned about what legislators were voting on in Washington than what happened on Jones Street in the Legislative Building in Raleigh.

In an effort to keep the big banks abreast of his group's work, Stock met weekly with the banks' lobbyist, but it was clear to Stock that most of the major banks were not paying attention. The only institution that was not a member of his association and expressed any interest was First Citizens, a conservative bank just on the cusp of its second century of operation. It had deep financial and political roots in North Carolina and only recently had begun to expand beyond the state's boundaries. James E. Creekman, a senior attorney with First Citizens, soon began meeting with Stock's group. Once negotiators settled on an item to go into the bill, it was Creekman, Calhoun, and Philip Lehman from the attorney general's staff who wrote the language to make it all work.

Creekman's role was to keep the bill on target. He accepted that Eakes knew the world of lending to homeowners and small businesses, but Eakes lacked experience in the full range of finance. Creekman was on guard against turns in the language that could complicate legitimate, large-dollar busi-ness transactions. He also wanted any new law to be clear and unambigu-ous. At the time, there was debate over features of a loan that qualified as "predatory." The financial world was highly competitive, and it was not just a matter of competing on interest rates alone. Modern-day lending used all manner of devices to make deals attractive to customers. "We didn't want the state mandating terms that were inflexible," Creekman recalled. "That would dry up the market."[7]

The group working on proposed legislation agreed that more rules re-quiring more disclosure of information were not the answer: that just pro-duced more paperwork. Disclosure had been the foundation for the reforms adopted by Congress in 1994 with the passage of the Home Ownership and Equity Protection Act, and it had not inhibited abusive lenders one bit. If anything, disclosure documents gave unscrupulous lenders more papers in which to hide shady items that they did not want customers to understand. The exhaustive number of forms requiring signatures on closing day only blurred a buyer's vision. There had to be another way.

The result was a bill that targeted the most flagrant abuses. Three important prohibitions were to apply to all home loans: prepayment penalties on all loans of $150,000 or less; "flipping," or repeated refinances by a lender of an existing loan that added more up-front fees; and financing single-premium credit insurance. A new section of law was created for what were called "high-cost home loans."

The most creative feature of the bill was that it did not put a cap on interest rates or fees. That was beyond the reach of state law. Instead, the proposed law created a new category of riskier loans that required certain actions to protect consumers. These provisions came into play when the up-front fees were greater than 5 percent of the loan amount or when the interest rate was 10 percent or higher (dropped to 8 percent in 2002) than the rates of U.S. treasury bills. If either of these conditions was met, borrowers would have to consult an independent credit counselor, who would advise them on the deal. Balloon payments, providing for a large lump sum due at some point, and negative amortization, where monthly payments do not cover loan costs, were prohibited. The requirements made it difficult for such high-cost loans to be worthwhile to the lender. And that was the purpose of measures Stock later described as "draconian." A final dose of common sense was included in the bill. Lenders would be required to consider a borrower's ability to repay.

It was not a perfect bill. Eakes had pushed for lower "triggers" that would push a loan into the high-cost category and make them less palatable to lenders like Associates First Capital. The state triggers were lower than those in federal law, but he still was not satisfied. Eakes finally resigned himself to the compromise, but that night, when he got home, he felt physically ill over the realization that he had not been able to do something better. His disappointment was tempered by provisions prohibiting single-premium credit life insurance.

Those who had thrashed out the details further agreed that after the bill was introduced, they would dissuade any who attempted to tinker with it in committee or on the floor. There was a concern that any changes to this delicately balanced compromise made amid the hustle and bustle of the legislative session might undo the entire package. In order to avoid any such trouble, the negotiators agreed to keep their legislative friends in check and oppose any amendments.

Everything seemed ready to go in early April 1999, when Attorney General Easley, who had his eye on winning the governorship in 2000, announced that a predatory lending bill was coming. At the same time, Eakes introduced a new citizens group called the Coalition for Responsible Lending. It included the bankers association and others that had participated in the negotiations along with those organizations—NAACP, consumer activists, AARP—in the Coalition for the Public Trust that had been so effective in bringing pressure to bear in the battle with N.C. Blue.[8]

At the Legislative Building in Raleigh, the bill's principal sponsor was Roy Cooper, the senate majority leader. He was eager to succeed Easley as attorney general, and this piece of legislation looked as good as any to ride into office. When Easley made his announcement, he was already lining up a majority of the senate as co-signers so the bill would include a formidable front when it was formally introduced.

Then, virtually overnight, Cooper's co-signers lost their nerve. It was as if someone had flipped a switch, and he soon discovered that that "someone" was the lawyers for the big banks that had sat on the sidelines throughout the past six months, confident that nothing would come of the tug-of-war going on at the bankers association offices. Cooper heard from the chief counsel for First Union, who tried to pull the plug on the entire process by pressing Cooper to introduce a shell bill with the details to be worked out in committee. For Eakes, it looked like N.C. Blue all over again. He was furious. "His face got redder from one day to the next," Cooper recalled.[9]

Cooper balked at the presumption of the big banks. So did Easley. The attorney general called those he knew in the upper echelon at Bank of America and First Union, the two banks that had used their muscle to scare off co-signers. "Tell me what you do not like about the bill," Easley requested. They came back a day or two later with objections, most of which Hirsch batted down with satisfactory answers. In the end, it appeared that the bank's lawyers hadn't really studied the bill and were unaware of what was included in it. They did not have any sound arguments, at least not any that would withstand public scrutiny, against curbing bad behavior in the marketplace.

There was still one major hang-up, and this one proved exasperating. The big banks argued that the limit on prepayment penalties was too low and would inhibit lending. Eakes had wanted these penalties eliminated entirely; the bankers insisted that they were necessary under certain conditions. Hirsch and Eakes went to see Cooper, who was about to introduce the bill. In the end, prepayment conditions were allowed on loans of more than $150,000. Cooper accepted the change rather than risk the major banks opposing the bill altogether. Hirsch claims he saw a tear form in Eakes's eye.[10] He did not admit to the display of emotion, but Eakes said, "I felt like I had let people down."

"For Martin, the world is often black and white," said Hirsch. "There are the good guys and the bad guys. That allows him to bring remarkable energy."

Cooper's name was the only one on the bill when it was introduced. Nonetheless, the bill had support from the attorney general, and it had the bankers association and others from the financial industry behind it. Eakes displayed no regret as he trolled the halls of the General Assembly over the next few weeks, pulling aside legislators to watch a videotape of the broadcast news accounts of victims of predatory lending. He had arranged for seven thousand copies of the videotape to be reproduced and distributed to members of the coalition to be shown to their members. Eakes pulled a cart carrying a portable videotape player through the halls of the Legislative Building. His mobile theater was so ubiquitous that his friends began calling him Teletubby, a reference to characters in a popular BBC children's show who had video screens embedded in their midsections.

The video included portions of investigative pieces done in Georgia and supplied to Eakes by Bill Brennan, the Legal Aid lawyer in Atlanta. Eakes judiciously edited the reports to keep the focus on Associates First Capital and left out a segment that exposed questionable behavior of EquiCredit, a subprime lender owned by Bank of America. It was a strategic decision he borrowed from Dr. Martin Luther King Jr.'s campaign in Birmingham—pick out one villain and go after him. When Bank of America's legal counsel began pressuring Cooper to scuttle the bill, Eakes amended his spiel, but not the video, to include a recitation of the problems encountered with EquiCredit. He got a complaint from his contact at Bank of America, whom he reminded of the favor he had done when producing the videotape. "Yes," she told him, "but you told every goddamn person in the world that you took it out and that is just as bad."

At one point, Hirsch fielded a complaint from a representative from Countrywide, the mortgage lender with headquarters in California that would later come to be known as one of the worst of the lenders pushing bad deals. Hirsch was told that the company would pull out of North Carolina if the bill passed. When he passed that message along, Eakes told him that was fine if they did not want to play by the rules in North Carolina. Lawyers from the American Bar Association's section on mortgage lending also sent inquiries, sure that the drafters had overlooked something. They said that what was proposed in the legislation was not legitimate at the state level. After reviewing the fine points with Hirsch, they conceded that perhaps North Carolina was on to something.

Easley stood behind the bill. Before entering law school, he had worked at a savings and loan and remembered customers as hardworking folk who depended on his judgment to present a fair deal. "When you were closing a loan, you understood that they were trusting you," he said. He recalled one borrower who called to tell him he had money for his monthly payment but not enough to cover "the Eskimo payment." In the background, Easley could hear the man's wife calling out, "escrow, escrow, you fool."[11]

The bill's working group remained mostly intact. The major banks, mollified by the changes they got from Cooper and running out of room with Easley, finally acquiesced. Some legislators remained balky, but Stock and Calhoun often appeared together, all but arm in arm, at the committee hearings where they answered questions together.

A provision was added in committee that required the legislature's research arm to report back in a year on whether the law had made any difference. In the end, there was some grumbling, and some complained of legislative overreach in floor debate, but the bill passed the senate with only one dissenting vote. In the house, the vote was 108–2.

"None of the major players [in the legislature] wanted to take a chance that they would be fighting the banking industry in North Carolina," said Hirsch.

It was a major victory for Eakes, who with his videos and constant presence at the Legislative Building got much of the credit. This rankled other consumer advocates who had worked just as hard once the bill was introduced. Eakes gave the affable Paul D. Stock high marks for holding the coalition together, putting his association's reputation on the line, and, in the end, making the entire process possible. But, Eakes added wryly, "as Paul would say, 'in my world, getting credit for that is not a good thing.'"

Indeed, some of the bankers' friends in the legislature confronted Stock when he told them he was solidly behind the bill. "And, we'd say, 'Absolutely. There are some dreadful things happening in the marketplace, and it is our marketplace and we want it clean.' That was our party line."

The state's new law scared bankers in other states where any changes were regarded as an intrusion on a bank's franchise. Stock absorbed complaints from colleagues who complained that North Carolina had "let the camel get its nose under the tent." When he was challenged by otherwise loyal friends at meetings of the American Bankers Association and the like, Stock had a ready response, but it largely fell on deaf ears. "If you have bills coming forward in your state," he would tell the complainers, "my advice is to not take the traditional approach and say we think we can beat this, but sit down and try to enact it. You need to look at what's going on in your marketplace."

Stock's standing joke to lighten the mood among those used to throwing their political weight around, trouncing any opposition, was that he had predicted that if the bill passed, the attorney general and state senator who pushed it would not have their jobs after the next election. Sure enough, he was right. Easley was elected governor in 2000, and Cooper succeeded him as attorney general. The predatory lending bill had proved to be an excellent "run-on" bill for both of them. (After four terms as attorney general, Cooper was elected governor in 2016.)

Easley did not let the moment pass. Within days of the legislation's passage in the summer of 1999, his office began airing a spate of public service announcements telling home buyers about their new protections under the new law, certain provisions of which went into effect October 1, 1999. He also punctuated the message by opening an investigation of Associates First Capital in North Carolina, citing fifty complaints against the company.

Eakes would later claim that he was brought "kicking and screaming" into the legislative battle in order to rectify the injustice to Freddie Rogers, but the fight was one that, in the end, he was glad he had joined. Clearly, he had walked into near-perfect conditions for a legislative victory. Lending weight to the successful effort were politically ambitious public officials, the influence of the attorney general's office, conscientious bankers concerned about their public image, and a "villain" whose base of operations was a thousand miles away.

There was no discounting the energy and enthusiasm that Eakes and his colleagues brought to bear. He and others had invested their time over weeks of negotiations, with Eakes pushing himself and his own allies to moments of aggravation. There had been fifteen-hour days at the legislature and Eakes's chutzpah to all but stand on the corner and show his incriminating videotape to any passerby. "He wasn't going to let anybody rest," Hirsch said of Eakes, "until we solved this problem."

The credit insurance crowd returned in 2000 with an effort to weaken the prohibition on single-premium policies, but by that time the movement against the practice was growing nationally. After years of constant nagging from Eakes and others, Fannie Mae and Freddie Mac announced that they no longer would take loans that included these outrageous charges in the closing costs. The prohibitions included in North Carolina's new law added some necessary cover as a practice estimated to have touched ten thousand homebuyers came to a close.

For all of Martin Eakes's professed reluctance as a public advocate, he was now in it and making the most of his new popularity as a lender who did not mind kicking the shins of the financial establishment. He was asked to join a panel organized by the Federal Reserve that was gathering testimony on predatory lending. The morning session held in Charlotte in July 2000 turned into a public airing of the North Carolina law and included most of the principal players, including Paul Stock and Philip Lehman from the attorney general's office. For his part, Eakes tried to turn up the heat on the Federal Reserve, which six years earlier had been commissioned by Congress to police the home-lending marketplace. Under its current chair, Alan Greenspan, the Federal Reserve had done nothing, and Eakes found that remarkable. "It is not discretionary, it's mandatory," Eakes declared. "It says you shall come up with regulations for acts you find to be unfair."

He kept the pressure on the representatives from fast-credit lenders who had seats on the same panel. The chief executive officer of EquiCredit, a subsidiary of Bank of America, declared that her company could not work under the North Carolina law. She said EquiCredit would have to leave the state, and borrowers who could not find loans at traditional sources would suffer. "Come back in a year," Eakes said, "and see what the market is like. If you lose some loans, 30 percent, and they're picked up by someone else who says we don't need those fees, then I think that's a good thing for the market-place." (Bank of America would shed its EquiCredit operations in two years.) Indeed, a subsequent study of lending after passage of the law showed that subprime lending increased by 31 percent.[12]

Beyond the hearing, Eakes became Associates First Capital's most nag-ging nightmare. He had not forgotten the promise to drive the company out of the state and publicly criticized Citigroup when it announced in Septem-ber 2000 that it was buying Associates First Capital. Eakes and others raised enough of a stink that Citigroup's Charles O. Prince, who was soon to be-come the financial giant's chief operating officer, came from Manhattan to gritty little Durham to talk to the company's critics. Meeting in the offices of Mechanics and Farmers Bank, one of the oldest black financial institutions in America, Prince heard from Eakes, Peter Skillern of CRA-NC, and others. Bill Brennan came from Atlanta for the session. Altogether, Eakes, Skillern, and Brennan dumped case after case of abusive practices into Prince's lap. Prince promised to investigate them all, and the company actually followed up with Brennan when the details of the offending accounts were not sent to him promptly.[13]

Brennan made sure that the *New York Times* heard about the meeting, and reporter Richard A. Oppel Jr. was one of the first to introduce Martin Eakes to a national readership. Eakes was as blunt as ever in his criticism. He told Oppel, "It is simply unacceptable to have the largest bank in America take over the icon of predatory lending."[14] Eakes's constant carping about practices such as single-premium credit insurance and prepayment penalties was also beginning to have an impact and promised more pressure on companies giving shelter to offensive lending practices. He told another *Times* writer that African American ministers planned to make abusive lending practices the civil rights movement of the decade.

By the time the Sandlers caught up with Eakes in the summer of 2001, the tide was on the way out for the Associates, as it came to be known after the Citigroup merger. In March, the Federal Trade Commission had opened an investigation, and in the fall of that year, Citigroup, on behalf of the Associates, agreed to pay $20 million to settle the state action begun under Attorney General Easley two years before.[15] The money went to customers who had purchased single-premium credit insurance between 1995 and 2000. About nine thousand residents were eligible. The Federal Trade Commission would later settle its case for ten times that much.[16]

The offer from the Sandlers to expand the success in North Carolina to a national stage was provocative. Self-Help was already considering such a move. Once the North Carolina law passed, Self-Help staffers began fielding calls from around the country. How did the North Carolina law work? What was in it? Could the same bill work in New Jersey or Georgia or Illinois?

At the same time, the Coalition for Responsible Lending, the ad hoc group behind the 1999 predatory lending bill, had waded hip-deep into other legislative battles. Wib Gulley, Eakes's former law partner and now a state senator, had introduced a bill to regulate mortgage brokers. Meanwhile, consumer advocates were trying to put an end to so-called payday lending—short-term consumer loans made at high interest rates—in the state.

Payday lending became legal in North Carolina in 1997 with a bill to legalize a simple check-cashing scheme. At the time, Eakes was suiting up for battle with N.C. Blue, and nobody had raised a hand against it. Within two years, there were 840 payday lending outlets open in the state making upward of three million loans a year. The number of outlets was up to more than 1,370 in mid-2001.[17] The storefront operations made small loans for interest and fees that could amount to an annualized interest charge of as high as 400 percent. The business trapped many borrowers in a cycle of never-ending debt if they took out subsequent loans to pay off outstanding balances. Research showed that more than half had between two and ten loans each. The 1997 bill passed with a sunset provision and was due to expire in 2001 unless it was renewed by the General Assembly. The payday crowd was determined to see it continued in effect.

The battle raged through the summer of 2001, but the industry failed to get the extension. That was not the end of the story, however. While some operators closed, others remained in business cashing checks for a fee. Still others, particularly those that were part of one of the large multistate outfits such as Advance America of Spartanburg, South Carolina, continued on as before, claiming that their affiliation with national banks made them exempt from state regulation.[18] It would take legal action by the state attorney general and four years of legal wrangling before the last payday lender closed shop in North Carolina.

When the Sandlers met Eakes for dinner in Chapel Hill, the payday lending fight was in full swing. Eakes's attention was focused on Raleigh, but the meeting left an impression. What he saw was a devoted couple that often finished each other's sentences. They had worked side by side for nearly four decades, turning a small California savings and loan they bought for $4.3 million into a business worth billions.

Herb was bald and a bit popeyed. Marion was short and could be curt in her comments and questions. During business meetings, she often busied herself with knitting, but she absorbed every syllable of the conversation. They were without pretense or inhibitions. He could swear like a sailor; she would finish a fellow diner's meal if there was food left on the plate. They did not do things in half measure. Sandler had already put together a small portfolio on Eakes that included high marks for Self-Help's record in home lending with the Ford Foundation. The Sandlers ran their business with tight controls. The couple would later complain that Self-Help's pay scale was far too low, but their own administrative costs were half those of other banks, and their offices were spartan.

The Sandlers were old hands at lending money and making things happen. Their Golden West Savings and Loan was one of the most profitable in the business. Long before others got into the market, Golden West was making nontraditional loans. Most were adjustable rate mortgages (ARMs). The starting rate may be lower than a thirty-year fixed-rate mortgage, but it could rise as the market changed. ARMs were created to help institutions avoid the trap of unfavorable rates. Between 1981 and 2005, when they sold their business, the Sandlers booked $274 billion in ARM loans. However, unlike a competitor, Countrywide, which sold its loans to Wall Street, the Sandlers kept their loans in their own portfolio. That meant that the company was dependent on proper vetting of these loans in order to keep their losses to a minimum. The Golden West loans were not trouble-free, however, and in later years, after abuses of ARMs were reported, some of Self-Help's allies with cases pending against the lender questioned Self-Help's alliance with the Sandlers.[19]

The Sandlers had done well over the years, and much of their wealth was in a foundation founded in 1991 to back progressive causes. Usually, they would identify an area of interest, find organizations that might be capable of addressing a problem, ask for research proposals from the candidates, and then settle on the one they liked best.[20]

"I have always had an intense interest in the issue of people being screwed," Sandler said in 2015. "When I was in the financial business, predatory lending, and all the things associated with that, drove me crazy." When he found out he was going to be in North Carolina, he invited Eakes to dinner.

Over the course of their evening together, the Sandlers decided that Eakes was the man they wanted to support. There would be no solicitation of proposals from others. "While there were a number of very good organizations," Sandler recalled, "there was only one person who had leadership qualities who could put together organization that could be really effective."

The Sandlers not only liked the work that Self-Help was doing; they also liked Eakes. "He is one of the most unforgettable characters I have ever met," Sandler said. "He has this combination of leadership quality, strategic thinking, high intelligence, and a burning, burning passion to stop poor people, especially poor people of color, from being screwed. And I love him for it."

"I have to tell you that a large key to success in philanthropic efforts emanates from focusing on extraordinary leaders," Sandler said. "You can love the mission and believe in the mission, but if you don't have extraordinary leadership with the capacity to do what you have to do, you won't accomplish anything. You can feel good, but you won't get anything done."

Other Sandler-funded initiatives to come would be the Center for American Progress, a left-leaning alternative to conservative think tanks such as the Heritage Foundation and the American Enterprise Institute. The Sandlers also provided initial funding for ProPublica, an independent nonprofit supporting investigative journalism.

The Sandlers pressed Eakes for an estimate on how much money he would need. Eakes put them off, his mind recalling a similar request from Julian Price in Asheville. The dinner ended with Eakes agreeing to submit a proposal.

There was too much going on that summer to respond immediately. Putting together a full proposal required carving time out of everything else that was going on, and that meant more late nights, more double-duty from colleagues, and more writing and rewriting of something that they called the Responsible Lending Law and Policy Center.

"We were busy, and Herb kept calling me, saying 'I am serious. What would it take? Write it down,'" recalled Eakes. "So we finally got together and came up with a plan, and we had a couple of assumptions. We needed sixty-plus staff members that would fan out across the states, North Carolina and twelve to fifteen additional states, in order to pass state legislation, and the budget to do that would be $9 million a year.

"The work would be extremely controversial. We already knew we were in a blood-bath fight with the national mortgage bankers and the big banks, with payday lenders. It was a free-for-all. We would need this to be endowed from day one. To endow a $9 million budget that would pay out 5 percent, you have to have $180 million. We actually looked at each other and said, 'Do we have the guts to send a proposal to someone we have never met except for one dinner and ask him for $180 million?' Which is what we did. We said, 'What the heck. Easy come and easy go.'"

By the time Eakes sent a proposal to the Sandlers, it was February 2002. More than six months had passed since their dinner meeting in Chapel Hill. Now, they had what they had been asking for. Eakes gathered the staff members who had produced more than forty pages of ideas, plans, and appendices around a table that all but filled a windowed conference room called the "fishbowl," just down the hall from Eakes's office on the sixth floor of Self-Help's Durham office building. A speakerphone sat in the middle of the table. They dialed Sandler's number, he answered, and Eakes asked Sandler if he had read their handiwork.

According to Eakes, Sandler said, "'Yes, I read it. Are you out of your *fucking* mind?' There was no introduction, no nothing. For about five minutes, he just abused me on the phone. I am sort of laughing; as a matter of fact, my friends tell me that the answer to that question is 'yes.'

"He just goes on and on, berating me," Eakes said. "After the end of five minutes, he just runs out of . . . they say every storm just runs out of rain. Well, he just ran out of rain. He said, 'Well, I'll tell you what I'll do. I am not going to give you $180 million. That is ridiculous, but I know George Soros and I know a bunch of other wealthy philanthropists, and we will put together a consortium that will fund your annual budget [$9 million] for the first five years.'

"So I am sitting there on the phone, and I said, 'Let me make sure I've got this. To our request for $180 million, the answer is hell no! That either we take $45 million or nothing.' [Sandler says] 'That is exactly what I am saying.' I said, 'Yes sir, I think we have a deal.'"

Before the day was out, Eakes had assigned Mary Mountcastle to begin putting together operating plans for what would become the Center for Responsible Lending.

CHAPTER TEN

A Box of Rattlesnakes

In February 2003, Angelo Mozilo, the CEO of the mortgage giant Countrywide, delivered the John T. Dunlop lecture at Harvard University's Joint Center for Housing Studies. Mozilo's company was racing to become the nation's leading underwriter of subprime mortgages, and he dismissed new predatory lending laws as impediments to low- and moderate-income borrowers realizing the dream of homeownership. In an astonishing turn of the numbers, Mozilo said that America was too focused on the 20 percent defaulting on the exotic loans, such as those made by his company, rather than on the 80 percent paying on time. "Shouldn't we, as a nation, be justifiably proud that we are dramatically increasing homeownership opportunities for those who have been traditionally left behind?"[1]

Mozilo threw in a few jabs at states such as Georgia and North Carolina that had passed laws regulating Mozilo's business and that of brokers who filled Countrywide's mortgage stream with loans doomed to fail and that would bring down the nation's financial markets in 2008. Then, with the evangelical fervor of Martin Eakes, a man who helped make North Carolina uncomfortable for Countrywide, Mozilo declared: "The most important point is that low-income and minority households, who are so proud to be homeowners and who will do whatever it takes to meet their mortgage payments, deserve our undivided attention. And our nation requires it."

Certainly, Countrywide was doing its part. It was a mortgage factory, running full tilt, and would issue $1.5 trillion in loans between 2002 and 2005.[2] The subprime mortgage industry was in flood in 2003, with businesses like Countrywide driving packages of mortgages to Wall Street in a volume like nothing that had been seen before.

Wall Street investors could not be satisfied. They took these loans, rolled them into mortgage-backed securities, and sold them in pieces to investors who clamored for more. "We had our loans sold three months in advance, before they were even made at one point," an executive with New Century, one of the other big players, later declared in testimony before the Financial Crisis Inquiry Commission.[3]

In 2007, these nontraditional loans made by Countrywide—and its fiercest competitor, Ameriquest—began to fail, and the housing market collapsed, ending the boom times and creating the most serious financial crisis since the Great Depression. It would take years for the nation to regain its financial footing.

Such an outcome seemed preposterous on that evening in 2003 in Cambridge, on the Harvard campus, where Mozilo was toasted as a "housing leader." Countrywide was on a mission to provide homes for those who heretofore had been unable to afford them, Mozilo told his audience. He declared proudly that "homeownership is not a privilege, but a right," and he believed that his company was on a mission, one that served the nation by easing class tensions between the haves and the have-nots. "We had an obligation," he would later say. "It was clearly a social issue in the country that was going to explode. The number of have-nots was growing, and the 'have-not' was primarily in the area of home ownership." The housing gap in America was "intolerably too wide," he told his Harvard audience.

Housing values were rising steadily from year to year, and with each click upward, more and more people joined the ranks of homeowners. Existing owners refinanced loans to draw out cash to be spent on enhancing their lifestyles. Homeownership would reach its highest level ever—69.4 percent—in 2004. This kind of growth was considered good for business, good for the nation, and good for proud new homeowners, according to the policy makers and legislators in Washington. The last thing anyone wanted to do was to stall this powerful economic engine, the most robust in an economy coming off the bursting of the dot-com bubble and colossal failures such as the energy giant Enron. In one congressional hearing after another, mortgage bankers and their friends pushed back against anything they saw as limiting their opportunity to find more customers, lend them more money, and send this train of prosperity farther down the track.

The last thing the industry wanted was more restrictions like those in North Carolina. Its passage of a predatory lending law had emboldened state legislators elsewhere to try the same thing. By the end of 2003, sixteen other states or municipalities had adopted similar legislation. Some advocates had simply taken the North Carolina language and submitted it, almost verbatim, for legislative approval.

After being caught unawares in North Carolina, the financial industry went on full alert, using the examples of legislation there and in Georgia as cautionary tales. Most important, a Mortgage Bankers Association presentation said that there was no room for compromise such as the accommodation in North Carolina.

Publicly, the industry's response was to acknowledge the existence of a few bad actors and rogue operations that used high-pressure tactics and outright deception. Certainly, these were methods and practices that no one condoned, spokesmen said. In congressional hearings and elsewhere around the country, dignified corporate officers were disappointed by the abuses reported with greater and greater frequency by witnesses at congressional hearings and in the press. "That's not us," they said. "We do things the right way."

Testifying at a U.S. Senate Banking Committee hearing in 2001, seated just down the table from Martin Eakes, was the chairman of the board of Ameriquest, who read from his company's standards of best practices and drew compliments from committee chairman Senator Paul Sarbanes of Maryland. No mention was made of an Ameriquest tactic of spamming potential customers with phony emails. Subsequent lawsuits filed after the market collapsed would demonstrate that declarations of ethical behavior like the one from Ameriquest were so much eyewash.

Consumer and civil rights groups brought witnesses to hearings like this one. The industry routinely dismissed as anecdotal the repeated stories of the elderly and semiliterate trapped into loans they could not repay and that had cost them their savings and, often, even their homes when mortgages went into foreclosure. Industry advocates claimed the best way to rid the nation of abuses was vigorous enforcement of existing state and federal laws. New regulations would only inhibit investment, stem the flow of cash that was boosting the economy, and deprive those most worthy of the chance of owning a home.

More state laws, or more regulations from Washington, would lead to the end of credit for those just in reach of owning a home, the industry said. That night at Harvard, Mozilo cited a 2002 study by the Credit Research Center at Georgetown University that reported that credit became less available for low- and moderate-income borrowers after North Carolina's law went into effect. The Georgetown figures indeed showed a decline in overall lending, but that was not the full story.[4] A subsequent 2004 study by the Center for Community Capital, which used a vastly larger database of 3.3 million loans made between 1998 and 2002, reported a sharp decline in the refinancing of existing loans, which were the kinds of transactions most fraught with abuse. According to this analysis, the data showed that the law "is doing what it was intended to do: eliminate abusive loans without restricting the supply of subprime mortgage capital for borrowers with blemished credit records." Indeed, the law had not inhibited the flow of money that enabled subprime borrowers to take out their first loans. The data showed the opposite; it had increased.[5]

As Wall Street investors fed on the growing subprime market in 2001, before the creation of the Center for Responsible Lending, Self-Help was continuing its fight with unscrupulous lenders in an industry that it said was all but stealing $9.1 billion from the nation's homeowners every year. That was the amount that Eric Stein, Eakes's deputy and chief operating officer at Self-Help, had calculated as the cost of predatory lending in a paper released in 2001.[6]

Stein's study, "Quantifying the Economic Cost of Predatory Lending," was the first hefty piece of published research to come out of Self-Help. It was also the first attempt to put numbers behind victims' stories that had been aired in congressional hearings and in lawsuits. It followed on the report by the U.S. Departments of Treasury and Housing and Urban Development task force warning of the dangers inherent in the mortgage market.[7] For the first time, however, Stein's paper assigned dollar losses due to equity stripping, excessive interest rates, and the foreclosures that went hand in hand with predatory lending. The number was stunning, and Stein's estimate of $9.1 billion in losses began showing up in public testimony. Eakes had it inserted into the record the day he appeared before

Sarbanes's committee. It was picked up immediately by those concerned about the growing menace.

The strategy behind producing the study and getting it into the hands of policy makers was right out of the Self-Help playbook. Solid research and demonstrable evidence were far more persuasive in the public arena than yet another story of woe from a defrauded homeowner. The strategy was not that different from earlier demonstration work in North Carolina. Using its own lending as evidence, Self-Help had convinced the state's bankers that making home loans to marginal borrowers could build a record of creditworthiness. Develop a record, advertise the results, expand the opportunity.

Stein's research backstopped the value and necessity of the North Carolina law. By assigning a piece of the $9.1 billion loss to each state, the report helped advance the work of advocates for similar legislation elsewhere. Georgia governor Roy E. Barnes quoted Stein's study—calling out the $300 million cost to his fellow Georgians—in a speech to the National Consumer Law Center.

The report was still gaining circulation as Self-Help's newest subsidiary, the Center for Responsible Lending, was in its formative days. When Mary Mountcastle began putting the new outfit together, she picked one of Self-Help's utility infielders, Mark Pearce, to work as her deputy. Mountcastle was skilled in organizational management, understood the Self-Help culture, and was someone Eakes trusted to move right along with him and not get too far ahead. "I told Mark I didn't want to be doing this too long," she said some time later.[8] Within a year, Pearce succeeded her as president.

Pearce came from Self-Help's real estate development team. That included management of the array of commercial buildings that Self-Help owned in Durham and elsewhere in North Carolina, as well as an ambitious and innovative neighborhood revitalization program in a part of Durham called Walltown, which Self-Help, in a partnership with Duke University and the city of Durham, was helping to transform into a place where folks wanted to live, rather than avoid. "That was the work I thought I would do for my career, helping people become homeowners, doing community development law, helping nonprofits, and doing affordable housing development," Pearce said.[9]

Finding a name for this new organization got more consideration than when Eakes and his friends had created the Center for Community Self-Help in 1980. Some had argued for something that had an edge to it and included a phrase like "economic justice." Eakes wanted a less partisan name that would not disturb potential supporters who might subscribe to a more conservative agenda. Center for Responsible Lending was balanced, and it came with a handy acronym—CRL—that conformed to one already in use by the Coalition for Responsible Lending, the collection of allies behind the 1999 predatory lending bill.

Deborah Goldstein was another Self-Help staff member assigned early to the CRL. She was a Harvard-trained lawyer who, by the time she got to Durham, had a paper published by the Harvard housing institute that had honored Mozilo. Her study, which was released as the North Carolina law was being written, strengthened the discussion about what was, and what was not, predatory lending.[10] Eakes hired Goldstein in the summer of 2001, and she spent much of her time in her first few weeks on the job working in a cubbyhole off the hallway outside his office. Mostly, she fielded out-of-state calls from those wanting to know more about the new North Carolina law.[11]

With the Sandlers insisting on a proposal, Eakes assigned Goldstein to put the pieces together. The drafting went on for several months, with language and propositions shuttling between Eakes, Stein, Michael Calhoun, and others in the executive circle. The result was a proposal that included everything but the kitchen sink. It called for a staff of sixty-six lawyers, a team of research professionals, and a support staff. The center would have a litigation department, an investigative reporting component, and a team of sixteen—twelve lawyers and four support staff—to concentrate on legislative lobbying in a dozen or more states and on Capitol Hill. The center would have one office in the District of Columbia and another on the West Coast. The Sandlers were most keen on the latter. A communications section was part of the plan along with a separate unit to build coalitions and work with existing, like-minded organizations.

"We [proposed] what we thought we needed to be successful," Goldstein recalled. "I thought it was crazy. There is no way that this man is going to give us this. But it was also an all-or-nothing proposal. This is what we need to be successful."

The enterprise bore the cultural stamp of Self-Help. The center would be a collaborative effort and work with other advocacy groups, contributing its financial stability and knowledge of the financial markets developed over nearly twenty years of lending. "We no longer feel the youthful need to prove that we can accomplish goals on our own," the proposal read with a touch of hubris. At the same time, the center would remain nimble and seize opportunities as they arose, "avoiding 'strategy by committee.'" In short, the CRL welcomed allies, but it was not going to be dragged into doctrinal infighting. It was going to focus on what worked, not just on what was compatible with some purist credo.[12]

CRL's senior management would come from within. Eakes insisted on growing his own leaders, and he had no room for imported superstars. Self-Help's history was replete with examples of hiring bright people, allowing them to develop within the organization, and then turning to them to manage the various teams in the organization. A good example was Randy Chambers, Self-Help's chief financial officer in 2001. Four years earlier, Chambers had a new graduate degree in public policy and a desire to work in community development. After servicing mortgages and working long hours in the credit union's accounting operations, he was surprised to learn one day, as Eakes introduced him without ceremony to a group of visitors, that he was Self-Help's chief financial officer. At the time of his "promotion," Chambers explained, the accounting department included one full-time accountant and one other guy. "I was the other guy."[13]

A paramount consideration was financial independence. The CRL would be taking on powerful institutions with very deep pockets. There would be no time to stop in the midst of a legislative fight to conduct fund-raising for next year's salaries. Eakes had already experienced an effort to leverage Self-Help out of the debate over payday lending in the summer of 2001 when an influential state senator declared that if Self-Help did not back off, then it would never see another dollar of state money for housing. Fortunately, Self-Help had sufficient resources to ignore a threat that proved to be real. State support of Self-Help's programs indeed came to an end.

While the Sandlers rejected Eakes's request for $180 million—most colleges did not have endowments that large—they did guarantee the CRL for the first five years. At the same time, the Sandlers got a little more than they expected. They put Mountcastle through the ringer one day over administrative details associated with the center's formation. For all their due diligence, they had failed to realize that this was a tightly run organization that came complete with office space, payroll and computer systems, and a pool of talent, all the things a start-up could spend months putting into place.

The biggest difference for Goldstein after the money rolled in was that she and others answering questions from potential allies beyond North Carolina were no longer bound to their desks in Durham. A fully funded CRL meant a travel budget for staff members like Calhoun to spend more time in places like Atlanta, where he and Keith Ernst, a CRL staff member, all but took up residence after attention shifted to Georgia's new predatory lending law.

Georgia governor Roy E. Barnes had tried to get lenders and consumer interests to come to terms on a bill in 2001. All sides worked on a compromise, using many of the provisions of the North Carolina law, but, in the end, the lenders walked away from it. Barnes was not going to let that happen in 2002, and the resulting bill was a tough one with even more restrictive provisions than those in North Carolina. The governor was working arm in arm with Bill Brennan, with whom he had collaborated a decade earlier on lawsuits against predatory lenders. Brennan welcomed help from Calhoun and Ernst, who reported for duty in Atlanta on the CRL's dime. They lived for a time at Brennan's house.[14]

Georgia's law took effect in October 2002, and the state became *the* predatory lending battleground after the agencies that rated mortgage-backed securities, Fitch's and Standard and Poors, withdrew coverage of most of the loans covered under the new law. The rating agencies had a particular objection to provisions that shifted responsibility for the legality of a loan to the final holder of the note. Assigning legal liability for any misdeeds done during the making of the loan was more than the market could bear. With loans lumped together in a package of securities, it was difficult to know who would be responsible. No such alarm had arisen four years earlier in North Carolina when violations of the state antipredatory lending law were deemed to be violations of the state's existing usury law, which had long held assignees liable for usury violations. At the time, the securitization of home mortgages had not mushroomed to such prominence on Wall Street.

Georgia legislators were told that if the law were allowed to stand, then the building boom in the suburbs of the South's leading city would come to an end. Barnes had lost his bid for reelection in 2002, in part because voters were angry about his efforts to remove the stars and bars of the old Confederacy from the state flag. The legislature bowed to pressure from the financial industry when it reconvened with Barnes's replacement, Sonny Perdue, in office. Rather than satisfy Wall Street by tweaking the bill to respond to the narrow objections, the legislature gutted Barnes's law, and the flow of dangerous subprime loans resumed. If North Carolina had been a feel-good victory, then this was a bitter defeat. In the years ahead, Georgia home buyers would suffer like those in hot subprime states like California, Arizona, and Florida after the real estate market eventually collapsed.

The subprime industry was now organized like never before. *Inside B&C Lending*, a niche publication focused on the growing subprime market, reported a few days after Georgia's revised law took effect that any conciliation and cooperation with consumer groups to work out a national solution was off the table. The industry had a new advocacy organization of its own. The Coalition for Fair and Affordable Lending pushed federal legislation to preempt state laws and municipal ordinances, all under the guise of consumer protection and uniformity. It was the product of lobbyist Wright Andrews, who in April 2003 told one of his clients, the National Home Equity Mortgage Association, "We can use a lot more force and a lot more ground troops."[15]

The CRL was not even a year old, and it had people working in Georgia and New Jersey when Chris Kukla headed to New Mexico in early 2003. It was all quite opportunistic, another Self-Help character trait. New Mexico had not qualified in the original proposal as a state worthy of attention. The plan had called for efforts in the thirteen largest states, and New Mexico ranked thirty-six. That was before Kukla heard about Don Kidd, a community banker and Republican from Carlsbad who was giving his fellow bankers fits with a bill that he had introduced to outlaw abusive lending practices.

"I think what we came to realize was that the size of the state didn't matter," Kukla said later. "If we get enough states to pass laws, then it was going to be really hard for people not to take notice, especially if you can go and say, 'Even New Mexico figured out this was a problem. How come you are not doing something about it?'"[16]

Kukla was raised in the suburbs of Chicago and had a law degree from Notre Dame. Before moving to Durham with his wife—they liked the area—he had spent five years working in congressional offices. A friend of his wife worked at Self-Help and introduced him to Eric Stein. Kukla paid a call at the Self-Help headquarters, thinking the visit was just an introduction, and left with a job offer. He began work on June 1, 2002.

Kukla's initial assignment was to field calls about predatory lending legislation. That's how he heard about Kidd and the co-sponsor on his bill, a Democrat and senate powerhouse named Manny M. Aragon. "You had this very liberal Latino Democrat from Albuquerque teamed up with a conservative banker from Carlsbad, both of whom were equally passionate about protecting consumers in the home-lending market," Kukla recalled. He booked a flight to Santa Fe and checked into a hotel.

"They sicced Chris on me," Kidd chuckled as he recalled his introduction to the CRL some years later. Kidd speaks with a pronounced drawl and punctuates his conversation with regional aphorisms accumulated from a lifetime of doing business with ranchers and small-town businessmen. Balding, with glasses, Kidd had run his Western Commerce Bank since the early 1970s. The bank was not especially large, but it was profitable, and it had expanded beyond the town of Carlsbad to three nearby communities. Kidd's credentials in business and Republican politics were impeccable. A couple of decades earlier, he had helped organize the state's community bankers association. Though a member of the state's minority party, he had been elected and reelected to the state legislature dominated by Democrats for a decade. He was not the sort to immediately warm up to activists like Eakes and the CRL crowd.

The subprime market was just gathering steam in the Southwest when Kidd asked a fellow legislator, a realtor who had an office near one of his bank's branch locations, why Western Commerce was not being asked to write any home mortgages for his home sales. His colleague told him that Western Commerce could not turn business around fast enough to satisfy his buyers, so they were doing business with a mortgage broker. "I started looking into it and found out they were doing subprime loans and getting ten points up front," Kidd said. "No, the realtor wasn't; he was just selling the house. I guess he didn't tell 'em how to kill 'em. He just wanted them dead."

This whole business offended Kidd. "It was the most thieving thing that I had ever seen," he said. He said the lenders he discovered taking his customers away did not even follow his own belief that a borrower should be capable of repaying the loan, something he had learned a long time ago. It was one of the fundamentals that had helped grow Western Commerce from $14 million to more than $400 million in assets. He said what these mortgage brokers were doing was peddling a "box of rattlesnakes. That worked pretty good as long as you didn't let them out." Kidd was no friend of more government regulations but he believed this kind of business was just wrong. "If you know you are going to have to look at that lady in the eye for thirty years," he said, "you aren't going to mistreat her."

Kidd liked his new sidekick, Kukla, a mere pup who had not been born when Kidd became a banker. Kukla liked Kidd, too, but he later confessed that he arrived suspicious that Kidd may be talking the talk but would walk out at the last minute like the lenders in Georgia. It did not take long for

Kukla to realize that Kidd was a man of his word as well as a wily legislator who knew how to get things done. Kidd did not want a fancy bill with lots of words that could be turned inside out and used to sidestep the intent of the law. He wanted simple limits on points and fees—3 percent, not 10 percent—and a law that prohibited such things as flipping and the financing of credit insurance premiums. He also included a provision that required lenders to document a borrower's ability to repay.[17]

As the legislative fight got under way, Kukla brought to Kidd a wealth of background information, details about lending legislation pending elsewhere, and the research that the CRL could put on the table to deal with tricky issues such as assignee liability, the provision that blew up the Georgia law. Kidd also was introduced to consumer advocates and other new allies, most of whom he'd never broken bread with before. "Little old nonprofits in Albuquerque found out about the bill, so they would come to hearings with me," Kidd said. "It was such fun to sit with four or five ladies with switchblades. They were going to kill them if it didn't pass."

Kukla was laboring away in the deep Southwest, a long way from Durham, shuttling back and forth on weekend flights and working with a crowd that had no idea what Self-Help was. At least the desk clerk at the Santa Fe Hilton knew him; he registered frequently enough to qualify for a discount. He finally established Self-Help's bona fides with Kidd's Democratic ally Senator Manny Aragon after Aragon's top assistant came east to visit family in Greensboro, North Carolina. Kukla met him in Durham, just fifty miles away, and gave him the Self-Help story, making sure he saw the real estate that Self-Help owned in downtown. At least the guy now knew that the CRL was not a bunch of over-caffeinated activists working out of a storefront in a strip mall. It was a fully functional component of an organization with assets, substance, talent, and resources.

Kukla assumed a supporting role, bringing to bear what Self-Help had learned in North Carolina. "The folks on the ground picked the right people," he said, "and they knew what they needed to get legislation done. I was there to provide technical support. What they needed was someone who knew this law backward and forward and to help them navigate it out with [answers to] questions. That is what I did."

The opposition certainly knew who Kukla was and what was happening in New Mexico. Calhoun warned Kukla that he had overheard industry lobbyists in Atlanta talking about Kidd's bill and alerted Kukla that they were headed his way. Kukla's mother even gave him a heads-up. She worked for a mortgage company in Chicago, one that was peddling loans like those he was trying to make illegal. She called one day and said, "I can know where you are when someone comes by [my office] and puts their head in and says, 'What the hell is your son doing now?' You thought maybe they didn't know who you are. Trust me. They know who you are." The New Mexico Home Loan Protection Act passed, with comfortable margins in both houses, though Kidd's banker friends went the other way.

The industry did not fold or leave Santa Fe when Kidd's bill became law. Rather, they lobbied the lieutenant governor to leave some room for changes, perhaps in an upcoming short session. The opposition then raised a howl and badgered Kidd and Aragon into a public hearing so they could air their complaints, along with threats and warnings of dire consequences for the housing market if something was not done before the law went into effect. When Kukla arrived at the hearing, Kidd told him that he was responsible for answering any difficult questions that might arise.

Kukla recalled that one of the speakers that day was the head of the community bankers association, the same organization that Kidd had helped organize years before but which had recently revoked his membership. The association's president complained about how onerous the new provisions were and how lending would dry up as a result. Kidd finally had heard enough. He raised his hand and said, "Jerry, I've known you for twenty-five years, and you have never screwed somebody. You are not screwing people now, are you Jerry? Well, then I don't really understand what you are worried about because this is only for people who are screwing people, and I know you are not screwing people."

Continuing his recollection of the day, Kukla said Kidd told the president, "I can live with it, and so can you. You know I asked the head of my mortgage operations to tell me what we are charging, and she said we are charging 2 percent in points and fees. I said, 'Sweetheart, we are leaving money on the table.' He was making the point that if you can't get by with 5 percent in points and fees, you ought not to be in business."

There were a few minor adjustments made to the law, but it survived virtually intact. Kidd called it his best work in more than a decade as a legislator. He got the last laugh. "The bankers association excommunicated me. Took the buttons off my coat and everything," he said many years later, after the subprime industry collapsed, leaving devastation in its wake. "Now they tell me I saved New Mexico from becoming California or Arizona." Eakes would later ask Kidd to become a CRL director, where, Kidd said, "I am the only redneck on the board. Talk about being outnumbered."

"The Self-Help philosophy is this country," he said. "They are trying to give people an opportunity to help themselves."

The success in New Mexico helped ease the pain suffered in Georgia. It was the first notch for Kukla, who would later lead the CRL's lobbying work in North Carolina. The win added some impetus to work in New Jersey, where Deborah Goldstein was on the ground and working with allies such as AARP (American Association of Retired Persons).

In the spring and summer of 2003, the battle was shifting from the states and municipalities to Capitol Hill. "We recognized that we couldn't solve the issues of predatory lending just by focusing at the state level," said Pearce. Eakes began looking for a building in which to install the newest outpost of Self-Help. He found what he wanted in a handsome, prewar office building in a prime location near the White House. But, it would be the CRL's research, along with its Washington address, that would raise its national profile in the next few years.

CHAPTER ELEVEN

The Emperor's Naked

The numbers were too stunning to be true. The nation's housing market appeared to be chugging merrily along in the early part of 2006, with television reality shows hyping the bundles of cash that speculators could make by flipping houses as prices rose faster than at any time since the 1920s. But, if the analysts at the Center for Responsible Lending were right, more than two million homeowners with subprime loans issued since 1998 were either in foreclosure or headed there soon. That included nearly 20 percent of all subprime loans issued in recent years. The total bill would be staggering, $164 billion in lost wealth. The worst foreclosure crisis in thirty years lay just ahead.

Of course, the report was *wrong*, but not in the way those making fortunes off home mortgages insisted.

The looming financial disaster would turn out to be at least *twice* as bad—with more than four million borrowers losing their homes—as what was predicted in *Losing Ground: Foreclosures in the Subprime Market and Their Cost to Homeowners*, a report prepared by the CRL and released in the latter part of 2006. "Holding a subprime loan has become something of a high-stakes wager," the report said.[1]

The report's dire prediction seized the attention of national news outlets. The *New York Times* would provoke further commentary four months later in business writer Gretchen Morgenstern's Sunday column. She was following up on testimony delivered by Michael Calhoun, Mark Pearce's successor as president of the CRL, at a hearing on March 27, 2007, before the U.S. House Financial Services Committee. The mortgage bankers called the report "overly pessimistic." Yet, only a few weeks before Calhoun's testimony, Lehman Brothers, a New York banking house, had estimated a foreclosure rate of 30 percent on the newfangled loans that gave borrowers a low introductory interest rate before resetting to a higher adjustable rate with monthly payments many of these borrowers probably could not afford.

After launching the CRL with plans for multiple components—litigation, investigative journalism, coalition building, and advocacy—the organization found its niche as a research and policy group. The staff never reached the sixty-plus members originally projected, settling in at around forty or so four or five years in. As the original guarantee of income from the Sandlers decreased, the CRL secured other grants from foundations such as Ford, Pew, and MacArthur, and broadened its funding base to secure its future. And while other reports had preceded *Losing Ground*, it was this report, which followed on Eric Stein's 2001 estimate of $9.1 billion as the cost of predatory lending, that gave the CRL a national reputation as an outfit whose work would bear watching as the mortgage market declined in 2007 and ultimately collapsed in 2008.

"We were not just another do-gooder organization thinking we knew how the world ought to run," recalled David Wiley, Martin Eakes's deputy in Washington. "We could prove how [predatory lending] was actually being run and how and why it was hurting the borrower. Those research reports were critical. In terms of bodies on the ground, we were outgunned, and we would always be outgunned. But, in terms of the facts, they could not prove our facts wrong."[2]

The online news magazine *Politico* would soon post a story calling Self-Help "the main intellectual engine driving Democratic responses to the housing crisis."[3]

Wiley was one of Eakes's Davidson College classmates who had made a pact in their postgrad years to improve the world they had inherited. Wiley had put his name down as one of the incorporators of the Center for Community Self-Help back in 1980 but had never played an active role in Self-Help's affairs until Eakes called him in 2002 and asked if he would be willing to organize the Self-Help office in Washington, D.C., which was to be its first base of operations outside North Carolina.

Wiley had spent nearly two decades developing affordable housing in the District of Columbia. At the time of Eakes's call, he was putting that experience and his early training at the Yale School of Management to work as a consultant in community development. His wife, also a Davidson graduate, was one of Bonnie Wright's best friends. She was working as a midwife at a Latino health clinic in Washington when she and Wiley reunited seventeen years after leaving college. They began dating and eventually were wed. She told her husband not to think twice about accepting Eakes's invitation.

"I didn't know a whole lot about lobbying, but I know how to create systems, and he thought I would be a good person to have creating the office," Wiley said. Going unsaid was a solid foundation of trust.

The Sandler money certainly helped, but Wiley said a Washington office had always been on the Self-Help agenda, regardless of whether a pile of cash came available. As he and Eakes talked ahead of his joining the CRL in January 2003, the lending industry's focus was shifting to Congress and away from the exhausting work of fighting state legislation and municipal ordinances. The industry wanted comprehensive nationwide protection from a patchwork of laws threatening to restrict their business. That meant congressional action. Eakes wanted Self-Help to be there when the bills starting arriving on Capitol Hill. Wiley had been on the payroll less than a month when the industry's lead lobbyist, Wright Andrews, created the Coalition for Fair and Affordable Lending.

In time, the Washington office would become the hub of Self-Help's lobbying, blending what had been learned while helping write legislation at the state level with a growing library of research reports. But Eakes had a much more ambitious goal in mind for his first out-of-state location.

Self-Help would not use the Washington office merely as a place for employees to hang their coats while pursuing policy makers. Eakes wanted Self-Help to become a part of the District of Columbia and establish as deep a footprint as possible. In the nation's capital, a city with a majority African American population, there were pressing needs for community development, affordable housing, and small business lending, all part of Self-Help's portfolio. That was the way Self-Help operated in its branch offices in

Asheville, Charlotte, Greensboro, Wilmington, and Greenville, North Carolina. Washington would be no different.

With this plan in mind, one of David Wiley's early hires was George W. Brown, a former deputy mayor in the District of Columbia. The two had worked together on various projects for more than twenty years. Brown had founded a community development corporation that revitalized a commercial strip in the district and had served as the mayor's economic development chief. Brown's experience, combined with Wiley's own work in the city, immediately connected Self-Help to neighborhood groups and community development organizations, and brought political resources to Self-Help that would otherwise have taken years for the organization to develop.

Brown had never seen anything like the crowd to which Wiley introduced him. On his first visit to Durham, Brown was advised to leave his usual workday uniform of a suit and tie at home. "Dress casual," Wiley told him. It was summer in Durham; Eric Stein greeted Brown wearing shorts. Brown took to this wonky bunch with their advanced degrees and offbeat, casual manner. He sensed what he called "an atmosphere of just folks who had an air about them, who wanted to do stuff, like a family." After listening to Eakes's biographical monologue, Brown was sold. A few months later, he was the new face and voice of Self-Help on Capitol Hill at a committee hearing in the fall of 2003. Brown said that Eakes told him, "We are going to make the District of Columbia part of our program. From day one, that was his approach."

Brown knew his way around the dozen or more community development financial institutions operating in Washington. His focus was on lending in neighborhoods and communities that most traditional banks would not touch. He explained that Self-Help's strategy was not to elbow its way in and throw its financial weight around but to backstop local efforts and serve as a secondary lender, providing stability to projects local organizations had in their lineup. One of the best of these, which brought nearly thirty apartments on line to be leased at affordable terms, would not have been possible if Self-Help had not provided two early loans to help reestablish a neighborhood. "Our job was never to compete," Brown said, "but to complement and fit in, to be a lender to other lenders to make a deal work."[4]

Wiley first operated out of his home before moving Brown and two new hires assigned to research and lobbying chores into temporary space on loan from a company that happened to be a Self-Help tenant in Durham. The quarters were little more than an open floor with a handful of borrowed desks hidden in cubicles. If not wholly adequate, the office was well located near Capitol Hill. Along with his other duties as Self-Help's principal emissary in the District of Columbia, Brown was also on the lookout for more suitable permanent quarters.

The CRL headquarters remained in downtown Durham with the rest of the Self-Help staff. It eventually moved across Main Street into what was called the Temple Building, another of Self-Help's recently acquired holdings that had been refitted for office service.

The Temple Building predated World War I and had been built by John Sprunt Hill, a Durham financier and capitalist. At the turn of the last century, Hill called himself a Jeffersonian Democrat and was as dedicated to helping small farmers as Eakes was in settling African American single moms and their families into homes of their own. Hill's banker friends were dumbfounded when he became a champion for rural credit unions and opposed crop liens, that era's equivalent of predatory lending. Working with some Durham County farmers, Hill helped establish the state's first credit union in 1916 at a crossroads community called Lowes Grove, about a dozen miles south of Durham in what would later become North Carolina's Research Triangle Park.[5] The irony of recycling the Temple Building was not lost on Eakes.

At about the time of the move into the Temple Building, Self-Help found its permanent office in Washington in the Barr Building, eleven stories of pre–World War II limestone elegance with a top crenulated by architectural touches that was bought for $23 million. One side opened on K Street, the preferred address for the Washington lobbyists, but the front door was on 17th Street on the west side of Farragut Square, just three blocks from the White House. It was prime space at a relatively good price, and Wiley convinced Eakes that the economics of ownership beat anything available in a city known for outrageous rents. Self-Help took over one of the floors and leased the rest. For Eakes, the location and the investment made a statement: Self-Help was in Washington, D.C., to stay.

Some within Self-Help argued that buying the building was a mistake. They believed that the CRL people could easily reach Washington from Durham, without the expense of permanent offices. Critics also held that it was best to remain out of the Washington milieu and close to Self-Help's roots in North Carolina and its customer base, whose experience informed its research and policy direction. Wiley and others argued that officials in Washington would not wait for someone from Durham to find a plane or car to travel to Washington for a meeting. When a congressional aide called and asked for information, delivery was expected within the hour. The price of the Barr Building was steep, but like other properties Eakes had acquired over the years, this one, too, would increase in value and improve Self-Help's bottom line as an income-generating asset.

With its new advocacy unit, Self-Help was eager to become an equal partner with the diversified and established field of national consumer and civil rights groups that had already compiled impressive records of their own. Eakes had always considered Self-Help to be a civil rights organization, although nearly twenty years of work primarily as a financial institution did not readily suggest the image of a successor to the work of Dr. Martin Luther King Jr. The focus on expanding financial services to women and the poor certainly demonstrated a commitment to the cause, and early board members of the CRL reinforced the civil rights mission. The list included two well-known names: Julian Bond, the chair of the NAACP, and Wade Henderson, the president of the Leadership Conference on Civil and Human Rights.

It would take more than a simple declaration of intent in order to build a reputation and credibility in Washington, where the lending industry was already lining up behind a bill prepared for the 108th Congress. Their man was U.S. Representative Robert W. Ney, an Ohio Republican who introduced what he called the Responsible Lending Act of 2003.

Ney's bill was the mortgage industry's answer to what the congressman derided as "feel-good" legislation being passed in various states that he said threatened to disrupt the steady flow of mortgage money to worthy homeowners. The bill contained a few provisions prohibiting the most egregious abuses, but its fundamental purpose was to preempt local regulations and state laws, like the one in North Carolina. Even before Ney's bill was introduced, Eakes co-signed a letter with leaders of a dozen other consumer and civil rights groups declaring opposition to Ney's plans for mortgage lending legislation.

At the time, some problems were already beginning to appear in the wave of subprime mortgages washing up on Wall Street. In its initial story on Ney's bill, the *Wall Street Journal* reported that 8.5 percent of subprime loans had ended in foreclosure in the third quarter of the previous year. That was compared to 1.15 percent of all loans. The Mortgage Bankers Association, whose data were quoted by the *Journal*, warned that the numbers were merely a sample and not a reflection of the entire market.[6] Yet, these early failures included trouble right in Ney's home state. His congressional district in the northeast corner of Ohio was not far from Cleveland, where the number of foreclosures had doubled between 1995 and 2000. They would quadruple by 2007 and devastate entire neighborhoods. In 2003, the problems in Cleveland were an early warning of what was to come, but few outside of northern Ohio paid attention.[7]

The groups that the CRL allied itself with were all better equipped to deal with the day-to-day business of influencing legislation. The NAACP had chapters throughout the nation and decades of experience on Capitol Hill. Consumers Union, with its popular magazine, *Consumer Reports*, in its portfolio certainly enjoyed a higher nationwide profile. The Association of Community Organizations for Reform Now, a group known as ACORN, was putting boots on the ground and arousing voters when Self-Help was just aborning, while the National Community Reinvestment Coalition (NCRC) had six hundred member organizations across the country that knew how to organize letter writers and fill congressional boxes with their views. The AARP claimed more members than the population of small states.

For far longer than most, the NCRC's John Taylor had been in the trenches browbeating bankers and policy makers into making fair and equitable lending available to low- and moderate-income borrowers. While Taylor appeared to be a soul mate with Eakes, Wiley had some fence mending to do. Taylor remained upset with Eakes's refusal to join the NCRC's push to have credit unions file reports under the Community Reinvestment Act (CRA) in the same way as banks. Taylor said a NCRC study found that very large credit unions had records on lending to poor people that were worse than some banks.

It also irritated Taylor that Self-Help's remarkable growth in home lending had been enlarged by banks after the NCRC helped turn up the heat over their CRA scores. These critics included Peter Skillern at CRA-NC (later Reinvestment Partners), who was still bothered that Self-Help's good press in North Carolina overshadowed the successful work of his own organization. Skillern's book *Payday Lending: Too Much Month at the End of the Paycheck* had catalyzed opponents to predatory lending in 1999, with seminars, public demonstrations, and organizing, as well as the fight over extension of the payday lending law in 2001.[8]

Self-Help, and Eakes, often got much of the credit in the efforts, with published accounts giving short shrift to the work of Skillern and others. "It tends to be a narrative that focused around one person or one component, and the more textured story line is left off," said Skillern. "Again, why Self-Help has been so successful is its really good ability to tell that story, not only to provide that leadership, but to tell that story which garners more attention, which then garners funding, which then more garners power, which then garners something bigger. It is a story about being successful. It is about playing to win, and that is what Self-Help is really good at."[9]

Wiley was close enough to Taylor and Eakes to know that they were bound to clash, at least at some point. Regardless of past differences, it was essential that Self-Help's expansion into Washington not be misunderstood. Wiley helped convince Taylor and others that it was a part of Self-Help's DNA to collaborate with like-minded organizations. The new money backing the CRL certainly had to be good news for those seeking fresh new resources. "It was very important that we stayed in close communication," Wiley added, "and we knew what the other was doing and what our respective positions were on state and federal legislation."

New to town, old frictions to be resolved, and with its reputation still to be defined, Self-Help had big challenges. At the same time, the organization's pack was not quite as empty as it may have appeared. Self-Help had helped produce the landmark bill in North Carolina, and CRL's staffers were scoring some victories in state legislatures, both with predatory lending bills and in opposition to payday lending. The mortgage industry, and the principals at Fannie Mae and Freddie Mac, had also discovered, as they worked their way through the details of legislation, that CRL lawyers knew the mortgage business as well as, or even better than, they did.

That respect grew largely from Self-Help's two decades of lending. From the first loans in the mid-1980s to the present, Self-Help's record in 2003 was measured in the billions, $2.6 billion to be exact, with customers in forty-eight states where 33,400 families had bought homes that they were working hard to own.[10] The Self-Help Ventures Fund was underwriting expansion of small businesses and providing financing for child care operators and charter schools for eight thousand children. Most important was that even with a huge customer base unable to qualify for prime loans, Self-Help's loss rate was less than one-half of 1 percent per year. No other organization, and for that matter no other lender to low- and moderate-income borrowers, could bring that sort of record to the table.

Self-Help's broad background in lending lifted the congressional testimony of Martin Eakes out of the ordinary. In one of his appearances before the U.S. House Financial Services Committee, Representative Maxine

Waters, a California Democrat, encouraged Eakes to keep talking after his allotted time had expired. "You are like a breath of fresh air," she told him, applauding his testimony that dealt in specifics, not in the broad generalities offered by the lineup of industry representatives who had preceded him. "You came here to offer some very constructive ways we need to address this problem and to say what you have done."[11]

Self-Help's volume of lending may have been relatively modest—about the same as one branch office of a major money-center bank, Eakes would say with a smile—but the hands-on experience and a record of making non-traditional loans work with regular payments on basic thirty-year terms without gimmicks and expensive add-ons was undeniable. Over the coming years, from one committee hearing to another, Self-Help witnesses always introduced themselves first as lenders and second as advocates.

Self-Help also enjoyed another advantage that set it apart from its allies. The CRL had the luxury of being able to focus on a limited number of issues, such as mortgage lending, while other organizations had broader agendas to follow and support. Plus, Self-Help was led by a single-minded, determined, and unfettered chief executive officer who refused to quit until he had bagged his target.

Eakes had done just that with single-premium credit insurance, a feature that few others had given much attention to in the early days. By 2003, it had all but disappeared from the marketplace. The nation's major banks had discarded it, and Fannie Mae and Freddie Mac declined loans that carried such baggage. Those who were paying attention gave the credit for its demise to Eakes. "I got excited about it once I understood it from Martin," recalled the NCRC's John Taylor, one of the leading early voices in the fight against predatory lending. "He really led the charge on that."[12]

In the coming months, the CRL would begin to distinguish itself in one other important way. It would become a source of credible data-driven research that quantified the cost and impact of predatory lending in even more telling detail than Stein's 2001 study. It was a strategy discussed in the formative months as Mary Mountcastle and Mark Pearce sorted through the incoming applications for jobs and talked about how the new center would make its mark.

According to John R. Farris, one of the early hires at the CRL, the challenge was how to convert policy issues into something legislators, policy makers, and ordinary citizens could relate to and understand. The mortgage market had become far too complicated for laymen—"What did my home loan have to do with Wall Street?"—and what the CRL wanted to do was to "put a face on the problem," according to another early staff member, Deborah Goldstein. Moreover, the resulting reports had to be solid and based on data but not be constructed in a wonky fashion that only academics could understand.[13]

When Farris joined the CRL in 2001, he had been in and out of Self-Help's Durham offices since finishing at Princeton University. He had been enrolled in the Woodrow Wilson School, where Eakes had studied twenty years earlier. That connection led Farris to Durham for a summer as a Self-Help intern, where he had worked with Stein on some of the statistical modeling that went into the 2001 report. He was looking for a full-time job when the Sandler money came in. "We needed to make a splash with some sort of concept that people could quantify," he said some time later.

The first CRL report came in early 2004, two years before the *Losing Ground* study, and went straight for the jugular. The nation's leading banks had been contending they were not doing all those naughty things their lobbyists attributed to outliers and undisciplined mortgage brokers. The CRL's April 2004 report, tamely titled *A Review of Wells Fargo's Subprime Lending*, disputed that. Wells Fargo was a major money-center bank, with three thousand branches and operations across North America bearing its storied stagecoach logo. Yet, the financial products that had given a huge boost to the bank's bottom line were as abusive as any in the industry. "Lulled by favorable analyst reports," the report concluded, "Wells Fargo investors may not realize they are subsidizing a predatory lender. In addition, limited regulatory oversight and loopholes in regulations have enabled Wells Fargo Financial to hide predatory practices from federal regulators."[14]

Other reports followed within the year. They focused on the perils of credit card debt, the payday lending industry's concentration of storefront operations in African American neighborhoods, and the risks for borrowers who put their car titles up as security for short-term loans. Auto-title lending was a close cousin to payday lending. The latter could be just as devastating for borrowers threatened with the loss of their automobile, which, for some, meant the loss of transportation to a job. The range of topics demonstrated that the CRL could sing more than one tune and promised to take its opposition to the payday lenders beyond the boundaries of North Carolina.

Those targeted by the reports countered with their own studies by underwriting research from a variety of academic sources. It was all part of the comprehensive strategy created by Wright Andrews, the Washington lobbyist, who told a gathering of mortgage brokers in 2003, "It is critical that we get data," and he wanted more and more money to pay for it. "These professors don't come cheap," he was quoted as saying in one *Inside B&C* report.[15]

The CRL took up the challenge and answered a study out of Georgetown University that challenged the benefits to homebuyers from the North Carolina law. It also refuted a critical analysis of the CRL's accusation that payday lenders targeted African Americans. Clearly, the industry was paying attention to this upstart group down in Durham, even if its shadow in Washington was not that long.

After release of the Wells Fargo study, Goldstein said substantive conversations with the bank followed and that led to some revisions of Wells Fargo's lending. Throughout it all, Wells Fargo continued to participate in Self-Help's secondary market program. "More than any other group that I know of," Eakes said, "partly because of our branding and mission, we had gotten big enough that we can have a good cop and bad cop within the same organization. We have somebody who is trying to work with Wells Fargo, and they hate me with a passion, and [the Self-Help person says,] 'That is how Martin is. You can't hold that against us.' I've always had a foot in both worlds."[16]

The payday lenders were not so ready to sit down to talk. They had lost their fight in North Carolina, but the industry was doing quite well in other states and was determined to keep it that way. Just across the line in South Carolina, storefront operations touting auto-title loans and short-term credit crowded one another on the corners of busy commercial districts filled with strip malls and one-story office buildings. The home offices of two industry leaders were close by. Advance America was in Spartanburg, South Carolina, while Check into Cash Inc. had its home in Cleveland, Tennessee.

Payday lenders fought back, hard. At one point, Eakes said he was told that the industry had raised $10 million to mount a counter campaign that would ruin him personally and drive Self-Help off the map. Eakes turned the threat into a standard line in subsequent public appearances. He would tell people that his mother warned him that pride was one of the deadly sins. But, he could not help feeling good about the target that the payday industry had put on him and his organization. "I'm only worth $10," he would say. "What are they going to do with the rest of the money?"

The payday lending industry would later organize a lobbying group called the Consumer Rights League, with an acronym designed to confuse the source of information. When that happened, said one of the CRL lobbyists, Josh Nassar, "I knew we had arrived."[17]

Nassar was typical of the new hires in the Washington office. Most had never worked in Durham, seen a loan application, or been immersed in the Self-Help culture. Nonetheless, he was as dedicated as any veteran in Durham to the Self-Help mission. He used his five years of experience in congressional staff work to navigate the warrens of official Washington.

As Wright Andrews had observed, data-driven research was not cheap. It required time and demanded experienced talent, along with the computing power to handle very large databases. Shortly after he had come aboard, Farris talked to Stein about finding a comprehensive database that could be used to dig below the surface of the mortgage market and determine what was really going on with the new wave of adjustable rate mortgages. They landed on one managed by Loan Performance, a private organization that aggregated the details of home mortgages and kept track of payment histories using data provided by participating lenders. As a lender, Self-Help qualified as a Loan Performance client, but joining the group was expensive. The retail cost of the database was about $500,000, plus Self-Help would be required to contribute records of its own lending and pay to have it wiped clean of identifying information, like the rest of the data set.

The cost was well beyond what Self-Help had paid for anything, short of an aging downtown office building. Eakes was notoriously cheap, and he turned down initial proposals from Stein and Wiley, who urged him to approve the purchase. Eakes finally agreed to put up Self-Help's share, after negotiating the price down to $250,000, but only if another organization would pay half. One of his new allies in Washington, AARP, which had a strong research component of its own, agreed to share the cost. Self-Help also included in the contract permission to use the data in published reports, a feature that caused no small amount of concern in the days ahead, when bankers discovered that Self-Help was using the data to publicly undermine what Wall Street considered a profitable line of business.

Farris left Self-Help in 2004 to become budget director for the governor of Kentucky before Keith Ernst, the CRL's lead researcher, and his colleague Wei Li began working with the Loan Performance data set. Ernst came to the task with broad experience that informed his research. He had been a member of Self-Help's secondary market team; he had helped Stein put together his $9.1 billion report; and he had spent time in the trenches at the Georgia legislature with Calhoun when that state's lending bill was being smashed to bits. David Wiley admired Ernst's facility to move smoothly from policy development to research.

When Ernst got his hands on the new data set, one that included information on hundreds of thousands of mortgages from coast to coast, he and Li began building statistical models to determine the trends in delinquent mortgage payments. The softest region, the one showing real signs of trouble, was the Midwest, where housing prices had never reached the peaks building on the West Coast and in the Sun Belt. Once they had those numbers, Ernst and Li took the research a step further and asked the question "What would happen if housing prices fell in California or Florida just like they had in distressed markets like Cleveland?" That required another data set, a commercial forecast of housing prices, and when the information from the two was combined, the results formed the foundation for *Losing Ground*.

Ernst and Li checked and double-checked their analysis. They were studying the results early in 2006, just as the run-up in housing prices, a trend that had begun in 1997, was reaching its peak and home building was at a thirty-year high.[18] At the time, a few economists had warned of a "housing bubble," but these early warnings were buried in what appeared to be never-ending good news in the housing market. Even Alan Greenspan, the chair of the Federal Reserve who had presided over the longest stretch of economic growth in the nation's history, said he wasn't worried. He acknowledged the problem but said the financial system was capable of handling any disruption caused by faulty mortgages.[19]

As Ernst worked through the numbers, he hedged toward the conservative side, whenever he was given a choice. Yet, even with this tilt, the future for home mortgages looked gloomy, and the results remained the same, even as the data and models were tweaked and adjusted. While the purpose of the research was to consider Self-Help's claims about the devastating impact of subprime lending run amuck, Self-Help had no need to add any spin to prove the point, even if Ernst had been so inclined.

Ernst was nervous. "If you think about it," he said some years later, "it was a little bit like standing up and saying the emperor has no clothes. If you are right, this is going to be very insightful. If you are wrong, it is not going to help our credibility one bit."[20]

Ernst gave the results of the *Losing Ground* study a test drive during the late spring and early summer of 2006, including a presentation at a state legislative conference. He was told that the results were overly pessimistic. After one such session, he received a call from a staff member of the California legislature. "She said, 'This is terrible news if this happened, but you can't prove it,'" Ernst recalled. "We had to say we couldn't prove this would happen, but we have a lot of confidence in this analysis." She thanked Ernst for not arguing more than what the data showed. When he hung up the phone, he was thinking, "I am not sure how she is going to feel a year from now."

Members of the CRL staff heard about the results and were eager to put the information in the hands of legislators and others considering predatory lending bills. Without a written report, however, they were left mute as Ernst and the writers of the report prepared a final draft.

Eakes was one of those for whom the future looked far darker than the one forecast in the report. The impact of risky mortgages with low teaser rates and provisions designed to get customers to sign without considering the consequences remained unknown. Growing in popularity were thirty-year loans that had very low interest rates for a short period of time, say two or three years, before they reset to a much higher rate. They were fine for people who hoped to buy a house, live in it for a short time, and then resell it and take advantage of the constant upward climb on home prices. They could be devastating for those unable to withstand the shock of higher interest rate. Eakes had been preaching against the so-called 2/28s and 3/27s for some time, refusing speaking engagements unless he was allowed to warn against their danger for customers whose incomes and resources would suffer in the long term.

Self-Help had discovered that loans like these were especially hard for some homebuyers to handle. Michael Calhoun remembered that early lesson. "We quickly found, and it was one of the things seared into our value system, that low- and moderate-income people cannot absorb payment shocks. I don't know how many years it took, but we switched to fixed-rate loans. That was a huge lesson learned fast."[21]

Now, loans with shifting rates in all shapes and sizes were all the rage in markets with rapidly rising housing prices. Eakes knew that 2/28 and 3/27 loans written a few years earlier were about to convert, and borrowers would be faced with unmanageable monthly payments, the first step to defaults. He suspected that Ernst's numbers had not adequately accounted for the popularity of these loans, especially as housing prices were beginning to fall.

Losing Ground was released in December 2006. The phones at the CRL offices began lighting up with calls for interviews with reporters with national audiences. Producers from CNN, MSNBC, and National Public Radio and re-porters from the *New York Times,* the *Washington Post,* and the *Wall Street Journal* all called to talk about the report. None of the center's dozen or so preceding releases had caught this kind of attention from news outlets.

"We happened to have a pretty compelling interpretation of the data to offer," said Ernst. "It did show that we didn't just have a point of view, but we had an interest in developing a factual record of what was happening that people could agree with or disagree with or do research on their own."

"Our media coverage shot through the roof," said Goldstein, the CRL's executive vice president. And it was not just news reporters calling. The report was posted on the CRL website, where analysts on Wall Street were reading it, too. Some of them called to say they were seeing the same faults in the system. More than one advised that predictions of massive defaults, dire indeed, were still too low.[22]

There were outliers in the financial markets who believed, as Eakes did, that the mortgage markets were heading toward a fall. As Michael Lewis portrayed in his book *The Big Short,* a clutch of investors had been bet-ting for two years or more that these very loans, the riskiest of the bunch in the mortgage-backed securities market, would begin to fail when the teaser rates expired. As the price of housing stalled, and then began to slide, it was only a matter of time. Some of the securities backed by these loans had begun to fail as early as 2006. In 2007, it became an avalanche as three-quarters of a trillion dollars in risky mortgages sold at teaser rates began resetting.[23] In December 2007, Morgan Stanley, the mighty financial house, declared a $9.2 billion loss in mortgage-backed securities.

Those who had read the fine print and understood the flimsy foundation of mortgages being thrown out to investors would reap dividends worth billions of dollars by betting against them. One of those who profited from the fall, John A. Paulson, whose firm Paulson and Company made $15 bil-lion in 2007, banked $4 billion personally.[24] In October 2007, the CRL an-nounced a $15 million grant from Paulson's firm. The money was used to form the Institute for Foreclosure Legal Assistance and assist homeowners facing foreclosure. The program was managed by the National Association of Consumer Advocates.[25]

Losing Ground did something earlier studies—including those from the CRL—had not done. According to Ernst, "It wasn't until *Losing Ground* that we had research that showed just how much risk was building in the system. When I think back on that paper, that is one of the things that distinguished it."

As the report gained wider circulation in the spring of 2007, the mortgage lending business was beginning to come apart. Eakes was attending a conference sponsored by the Consumer Federation of America, where he appeared alongside a representative from New Century Financial Corporation, the second largest subprime lender in the country. It had more than seven thousand employees and a market capitalization in the billions. Like Countrywide and Ameriquest, it, too, was based in California, where the bulk of the nontraditional loans were being issued.[26] As the session proceeded, Eakes noticed the face of the man from New Century turn ashen after he took a phone call. Eakes later learned that the call had alerted him that his company was no longer taking loans. A few weeks later, New Century filed for bankruptcy. A subsequent examiner's report showed that 17 percent of New Century's loans were in default within three months of the time that they were originated.[27]

Eakes was back in Durham a few days later and at his desk near the end of a busy day when his phone rang. It was a call from Jerry Brown, California's newly elected attorney general. Eakes had met Brown earlier, in the fall of 2006, when Brown was still the mayor of Oakland, California. Eakes had given him a preview of *Losing Ground*, but Brown was not impressed. Eakes thought him overly concerned about an abbreviation that appeared in a PowerPoint presentation illustrating the report rather than about the results predicting a disaster for his state, where a quarter of the most risky loans were being written.

Now, six months later, Eakes said Brown exploded. "He said, 'God damn it, you were right. It is terrible. The state is falling apart.' By now, he is in the attorney general's office and having to deal with all of these foreclosures," Eakes recalled. By the end of the year, most of the major subprime lenders would follow New Century into collapse or acquisition.

CHAPTER TWELVE

"We're Here Forever"

The Center for Responsible Lending finally found its footing as a research outfit with the release of the *Losing Ground* study. This crowd of policy wonks might be on to something—at least, that was what the CRL staffers were being told on phone calls, some of them with experienced Wall Street hands.

The CRL's legislative record was harder to measure, however. The payday lending crowd had suffered a setback when the U.S. Senate attached a cap on interest charges for service members to a defense spending bill. Even Republicans had voted for it, including North Carolina's Senator Elizabeth Dole, after commanding generals compared the lenders in the payday shops to sharks waiting just outside the gates of their military posts.

Eakes usually avoided public partisan political engagement. He had worked with Democrats and Republicans alike when arguing for Self-Help's interests in expanding affordable housing before legislative committees in Raleigh. Things were different in Washington. Republicans were firmly allied with the mortgage industry and considered limits on the mortgage industry to be bad for the housing market, and, ergo, bad for business and bad for the nation. Ohio congressman Robert W. Ney's 2003 bill died with the close of the 108th Congress, and then came back before the 109th Congress at the beginning of 2005. This time, after a session spent responding to the first Ney bill, consumer interests lined up behind an alternative introduced by two congressmen from North Carolina, Democrats Mel Watt and Brad Miller. Their proposal was closely modeled on the North Carolina predatory lending law.

Miller was from Raleigh and had served in the state legislature with Eakes's former law partner Wib Gulley. He knew Michael Calhoun from pickup basketball games at state bar meetings. Miller was elected in 2002 from a new 13th congressional district that the state gained after the 2000 census. Watt had been in Washington since 1993. He was also a beneficiary of the state's population growth with a whacky new congressional district. Its backbone was Interstate 85, through the state's midsection. The district captured African Americans who lived in the cities of the Piedmont section of the state. Watt's home was in Charlotte, but he had constituents as far east as Durham. He was no stranger to Self-Help. Adam Stein, Eric Stein's father, had been Watt's law partner when they both had worked with civil rights lawyer Julius Chambers in the 1970s at the state's first racially integrated law firm. In 2005, Watt's influence got a boost with his election as chair of the Congressional Black Caucus.

Both Miller and Watt were members of the House Financial Services Committee, along with another Tar Heel, Patrick McHenry, a Republican whose district lay in the mountain foothills west of Charlotte. McHenry was twenty-nine, about the age of some of Martin Eakes's young staff, when he was elected in 2002. A busy young man, he signed on to Ney's 2005 bill co-sponsored with a Democrat, Paul Kanjorski from Pennsylvania. The bill's title this time was the "Responsible Lending Act." It was presented as a compromise, but, as before, it preempted state laws, and then set about a reshuffling of fees and how they would be accounted for in "high-cost loans." It even endorsed single-premium credit insurance.

McHenry set Eakes on edge when he introduced a bill called "Credit Union Charter Choice." A favorite of the American Bankers Association, the bill would assist banks interested in acquiring credit unions by limiting the influence of a credit union's management in conversion elections. Forest City, North Carolina, where Eakes and Calhoun had come to the aid of dissident shareholders in a savings and loan sold to a bank, was in McHenry's district. Even predatory lending took a backseat to Eakes's interest in the integrity of member-owned institutions.

McHenry's support of the financial industry was well rewarded. In his reelection campaign in 2004, the one that sent him back to introduce the credit union bill, he grossed more than $100,000 in campaign contributions from banks and subprime lenders, despite his limited tenure and experience. By comparison, his Democratic colleague, Mel Watt, a legislator with more than a decade on the committee and far more influence through the Legislative Black Caucus, received half that amount.

McHenry would eventually pick up the industry banner that was dropped after Ney became embroiled in the 2006 Abramoff lobbying scandal. In a letter to the *Charlotte Observer*, McHenry rebuked Self-Help for investing in a Washington, D.C., office building and belittled its history of lending to low- and moderate-income borrowers. America needed less regulation in its financial markets, not more, McHenry argued, overlooking his own earlier votes in the N.C. General Assembly in support of the state's 1999 predatory lending law.[1]

McHenry seemed to enjoy his role as the point man for Self-Help's adversaries in the financial industry. During a hearing on the predatory lending bills in May 2005, McHenry tried to disparage Self-Help's record by insisting that the *delinquency* rate of Self-Help's borrowers—those thirty or sixty days behind in payments—was equivalent to the 20 percent of subprime borrowers whose loans were in *default* in 2004. McHenry pressed the point, even after Eakes explained the difference, almost to the point of embarrassment for the congressman who never acknowledged that delinquency and default were different. Before he relinquished his time that day, McHenry asked for permission to submit further questions to Self-Help.[2]

Six months later, the same issues that McHenry raised in his post-hearing query were the highlight of a lengthy, partisan critique of Self-Help written by John Hogberg for the Capital Research Center (CRC), a Washington-based group that presented itself as a watchdog of "left-liberal special interest groups." The article, titled "Self-Help Helps Itself," tracked the creation of the family of Self-Help entities. It began with Self-Help's early days aiding worker-owned businesses, shifted to its growth and development in mortgage lending, and noted Self-Help's more recent opposition to payday lending. This evolution, according to Hogberg, had produced a leftist organization underwritten by huge foundation grants and community development lending backed by loans from the federal government. More important, the article claimed, this crowd in North Carolina, based in a modest credit union, had somehow mustered sufficient political power to coerce financial institutions many times its size to do its bidding. Its weapons: "playing the race card" and promotion of "pseudo-scholarly research."[3]

Using McHenry's queries as a launching pad, but disregarding the responses posted by Eakes to the committee, Hogberg's article accused Self-Help officials of insider loan deals and forsaking its mission to aid the poor by buying an expensive Washington office building, all along using its tax-exempt status to lobby Congress and state legislatures to regulate payday lending and the mortgage industry. The alleged insider lending amounted to shifting of money within Self-Help accounts that resulted in an inaccurate regulatory filing. Self-Help had corrected the offending report, and regulators had approved it even before McHenry raised his question.

Had Hogberg bothered to ask for an explanation from Eakes, who was never one to shy from examination, he would have learned that what CRC found reprehensible—driving a liberal agenda—was the essence of Self-Help, not a conspiracy. Eakes had long described Self-Help using his bicycle metaphor, with the self-sustaining side of Self-Help (the credit union) driving a front wheel of mission. What the Right saw as something akin to fraud was Self-Help's basic business model, which Eakes had been declaring publicly for twenty years.

The opposition was now shifting the focus of its attacks. Earlier, the testimony of witnesses that Self-Help and others pushing for changes in the lending business brought to hearings was batted away as "anecdotal" and the work of bad elements in the industry. Now, the opposition to Self-Help was couched in terms of economic self-interest. The credit union opposed payday lending not because of bad policy that permitted high interest rates and allowed borrowers to become trapped in a series of flipped loans but because the payday operations were competition for the credit union. While this line was promoted with great energy, Self-Help had yet to open its first teller window or offer retail services that would come close to being an option for those who were attracted to thirty-day loans offered by companies like Check into Cash.

For the payday lenders, the fight had become personal. The Hogberg article was released in 2005 as a reporter for the *News and Observer* of Raleigh was preparing a lengthy profile of Eakes, who had been selected as the newspaper's "Tar Heel of the Year." The *News and Observer*'s Jim Nesbitt talked to Steven Schlein, a spokesman for the Community Financial Services Association, a group created after Denzenhall Resources Ltd., a Washington, D.C., crisis management firm, was hired by the payday lenders. "He really thinks he is the last honest man," Nesbitt quoted Schlein as saying.[4]

Five years later, with the CRL still dogging the industry, Schlein had not moderated his position. The payday lenders had had enough of Martin Eakes, Self-Help, and the CRL, Schlein told Gary Rivlin, the author of *Broke, USA*, a readable narrative account of the rise and development of payday lending, rapacious mortgages, and other devices inflicted on the poor. The legislative success in North Carolina left Eakes "enthralled with power," Rivlin quoted Schlein as saying. "Just listen to the guy speak. He oozes elitism out of every pore. He's the only one who knows what's best for everyone else."[5]

For Eakes, the payday lenders did not understand that Self-Help was not in the business of wringing every dime out of its borrowers and could actually survive and prosper with modest fees and equitable terms, much like New Mexico banker Don Kidd. "They don't understand idealism," Rivlin quoted Eakes as saying when the two talked. "They can't believe idealism exists. So they think 'you have to be doing this because you want our business.' They have the most cynical motives, so they conclude everyone else has cynical motives."[6]

Rumors circulated for a time that Eakes was not faithful to his aesthetic lifestyle, as published reports suggested. He may drive an aging Chevrolet with a cracked windshield, but he circumvented Self-Help's salary cap by drawing the highest allowable salary for each of the official posts he filled within the organization's structure. His pay was four times what was actually reported, it was said.

Within Self-Help, such stories about Eakes were laughable. The salary cap, with the highest-paid employee receiving no more than three times the lowest-paid, was inviolate. In 2005, when the industry was aiming all its big guns at Eakes, his annual salary was $60,000, at a time when lobbyist Wright Andrews was managing a budget of more than $4 million to represent the mortgage industry in Congress. Eakes had seen valued employees leave for greener pastures, yet the salary cap remained, even for employees living in the more expensive environs of Washington, D.C.

Antipredatory lending legislation did not move forward until November 2007, when the Miller-Watt bill, reintroduced in the 110th Congress, passed. It was not a perfect bill by any means. "By the time it passed the House," Miller said some time later, "I had really mixed feelings whether the Senate would take it up or not."

All along, Miller had worried that the civil rights and consumer groups pushing the bill could not deliver the necessary grassroots support to help secure passage. At one point, he expressed his frustration to fellow Democrat Representative Barney Frank from Massachusetts. "I told Barney they are 'horseless headsmen.' They can give you advice on every punctuation mark in a bill, but they can't get you a vote. They can't send anybody to work the halls. That was particularly true with civil rights groups."[7]

By late spring of 2008, further consideration of the Miller-Watt bill was fast becoming moot in the face of the crumbling financial empires at Countrywide, Ameriquest, and Bear Stearns. By summer, the very institutions that provided a backbone to home mortgage financing, Fannie Mae and Freddie Mac, were headed to receivership. The mortgage-backed securities that had fueled nearly a decade of Wild West–style lending were no longer simply a legislative concern. They were creating a full-blown crisis with potentially catastrophic results.

Those on the sixth floor of the Self-Help headquarters in Durham watched the collapse of the mortgage market. Randy Chambers, Self-Help's chief financial officer, said he found himself fixated on new reading material. "I have a master's in public policy, and I work for a community development financial institution, which is basically a mission-driven organization for people who care about mission and have technical skills and don't know where to use them. Here I am, every night at 10:30, checking the *Wall Street Journal Online* to see what the latest rumor is about Lehman Brothers."

On September 12, 2008, the financial crisis found Chambers in a profound way. He was on his way out of the building for an appointment in Raleigh when one of his assistants called him back to see an email just in from Morgan Stanley. The bank was one of several on Wall Street providing overnight lines of credit secured by Self-Help's own mortgage-backed securities. Self-Help's exposure to Morgan Stanley had been as high as $100 million, but on September 12 it stood at $35 million. The email notified Chambers that that amount was due by the end of the day!

Stunned by this surprise reversal of an arrangement that had been routine for more than four years, with the credit lines resetting day in and day out, Chambers called Morgan Stanley to confirm the notice. "Is there any negotiating room?" he asked when he got someone on the line. There was a pause for a minute or two. "He comes back and says, 'No. No room to negotiate.' OK, second question to you: When you say today, what time do you mean? I don't have $35 million sitting on my desk right now. Same thing.

Long pause." Three o'clock, Chambers is told. "Yeah, we are calling in all of our lines," the Morgan Stanley clerk continued.

This was not supposed to happen, at least not according to all the financial models and research that had preceded Self-Help's entry into the reverse repurchase agreement like the one with Morgan Stanley. "We had looked at the Long-Term Capital Management [debacle], the Mexican peso devaluation, the Russian ruble default, the Asian flu, the tech bubble bursting, and the recession in the early 2000s. Nothing happened," Chambers said. "We thought we had found a market that had a real low probability of ever undermining our business model. We were right, but we hit the one perfect Hurricane Katrina in the financial markets in September 2008."

There was no use appealing to anyone on Wall Street, where panic was being served for lunch. Every investment bank was calling in loans, regardless of the size of the company or the value of the relationship. Trust was gone. Only cash got respect. That Morgan Stanley had reached all the way down to Self-Help said something in itself.

With traditional sources unavailable, Self-Help fell back on a long-standing relationship with First Carolina Corporate Credit Union, a credit union for credit unions. "At the time, we owed them $100 million, and I said, 'Can we add $35 million to that?' This was old-fashioned, relationship banking," Chambers recalled. "I called the CFO, and he said, 'Let me get David and Fred together and see if we can do this,'" Chambers recalled. "They called back and said, 'Yeah, we can do this.'" Chambers shifted to First Carolina the same collateral that Self-Help had pledged at Morgan Stanley, paid off Wall Street, and everyone went home for the day, but not without some fancy financial footwork that ended up making money for First Carolina.[8]

Years of cautious investment, following rigorous attention to lending rules, and keeping clean financial sheets and audits, along with old-fashioned tithing for the rainy days, meant Self-Help recovered from the Morgan Stanley call with relative ease. Nonetheless, the impact of the day was not lost on Eakes.

"There was literally panic in the whole world," Eakes said. "And I would talk to some of my lefty friends who say this is not a big deal. I am telling you for us to get a call for $30-plus million to pay off, this is terrifying. If you are a little struggling electric motor company in upstate New York, and they call and say you have to pay off your line of credit by the end of today, you have to shut down. You can't do it. And that was what was happening in the last quarter when unemployment jumped because all of these companies couldn't meet demands of short-term credit calls. I have great sympathy for those [companies] because I know how they felt. If I had not been white-haired beforehand, I would have been by the end of that day."[9]

Brad Miller was right about the future of his bill. It never made it to the Senate floor, at least not in the way that he thought. Essential language in the bill did survive as an integral part of the mortgage lending provision of the Dodd-Frank Wall Street Reform and Consumer Protection Act that came as part of a congressional response to the Great Recession. When President Obama signed Dodd-Frank in July 2010, the protections and prohibitions aimed at predatory lending, plus more than what had been included before, became law. Moreover, the new law created the Consumer Financial Protection Bureau (CFPB), a new agency with far-reaching powers.

Dodd-Frank covered all the elements necessary to curb predatory lending that Eakes had proposed in 2003 before a Senate banking committee hearing and that the CRL's Kathleen Keest had offered as needed in December 2008, just as President-elect Obama was preparing his plans for a recovery.[10] The law removed incentives for fraud by prohibiting yield-spread premiums, eliminated prepayment penalties in subprime and nontraditional loans, required lenders to evaluate a borrower's ability to repay, codified duties of mortgage brokers, and set federal regulations as the floor, not the limit, of state regulations on lending.

The CFPB had been first proposed by U.S. Senator Elizabeth Warren of Massachusetts in 2007, when she was still a law professor at Harvard University. Putting the pieces together for the lending provisions in Dodd-Frank and later establishing the new agency was the work of Self-Help's Eric Stein. He left Self-Help in early 2009 with a presidential appointment as the deputy assistant secretary for consumer protection in the U.S. Department of Treasury. After feeding ideas and proposals to the president's pre-inaugural transition team on reforms needed in mortgage lending, Stein was hired to work on elements of the new laws. He remained in Washington long enough to help get the CFPB established and secure and then came back to Durham. The key provision establishing the CFPB's funding with money previously devoted to consumer protection by the Federal Reserve, rather than by congressional appropriation, was hatched in Eakes's office overlooking Main Street in Durham.

"The CFPB is a game changer. There is stuff that is getting fixed on car loans and debt collections," Eakes said some time later, after the CFPB had been in business for a couple years. "By having a forum where there can be data-driven assessment of what will perfect the market and not kill it, if it gets a chance to continue living, it will change the game, and America will be a lot fairer [of a] place."

All of the gains of Dodd-Frank came at a great price. This was especially true for millions of families whose lives were devastated by the loss of their homes to foreclosure. The final tally for foreclosures from 2007 to 2014 was somewhere above five million. Nearly three million homes went into foreclosure in 2010 alone. Then, there was the collateral damage. Homeowners not faced with foreclosure, who made it through the crisis without losing their homes, watched their neighborhoods decline as deserted foreclosed homes sat empty and deteriorating for lack of maintenance and attention. This was especially critical in African American communities targeted by subprime lenders.

The crisis wiped out recent gains made in closing of the wealth gap between whites and blacks. When Self-Help began lending, motivated by how home ownership could expand the accumulation of wealth, the difference in the net worth of blacks and whites was ten to one. As home-ownership among people of color grew, with overall home ownership increasing leading up to 2007, the difference had been reduced to about eight to one. In 2013, however, in the aftermath of foreclosures and unemployment brought on by the financial crisis, the gap had grown to thirteen to one.[11] According to Eakes, $500 billion in wealth had left African American and Latino communities through foreclosures and declining home values.

A 2012 study by the Center for Community Capital tracked 46,000 loans that were part of the Self-Help–sponsored secondary market. It found that these borrowers weathered the crisis far better than others, despite their limited financial resources. The median income in this group, where 41 percent were women heading a household and 40 percent were people of color, was $30,792. The study found that through the third quarter of 2011, 9 percent of these loans were in serious delinquency. That was alarming, but it was well below those in the market with prime adjustable rate mortgages (15 percent) and subprime adjustable rate mortgages (36 percent).[12]

Eighty-five percent of Self-Help's own borrowers never missed a payment, Eakes said, reflecting on that difficult period. Yet, the 15 percent who were not current remained a threat to Self-Help's future. Prior to the crisis, Self-Help had never ended the year in the red. In 2008, Eakes set aside more than $26 million in anticipated losses, and then increased that amount to more than $45 million in 2009. Eakes estimated that Self-Help's losses from the financial crisis could run as high as $150 million. At the time, Self-Help's reserves were at $100 million.

"We had moments in the spring of 2009," Eakes recalled. "I have always said that if we had layoffs, it was a signal of bad management. And I still believe that. We knew what was coming, but I didn't realize how hard it would hit the communities we were serving. We hung in there." Self-Help recorded its first loss in 2010, ending the year $13 million in the red due to the provisions made for credit losses. The balance sheet recovered in 2011.

Self-Help closed three branch offices, laid off thirty employees, and shifted staff responsibilities to meet the challenges faced by its borrowers, many of whom lost their jobs and were financially strapped. Loss mitigation became a top priority. Staff members who before the crash had worked to find new sources of loans from participating banks were reassigned to begin working with borrowers who were delinquent on their payments. Rather than press for foreclosure and risk loss all of its investment, Self-Help modified loans to keep borrowers in their homes, using a variety of programs offered through federal and state agencies.

At the same time, Self-Help began substituting money from an expanded depositor base to replace the working capital it had been borrowing previously on Wall Street. The credit union moved into the retail banking business—teller windows, consumer loans, and checking accounts—after taking on two struggling North Carolina credit unions where these services were standard. Conversations began about adding these services at other locations.

"Staff worked really hard, and at the same time we started thinking that if we can measure this right, we can also grow our presence on the West Coast [where a new federal credit union had been organized]," said Eakes. "We were using half of our resources to grow and half to shrink and survive. And it all worked out according to plan. But it didn't have to."

In 2012, the MacArthur Foundation presented the Center for Responsible Lending with its Award for Creative and Effective Institutions. The award came with a $2 million grant that went into the CRL endowment. "What I like most about this particular award," Eakes said, "is it lets us say to the bad guys that we are going to be here forever. We are going to build this into an endowment, and we are going to be in your face as long as time continues."

In late 2015, Eakes said,

My friends at Fannie Mae say we are the only entity in America focused on low-income home ownership lending that survived. The message that I have been delivering to staff is that we did survive, and Self-Help, when it is all said and done, will have $150 to $200 million in losses from recession, but during that same period we had gains greater than that, and we had reserves greater than that. At end of 2014, we were $100 million stronger than we were at the start of the crisis. It wasn't obvious that would happen, but it did happen.

The message is that the communities we serve and the families that we are working with, they are not out of this crisis yet. In fact, the level of transfer of wealth from families of color was the greatest in history. The low-income communities and communities of color are still struggling.

So I am saying we are doing OK, but we need to do more and take the privilege we have got. . . . We have more capacity in terms of financial reserves and people skills of just about any other nonprofit community development organization in the country. With that capacity is the duty to do more and more. We shouldn't be conservative now. We are through that. That was a stage. And now, next stage, we need to do more.[13]

CHAPTER THIRTEEN

Self-Help Federal—A National Institution

It was late afternoon before Martin Eakes settled into an old sofa in his office to talk. The overhead lights were off; Self-Help practices a severe regimen of energy economy. The illuminating glow from a computer screen was complemented by the rays of a setting late-November sun that reflected off the downtown Durham buildings in 2012.

Eakes was just back from a week in California, and West Coast culture had influenced his wardrobe. He was dressed in a black shirt and trousers with a light-green T-shirt showing at his open collar. He was wearing his usual footwear: comfortably scuffed leather moccasins. It had been a long day, following an exhausting week, but most days, weeks, and months usually were. In his late fifties, Eakes remained as energized as a teenager, especially as he recounted Self-Help's latest expansion of territory and mission.

He had arrived in Los Angeles a day early, on a Saturday, where he picked up a rental car and headed out on the freeway, only to be brought to a halt in a late-afternoon traffic jam. He inched along for two hours and covered seven miles before reaching his hotel. His accommodations were spartan and cheap, $59 a night. That did include a free breakfast, even if it amounted to only a carton of milk and two small boxes of cereal, both the same. On Sunday morning, he had driven to the Santa Monica pier for a look around. It was deserted and cold, but he found life at Venice Beach, even if it was only the "green doctors," who were writing scripts for medical marijuana. It was quite a sight for a Southern Baptist teetotaler whose idea of drugs was an aspirin.

Trips west had become more frequent by the time Eakes made this excursion in the fall of 2012. California was an emerging market for new and different operations of Self-Help. It was here that Eakes would forsake two of the cardinal rules that, for more than twenty years, had framed the work of Self-Help Credit Union: limit operations to North Carolina and leave retail services to the others.

This California expansion was taking Self-Help in new directions that were just as profound as the shift to home lending back in the mid-1980s. The move west would reshape Self-Help's financial model and turn it into a more conventional financial institution by expanding its base from about 16,000 member-depositors to more than 120,000 served by drive-thru windows, ATMs, and teller stations. Moreover, California was just the start. Locations in Illinois were on the horizon, and Florida would follow in 2016.

Eakes was in Los Angeles to look over five for-profit check-cashing stores that occupied modest spaces in an assortment of East Los Angeles strip malls. They were about to become part of Self-Help Federal Credit Union, which had been created in 2008. If things progressed as planned, Self-Help Federal would turn these check-cashing stores, or outlets very similar to them, into an experiment in outreach to unbanked and underbanked Latinos to help them build a credit record and accumulate savings.

Self-Help Federal's check-cashing operation was a form of do-gooder bait and switch. Check cashing is a lucrative for-profit business with storefront locations charging high rates to convert checks to cash, usually for those living from one dollar to the next. In Self-Help Federal's pilot operation in San Jose, at an office called Micro Branch, tellers cashed checks for customers at a considerably lower fee than the for-profit stores that had the same brightly colored, neon Checks Cashed signs hanging in the front window. Micro Branch was different. There, the tellers also nudged customers into considering other low-cost financial services, such as checking or savings accounts, as they presented an entry point to better credit or a financial nest egg. "I sometimes call it our sheep in wolf's clothing," said

Steve Zuckerman, Self-Help Federal's president and Eakes's man in California. "We meet the customer where they are and provide a path to the financial mainstream."[1]

So where did all of this come from? San Jose and East Los Angeles are a long way from Main Street in Durham. It is almost as great a distance, metaphorically speaking, as home lending to check cashing. Herb and Marion Sandler had a little to do with it. Their agreement with Eakes to fund the Center for Responsible Lending called for an office in California within three years, and Eakes had followed through on schedule. Even without the influence of the Sandlers, Eakes argues that California made sense as Self-Help's next stop.

"Part of our goal was to impact corporate and government policies that deal with poor people," Eakes said that afternoon at his office. "So having a bigger megaphone as a southern state doesn't really add anything for us. Having California, which is a leading policy state and is as big as a country, meant that we would have a West Coast and an East Coast policy stage. If you were going to have a platform on the West Coast, why wouldn't you have California? In terms of being able to build out, California was where we felt the foreclosure crisis would create opportunity for us to build something, and where the need would be the greatest."[2]

Finding a role for Self-Help in a state that sets national trends was another matter, however. Clearly, Self-Help did not need California to become a larger model of North Carolina, where its record of affordable mortgage lending had informed the legislative and policy fights against predatory lending. Instead, the work in California should be different. It should allow Self-Help to engage in new areas of financial services to gain experience and credibility to support policy positions and legislative lobbying that the CRL carried out in many states and in Congress.

Just what that role would be was yet to be determined when Eakes called Zuckerman midway through 2005. He announced that he was coming west to deliver a commencement address at the University of California, Santa Barbara, and he invited himself over for a reunion. The two had known each other since Zuckerman had been Martin and Bonnie's housemate in Durham, back in the mid-1980s, when they thought the future was in developing worker-owned businesses. Zuckerman stayed a year in Durham, and then left for business school at Stanford. Since earning his MBA in 1987, he had done well over the next fifteen years, building a handsome nest egg, along with a family. His wife was on the faculty at Stanford University when he left McCown De Leeuw and Company, a middle-market leverage buyout firm near Palo Alto, to take a "structured sabbatical," as he called it. When Eakes called, Zuckerman was a stay-at-home dad for three children. One night, as he and his wife shared the highlights of their day, his nugget to pass along was the thrill of saving $86 shopping at Safeway. She told him it was time to find a job.

Zuckerman is a talker, a man of medium build with a strong jaw, a busy head of graying hair, and blue eyes. He is infused with the Self-Help spirit and knows the story better than most, having been around in the early days and, later, a member of the board of directors. Knowing Eakes well enough to appreciate that he does not take on a task unless it looks impossible, he gave Eakes added confidence in considering a cross-continental leap.

By the time Zuckerman heard from Eakes, he was beginning to shift gears and reenter the job market, "preferably in the social benefit arena, something in economic justice. That is what I most cared about." They spent that day together in June 2005 riding around in Zuckerman's minivan while he delivered his kids to one spot and the other. Eakes brought the latest news from Durham and all that was going on since Zuckerman had left the Self-Help board.

That conversation led Zuckerman to think about taking his own plans for a start-up, social-mission company and blending them into Self-Help's efforts in California. Eakes asked Zuckerman to spend some time focusing on what Self-Help West could do best before becoming a part-time consultant in September 2006. Eakes told him to take his time and find an area of work consistent with Self-Help's mission that was not being addressed by any other organization and that was different from Self-Help's work in North Carolina.

Retail financial services, in particular finding alternatives to payday lending and the financial traps that drain wealth from those living paycheck to paycheck, quickly rose to the top of Zuckerman's list. Eakes and the CRL had been battling payday lenders for years and had helped shut down the business in North Carolina. Payday lenders, whose fees and interest drove the cost of money up by 400 percent or more, were thriving in California. In the two years that Zuckerman took to find the hook on which to hang Self-Help's West Coast venture, the total dollar volume of payday loans increased by a half billion dollars, and the number of transactions grew by more than 1.8 million.[3]

Retail services were new territory for Self-Help. At that time, the North Carolina credit union did not finance auto loans or make small loans to tide depositors over from one pay period to the next. Nonetheless, Eakes had begun to rethink Self-Help's twenty-year-old business model, which limited business to residential and commercial lending, after two traditional credit unions in North Carolina merged with Self-Help Credit Union in 2005. Clearly, if Self-Help had more experience serving retail customers, the experience could inform the development of public policy in much the same way that twenty-plus years of home lending had helped shape its positions on predatory lending.

"A lot of early CRL work was in predatory mortgage lending," said Zuckerman, "and we had the great benefit of being a mortgage lender for fifteen years and participants in $5 billion in mortgage loans. That gave Martin and Eric Stein and Mike Calhoun a lot of credibility when they were out testifying about mortgage issues. We didn't have that same kind of credibility when we were testifying about payday and some of the other consumer lending abuses that we were starting to pay attention to. This would give us that ability to build that expertise by actually being in that business."

The exact shape of that business did not arrive until after Zuckerman spent time listening to potential customers, kicking around a variety of ideas, and finding an innovative, but frustrated, entrepreneur who was wrestling with a similar notion. The result was Micro Branch. It was a check-cashing store, one that looked like all others that charged high fees but that offered a range of financial services, including check cashing at reasonable rates to people who did not want to use a bank or could not find one convenient to their neighborhood.

The nation's financial foundation was undulating like a California earthquake in late 2007 and early 2008 as Eakes and Zuckerman were sorting out the possibilities of a structure for the work in California. The idea of a for-profit bank, started from scratch, was considered, but discarded, considering the cautious attitude of regulators at the time. Expanding the state-chartered Self-Help Credit Union was discussed. Self-Help's charter was valid in California, but the North Carolina connection could present complications later on, especially if the California business grew as anticipated. They chose the option of a new federally chartered credit union.

Eakes had barely hung the charter of Self-Help's newest creation on the wall in June 2008 when Zuckerman received a call from a contact in San Francisco. He was asked to take a look at a small, struggling credit union in West Oakland and advise how it could be stabilized after suffering from a run of bad loans. Shortly thereafter, credit union regulators called and asked if Self-Help Federal would take over People's Community Partnership Federal Credit Union and save it from collapse. In September 2008, just as Wall Street was shutting down, Self-Help Federal was in business at an address in a lower-income neighborhood on the east side of San Francisco Bay.

This was not as much a surprise as it appeared. Zuckerman and Eakes had been watching the list of troubled credit unions in California grow longer and longer with each quarterly report on creditworthiness released by regulators. The conversation turned from the development of Micro Branch to the more urgent challenge of helping local institutions, some of which had been serving their communities for years. It was much like the rehabilitation work that the Self-Help staff had done over the years for small, rural credit unions in North Carolina serving African Americans. It was becoming apparent that Self-Help Federal might be able to salvage troubled credit unions, combine them to take advantage of economies of scale, and, in a short period of time, establish its presence and reputation. These new locations would also become part of the platform for the new business model—expanding the member-depositor base—that was a top priority back in Durham.

Watching these changes was Joe Duran, the chief executive officer of Community Trust Credit Union in Modesto, deep in California's Central Valley. A Mexican American, Duran had grown up in Modesto, the son of a single mother who spoke little English but who had raised a family with grit and determination, building a life for her family from wages earned at the local cannery. The family's first home was a condemned house she bought for $1,200. Born in New Mexico, Joe spoke little English when he entered the Modesto public schools at the age of five, but he learned quickly and became his mother's translator when she opened her first savings account, then a checking account, and later bought property.

Community Trust had been organized in 1961 to serve cannery workers in the Central Valley. In its early days, it was called Food Processors Credit Union. During the months of harvest in the vast fields surrounding Modesto, as many as ten thousand people worked in the canneries. That number then fell to two thousand in the off-season. Duran was fresh out of college in the early 1980s, wondering what to do with his bachelor's degree in sociology, when he was hired as a loan officer at Community Trust. After he took the job, he realized his life had come full circle when he saw a boy translating a loan officer's instructions for his parents, just as he had done for his mother years before. His new job was suddenly much,

much more. "I immediately knew what my life was going to be about," he said.[4]

Community Trust ran into trouble not long after Duran arrived, and regulators gave the board of directors six months to improve finances or face liquidation. The management named Duran, then thirty years old, as the new CEO and told him to make a difference. He began hustling new accounts from the cannery workers, with whom he had once worked while putting himself through college. The institutional death sentence was eventually lifted, and over the next twenty years Duran expanded Community Trust assets sixfold and added two branch offices.

Much of the growth came from accounts held by the low-income workers in the valley, a majority of whom were Latinos like him. Community Trust made home and automobile loans to ITIN borrowers, noncitizen immigrant workers who were paying federal income taxes under the individual tax identification numbers issued by the Internal Revenue Service. Duran's customers held steady jobs and, he discovered, were good credit risks.

All in all, Duran's ITIN borrowers were Self-Help's African American single moms of twenty years earlier that most commercial banks ignored. Regulators were getting nervous in 2009, however, and though Community Trust's solvency was not the issue, Duran was advised to limit the ITIN business that had served his institution and its customers well for years. Rather than curb lending for customers who were virtually closed out from other financial services, Duran went looking for a new partner to add some financial weight that would allow him to continue as before.

Through a friend, Duran heard about Self-Help and its plans in California. "I thought they were a little bit crazy," he said one morning in 2014 as he drove up the valley to a business meeting. His voice wafted in and out over an uncertain cell phone connection. Duran contacted Zuckerman, talked with the Community Trust board members, and after getting comfortable with what Self-Help was, he began serious consideration of a merger. The Micro Branch was still an idea, but Duran liked what he heard about the plans to extend financial services to the unbanked. "Those are the types of services that would resonate across California," he said.

Self-Help sounded like a good match, and Duran immediately took to Eakes. He still wanted to be sure that the cultural mix was right and if all of Self-Help shared his institution's culture and sense of mission. To find out, he asked three of his employees to fly east and spend some time in Durham. He singled out one teller, who was a new mother, and asked her to take her baby, just to add a bit of a twist to the normal visitation experience. His scouts came back "inspired," he said. "This is a DNA match. They are absolutely about the mission like we are. They just don't talk about it. They do it."

Community Trust, the institution Duran had grown from $4 million to $50 million in deposits, serving customers in four counties, merged with Self-Help Federal in June 2009. Self-Help Federal got 12,400 new members and an additional $42 million in assets. Duran stayed on even though the Self-Help salary cap meant a 33 percent cut in pay. "Martin Eakes is an extraordinary leader, incredibly authentic. He absolutely believes in and is convinced in his mission. He's somebody who I, without hesitation, would follow." When Duran talked about Self-Help to people in the Central Valley, he met skeptics, some of whom had heard the rumors spread by Self-Help's detractors that the salary cap was a sham. He told them, "One way he does mission is with his wallet."

Six months later, in January 2010, Zuckerman opened Self-Help Federal's first stand-alone check-cashing outlet in East San Jose. He did everything he could to make it familiar to what customers found at the locations run by the competition. Floors were covered with linoleum in a splashy, brightly colored pattern. There was an open counter, with a small side desk. A counter held forms for wire transfers of money to locations out of the country. A neon sign was in the window. A few plastic chairs stood along the wall and at the desk.

A child's play area in the corner might have been a signal that this store was different from the others. At the counter, new customers discovered that, in addition to cashing their checks, they could open a checking or savings account with as little as five dollars. The attraction for customers, many of whom kept coming back, was the low fees—1.5 percent for printed payroll or government checks less than $1,000 or 2 percent for handwritten checks of more than $1,000. The competition advertised 1.5 percent, but only for the most secure form—printed payroll checks. A housekeeper with a handwritten personal check might pay as much as 7 percent.

The old saw that people using check cashers were financially unsophisticated was simply wrong, Zuckerman learned. Customers living paycheck to paycheck had to be good money managers to survive and keep food on the table until the end of the month. Banks were not friendly; money from deposited checks was not immediately available. If they did open a checking account at a bank, they were liable to get clipped with overdraft charges when things got tight. That could cost more than paying the check casher.

Zuckerman's challenge was reaching customers who were either unfamiliar with banks or just disgusted with them based on past experiences. Zuckerman hoped the soft sell would encourage customers to consider opening accounts that could reduce their transaction fees, help them build some savings, or even allow them take out a loan and begin building a credit history. "We can give them time to build trust," Zuckerman said, "and to make the change [at] their own pace not because they're doing something wrong. We try to take a very nonjudgmental attitude."

Micro Branch (the name was later changed to Prospera as more credit unions became part of Self-Help) was just the beginning of a year that would leave Zuckerman exhausted. The paint was still fresh in San Jose when Self-Help Federal merged with the El Futuro (Portersville) and Kern Central (Bakersfield) credit unions. Unlike Community Trust, both were under pressure from regulators to increase credit ratios that had fallen below acceptable levels. By the end of January 2010, Self-Help Federal was the fastest-growing credit union in California, with an additional 23,000 members and $150 million more in assets.

Kern Central brought a touch of history that was almost poetic. Some of Kern Central's customers had been members of a credit union for farmworkers that had been co-founded by Dolores Huerta and Helen Chavez. In the 1960s, Huerta and Helen's husband, Cesar Chavez, led the United Farm Workers in a boycott of the California table grape industry that resulted in historic collective bargaining agreements.

The rapid expansion was facilitated by $25 million in secondary capital from the Self-Help Ventures Fund in North Carolina and a $30 million program-related investment from the Ford Foundation. The Ford money was one-third of a $90 million investment that Ford had set aside for programs to expand financial services to low-income people. Expansion continued in 2011 with the merger of Mission SF Credit Union in San Francisco and another 2,500 members. It, too, was facing financial pressure after a handful of bad loans reduced its capital ratio to a level unacceptable by regulators.

The mergers proved to be demanding for Zuckerman and Duran. The challenges included introducing Self-Help, especially its culture, to a host of new employees, few of whom had ever heard of something called the Center for Community Self-Help. Some officers of the Mission SF Credit Union had actively opposed the merger, which was closed by the National Credit Union Administration. One opponent spoke of Mission SF's tradition as a community development financial institution (CDFI) and feared its history of work in the community would be lost. He was apparently unaware that the very definition of a CDFI had been crafted twenty years earlier at a conference in Durham organized by Self-Help. It certainly was not an alien concept to the new management.

There were also systems to be integrated, phone systems to be connected, and operational boundaries to be defined. Procedures and policies were trimmed to conform to Self-Help's history of service. Some credit unions had been making money with overdraft fees. These charges were as noxious to Eakes as the evils of credit insurance. They came to an end. Most had never done mortgage lending, so new home lending options were introduced, while the lessons learned in retail service were transferred east to North Carolina.

Zuckerman had to convey the Self-Help culture of community development. That did not mean just treating customers with courtesy when they came in the door. That meant trying to find new ways to serve the unbanked population in the community.

"We had some [managements] that were very flat, egalitarian, and communicative, and we had others that were command and control, run by someone who everybody was scared of," Zuckerman said. "We inherited all this baggage and only one person in California who had spent any time working in North Carolina [and understood the Self-Help culture], and that was me."

Zuckerman was integrating all of these moving parts in the spring of 2012 when he got a call from Eakes telling him of "a project in Chicago that we have to do." Second Federal Savings and Loan, a community financial institution that was the foundation of home and business lending in the Little Village Latino community in Chicago, was in trouble. Self-Help could lend a hand, he argued. Zuckerman was adamant. Nothing more could be added to his operation, he contended. "Martin, you don't want to blow up the ship."

"Martin said, 'I think Joe [Duran] needs to come out and see,'" Zuckerman recalled. "Martin knew exactly what he was doing. Joe gets there, spends a day, and he calls back and says, 'Guys, we have got to do it.'"

For Duran, Second Federal's relationship with its community reminded him of his own institution, Community Trust. The Chicago institution had been organized in 1923 to serve an immigrant population from Eastern Europe, but a predecessor thrift dated to the late nineteenth century. More than eighty years later, Second Federal was the financial anchor for one of the largest urban concentrations of Latinos in the United States. A Mexican flag flew alongside the stars and stripes on top of the Second Federal building at Pulaski Road and 26th Street. Tellers greeted customers in Spanish. Up and down the streets, for miles in either direction, were business signs in Spanish, save for a few Asian restaurants. "I immediately fell in love with its community and mission," Duran said.

Second Federal's directors had been hit hard by the financial upheavals and had lost. The thrift had gambled on ITIN loans made through brokers and had not managed them well. It also had been lax in its own lending, depending on stated income of some borrowers rather than documenting a borrower's ability to repay. This kind of sloppy work had gotten a lot of institutions in trouble, and Second Federal's situation was compounded by the hammering that Chicago received in the run-up to the foreclosure crisis in 2008. Even ShoreBank, a beacon of community development lenders and an early inspiration for Self-Help, was in trouble, along with a host of other traditional banks in and around Chicago and northern Illinois.

Before the Second Federal option came along, Self-Help, with financial support from the MacArthur Foundation, was struggling to find a way to get families who had lost their homes due to foreclosure into homes that had been abandoned and were standing empty. The plan was to buy foreclosed houses and lease them to qualified families who would have a chance to regain their financial footing. If renters were steady in their payments and restored their credit, they would be offered a chance to buy the home. It was similar to the Turnkey Three program in Charlotte in 1986, which had helped launch Self-Help into home lending.

The relocation program did not work as planned. Self-Help could not find the intermediaries on the ground in Chicago to process the applications and arrange the resettlements. Eakes was ready to return the grant to MacArthur as Second Federal slipped closer and closer to default.

Second Federal was in the hands of the Federal Deposit Insurance Corporation (FDIC) in June 2012, and the agency was eager to sell its assets of $199.1 million and deposits of $175.9 million and recover what it could.[5] The thrift was holding more than a thousand home mortgages, a third of which were delinquent. The consequences for the community were dire if these homes went into foreclosure, a real likelihood for a buyer eager to get bad debts off the books as quickly as possible.

Raul Raymundo of The Resurrection Project (TRP), a community development organization, had done what he could to help raise capital for Second Federal, including an appeal to the MacArthur Foundation. He considered it to be the financial anchor for the community. Its loss would be felt for years. Raymundo had grown up in Chicago's Latino community and had helped found TRP in 1990 to rebuild an area in serious decline. In twenty-five years, the group had produced a record of community service, including managing property to provide affordable housing and financial counseling for borrowers.

The MacArthur folks sent Raymundo to Eakes. When the two finally got into the same room, one day in late spring 2012, Raymundo said they bonded like brothers. "We wanted to do what was right in the community," he said. "Sitting down, and meeting, we shared stories and we both knew we were doing the right thing. We needed them, and they needed us to get this done."[6]

Randy Chambers, Self-Help's chief financial officer, was vacationing with his family in June. As he periodically checked his email, he began to notice an ongoing exchange of messages about a troubled institution in Chicago. He had heard Eakes talk about Raymundo's efforts to get Chicago interests organized to buy Second Federal from the FDIC. At the time, he thought it was just another bunch of spaghetti thrown up on the wall to see what would stick. As the frequency of the email chatter increased, with Eakes leaning on staffers for various bits of advice and requests for Self-Help's legal counsel to take a look at some paragraph of an agreement in draft stage, Chambers turned to his wife and told her Eakes was talking about buying a failed bank in Chicago. "This has to be one of the dumber pieces of 'spaghetti' that has ever been tossed against the wall," he said.[7]

Chambers sided with Zuckerman. This was insane. On his return from vacation, he stopped in to see Eakes after the weekly Monday management meeting. "I said, 'Martin, we are stretched to the nines all over the country, we have got a whole lot of immigration stuff going on, and we don't know a damn thing about Chicago. And, by the way, I took a look at the demographic data, and the census tract that this bank is in, that you think is so hot to trot, has been losing population for the last decade.'"

Eakes's counterargument was that Second Federal was a larger version of the Latino Credit Union in Durham, an institution Self-Help had nursed to life more than a decade earlier that was now firmly planted in the state. "I was pissed," Chambers said. "I spent five years of my life helping [the Latino

Credit Union] get off the ground. It had better be good if you are going to tell me that. He said, 'Just go and take a look.'"

Chambers traveled to Chicago and returned with the same gobsmacked reaction as Duran. "It was the damnedest thing I had ever seen in my life. There aren't ten cities in the world that have this intense a Mexican neighborhood. You can drive for five miles and everything—the laundromats, the dress shops, the book stores, the restaurants, banks, car washes, everything—is in Spanish," he said. "And it is the coolest thing that this community exists."

Working with a California financial institution as a partner, Self-Help Federal produced a bid for Second Federal. It was declined. Instead, the FDIC sold Second Federal's deposits and its three branch offices to Wintrust Financial Corporation, a suburban Chicago bank holding company that had been busy buying failed banks and extending its franchise in Chicagoland. The decision was disappointing, even maddening to Eakes and Raymundo. Self-Help's bid was considerably higher than Wintrust's reported offer of $100,000, but it was different. Self-Help offered to take, at a deep discount, Second Federal's troubled loan portfolio, which had no appeal for Wintrust, as well as infuse $20 million in new capital to cover loan losses and provide cash for new loans.

"Our bid was based on the fact that we wanted to help and mitigate as many of the mortgages as the institution had so that families could stay in their homes," Raymundo said. In the end, Self-Help acquired the home mortgage portfolio and began working on loan modifications with borrowers.

At the same time, Raymundo began a political campaign to pressure Wintrust into returning control of the bank to the community. "I threw away the business plan and put together the organizing plan," Raymundo said. He worked political figures in Chicago and delivered a scathing letter to the FDIC. Urged on by the community, Chicago congressmen complained, and loudly, to the FDIC, which tried to defend itself.[8]

For Eakes, the FDIC's decision was a case of "reverse Robin Hood." From his point of view, it looked like the deposits of the low-income immigrants in Chicago's Little Village would be subsidizing Wintrust customers who lived in the city's wealthier suburbs. He did not see Wintrust bringing to the branches services like DREAMER loans, which covered the $465 application fee under the federal government's Deferred Action for Childhood Arrivals. These loans had become a staple of Self-Help Federal's service to Latinos in

California. While Raymundo worked Chicago, Eakes found allies in Washington and the MacArthur Foundation.

The foundation allowed Eakes to use money committed earlier to relocating those who had lost homes to foreclosure to assist in the purchase of Second Federal. The money was essential, Eakes said. "I am not sure the regulators would have approved us to do it if we had not had a new injection from MacArthur. The MacArthur board, to their everlasting credit, came together between sessions and voted on just that one action that enabled us to use that $15 million to support the Chicago expansion," Eakes said. "That was one of the best investments they have ever made and one of best we have ever made. It was totally unforeseen. Just happened that it was a failed investment that we could reprogram into something amazing."[9]

In November 2012, just a week or so after Eakes sat on the couch in his office relating Self-Help's role in the Second Federal saga, Wintrust's CEO Edward Wehmer finally got the message: a measured withdrawal could add some shine to the company's image, while holding the course could be damaging. He announced that it was best for Second Federal to remain whole, and Wintrust withdrew from Little Village, leaving Self-Help Federal as the new owner. It was the first time Wintrust had ever sold any of the businesses it had acquired in twenty-one years of operation. Raymundo praised Wintrust, who said of its former adversary, "Raul Raymundo is a very passionate and dedicated guy for his community."[10]

A year later, on a sunny Saturday in September 2013, Raymundo presided over a community celebration with helium-filled balloons, a street fair with games and music, and a host of dignitaries, including Illinois's governor and attorney general, to announce Second Federal's rebirth as a component of Self-Help Federal Credit Union. By that time, any nervousness of Second Federal's employees, produced by those worried about this new owner from North Carolina, had disappeared.

Among those on hand to celebrate were some of the 150 borrowers who had restructured home mortgages with terms they could afford. The delinquency rate, at 29 percent in February 2013, was down to 13 percent in 2014 and 10 percent in 2015. In mid-2014, only eight of Second Federal's 1,100 loans had gone into foreclosure while twenty changed hands in short sales. A bank known as "el banco del pueblo," or "the people's bank," remained open with even more services tailored to the immigrant customers it had served for more than a century.[11]

The acquisition produced winning results for the community and for Self-Help Federal, said Zuckerman. "By working closely with borrowers in a way that was fair and enabled them to repay, we think the collections over the life of the portfolio are going to be far higher than what we paid for it," he said in 2014. "By working it smart, we are going to make a lot of money on that purchase, which just fuels that back wheel [of sustainability]. Plus, if these three branches had fallen into somebody else's hands, it would have stopped the kind of services that the community relied upon. We came in and not only kept doing but added relevant services like mortgage lending again. We really preserved community lending for an immigrant community."

The creation of Self-Help Federal fundamentally changed Self-Help's financial structure. After just eight years, beginning in mid-2008, it was serving sixty-five thousand members from twenty-two branches in California, Illinois, and Florida, where the Community Trust Federal Credit Union in Apopka, Florida, was added in 2016. That was more than thirty thousand members and five more branches than what had been done by Self-Help Credit Union in North Carolina over thirty years.

By the end of 2015, Self-Help Federal had 241 employees, driving most of the growth of Self-Help's total workforce to more than 600 in 2016. Sixty-six percent of all Self-Help employees were working on the retail side, serving customers in credit union branches.[12]

Eakes achieved what he set out to do in 2008 when Self-Help was shaken by the impossible and Morgan Stanley called its loan. By the end of 2014, Self-Help's obligations to Wall Street investment banks had dropped from more than $564 million in 2006 to $48 million in 2015. Meanwhile, during this same time, member deposits had grown from $173 million in 2007 to more than $1 billion in 2015.

Not everything had gone as planned. Those early check-cashing outlets in California were later transitioned to branches of Self-Help Federal. Zuckerman found the operation not to be sustainable for an outfit like Self-Help, which provided employee benefits and an organizational minimum wage (it went to $12 an hour in 2016), particularly when competitors were using check cashing as a loss leader to enhance their payday lending business.

While Self-Help was opportunistic, it was not reckless, said Zuckerman. "People may say these guys are just a little bit out of control, when unbeknownst to them we have actually been pretty disciplined. And I think that is a culture skill that is one of Martin Eakes's strengths.

"If Self-Help had not built itself into the stable financial institution it was in 2006," Zuckerman said, "it couldn't have launched California. It certainly couldn't have embarked on such an aggressive merger strategy or created a brand-new kind of credit union model.

"Martin and others view that with capacity comes responsibility," Zuckerman said. "When these unique opportunities come along, that others really can't do and we can, that creates an obligation on our part to really stretch ourselves and do it because that is the luxury we have, and that luxury creates responsibility."

Retail service finally arrived at a downtown Durham office of Self-Help Credit Union in 2014 when one of the last of North Carolina's African American credit unions, which had been operating as Generations Credit Union, was merged into Self-Help Credit Union. Its small size and limited reach were not sufficient in the face of a changing market. The Generations merger was difficult for Eakes. He had worked with these African American institutions, some with long, rich histories, for nearly thirty years. But over the years, they had failed, one by one. He blamed himself for not doing more to help the survivors. "I waited too long," he said. "It was all in my own head that I didn't want to be perceived or to contribute to the image of a white leader taking over a black institution. Only in my mind was that an issue."[13]

Raymundo had no such qualms about Self-Help's acquisition of Second Federal in Chicago. "Things happen for a reason. It may be destiny, fate, or divine intervention. We all did the right thing. The partnership was never about what moneys could be generated or profits completed but [about] doing the right thing for the community."

CHAPTER FOURTEEN

The Mission

Once the property of the mighty American Tobacco Company, the collection of abandoned industrial buildings in downtown Durham, complete with steam plant, railroad siding, and a towering smokestack bearing the words *Lucky Strike*, was known for cracked walls, collapsed roofs, and wild growth the size of trees rising from sagging gutters. Inside, behind chain-link fencing topped with razor wire, it was worse. Water covered the basement floors and added to the environmental hazards of lead-based paint and steam pipes wrapped in asbestos. Police SWAT teams used the factory grounds, vacant for more than a decade, as a training ground. All in all, it was a fifteen-acre tableau of urban blight, a brownfield.

When Durham's minor league baseball team opened its season with ten thousand fans at an exhibition game in April 1998, team owner James F. Goodmon had his eye on this sad spread of industrial decay directly across from the proud, new Durham Bulls Athletic Park, which he had opened three years earlier. He could see the entire range of ten or more empty buildings—700,000 square feet or so of space under sagging roofs—from atop the $9 million office building he had built overlooking right field. He called his building Diamond View and filled it with first-class tenants and the studios of his company's Fox television broadcasting franchise. A year later, he had an option to buy the American Tobacco property.

As the chief executive officer of Raleigh's Capitol Broadcasting Company and owner of Raleigh's WRAL-TV, an NBC affiliate and one of the most innovative broadcasting outfits around, Goodmon was a known quantity with a record of accomplishing what he set out to do. Yet, nothing he had tried so far equaled his vision for the American Tobacco property, the largest historic renovation ever attempted in North Carolina. There was talk of a $250 million investment that would require money from the city and county, and would most likely prompt a tax increase. In exchange, Goodmon offered a catalyst that he argued would reverse the sagging fortune of Durham's center city with thousands of people coming to the restored buildings to work, live, and enjoy restaurants and nightlife.

Durham's elected officials finally backed the plan, promising to build two parking garages and dedicate new tax revenue for downtown development. Goodmon's bankers were less enthusiastic. While Capitol's credit was fine, this project appeared to have little more than optimism going for it. It would double first-class office space at a time when the city's economy was weak and seeking a solid footing. The property was far from Durham's more desirable addresses. Plus, Goodmon's company had no record for this kind of enterprise. The one lending package that Goodmon received was far from satisfactory.

The project was stalled in 2002 when it landed on Tucker Bartlett's desk at Self-Help. He was an intern on the commercial real estate team, working part time while he pursued a graduate degree at the University of North Carolina, Chapel Hill. The prospective $40 million deal—five times larger than any previous loan commitment—was a long way from the microlending he had done for two years with the Peace Corps in Africa before joining Self-Help. He was thirty years old.

The deal was as complicated as it was large, in part because Bartlett was figuring out how to use a new federal program that provided tax advantages for investment in depressed areas. Congress had approved the New Market Tax Credit program in 2000; the money was expected soon for qualified projects. Bartlett began putting together a lending package, bouncing ideas off his classmates in Chapel Hill. "I would sit in my real estate classes and raise my hand and say, 'Hypothetically speaking . . .'" His professor analyzed a proposed American Tobacco loan package before Bartlett took it to the Self-Help credit committee for review.

Self-Help had a vested interest in making Goodmon's dream come true. Martin Eakes was familiar with the American Tobacco property, having considered its purchase not long before Goodmon obtained an option. Moreover, the site was just across the railroad tracks that cleaved downtown from Self-Help's own office buildings on Main Street. A stronger, healthier downtown, with an exciting offering of attractions, could be transformative for a city long in need of good news. Greater prosperity could raise all boats, including Self-Help's substantial investment in the center of the city. At the same time, a misstep on a project this size could be troubling.

"We thought long and hard," Bartlett said. "It wasn't obvious that that project was going to be such a success. It was the largest loan we had ever done. I remember Martin saying to me, 'I don't care if you don't make any other loans this year, just don't mess this up.'"[1]

Self-Help arranged the permanent financing in April 2003, touted as the nation's first loan committed to the program. Wachovia and Self-Help were the only two North Carolina organizations—out of 345 that applied nationwide—to be selected.[2] The Ventures Fund provided long-term financing as well as money for construction that raised the loan total to $40 million. The additional money paid for converting a center concourse into an artificial river with a recirculating flow that sent water tumbling over broken blocks of concrete, spouting from fountains, and splashing over waterfalls. The waterway, which would become a popular attraction and photo backdrop, was a generous touch and fitting accompaniment to the refurbished 200-foot smokestack and the 150-foot water tower that was given a dose of simulated rust so it would show its age.

The first of American Tobacco's tenants started moving in during the spring of 2004, with construction still under way. More than four hundred employees came from GlaxoSmithKline, the pharmaceutical giant, which shifted people from its base in the Research Triangle Park. The Glaxo people were followed by employees from units of Duke University, the headquarters of the Triangle's top advertising agency, and a software company. Before long, American Tobacco's Underground, a repurposed subfloor in one block-long building, became a favorite of Internet entrepreneurs who rented desks and high-speed broadband connections.

A decade later, in 2014, American Tobacco proved to be everything that Goodmon and the city officials hoped it would be. It added $150 million in valuation to the city's tax base and brought nearly four thousand employ-ees to jobs downtown. That was more than double the number of workers at the plant when it was turning out cigarettes. One tech company started with fifteen hundred square feet of office space and, as it grew, expanded to a ninety-thousand-square-foot tenancy. When the company was sold for $200 million, the new owner retained the offices at American Tobacco and asked for more space to expand. In time, demands for office space meant some tenants were spilling over into one of Self-Help's buildings. A publicly financed performing arts center came next, along with a hotel and a burst of private investment to remake other aging buildings in Durham.[3]

Few would argue the impact of Goodmon's American Tobacco project on Durham. Most are unaware of Self-Help's role, however. "Martin got it," Goodmon's son Michael, the project's manager, said in 2015. "Their support was huge. It got us over the hump. It was really important for downtown Durham, and it was really important for his mission."[4]

In 2013, Self-Help began work on its industrial renovation in Greensboro, North Carolina, at Revolution Mill, a complex of buildings that dated to the early 1900s when six thousand to ten thousand Cone Mills Corporation employees reported daily over three shifts. The project was in foreclosure—with Self-Help Ventures Fund as a secondary lender—when Self-Help bought the twenty-five acres and its empty, deteriorating buildings. By 2016, the complex was on its way to accepting tenants and building out spaces for living, working, and dining.[5] Eakes hoped that the project would be the same sort of catalyst for his hometown.

Self-Help's work in community investment dates to its infancy. In 1986, Self-Help financed a group in Durham's Crest Street neighborhood to en-able the purchase of rental houses from absentee landlords. It was an effort to stabilize the community and the beginning of Crest Street residents' ef-forts to shape a future after a long and protracted fight over a potentially destructive highway project.

In the mid-1990s, Self-Help aligned with a community group to restore a former hospital, built in 1913 to serve African Americans in the eastern North Carolina tobacco town of Wilson. Mercy Hospital was all but ready to collapse when Eakes showed up one day with architect Eddie Belk in tow. Blue lights from a police cruiser were flashing out front as officers re-sponded to a drive-by shooting. The collaborative effort with the Wilson Community Improvement Association and Branch Bank and Trust Com-pany repurposed the old hospital, an iconic building for east Wilson, into a community center and business incubator and returned it to a source of local pride.[6]

Residents in Durham's Walltown neighborhood came to know Self-Help in 1996 after it began work in what was a hard-bitten section on the boundary of Duke University's East Campus. Working with city government and Walltown neighbors, and using an initial $2 million loan from Duke, Self-Help bought some thirty rental houses (a number that later grew to nearly one hundred of the seven hundred homes in the neighborhood), demolished those that were beyond repair and built new ones in their place, and renovated the rest. The homes were offered for sale to first-time, low-income buyers, with deed covenants designed to prevent speculators from reaping unjustified rewards. As part of the project, Walltown Elementary School, closed since 1976, was purchased and reopened after a $1.5 million renovation as a home for a church, charter school, and community library.

A subsequent study reported, "Self-Help's program's strength lies in the fact that they were invited in by the community to address a community need, that they were dedicated to the goals the community felt were important, and had a history of efficiently attaining those goals. Although there were issues along the way, I do not think the divisions could have been properly repaired if this relationship had not existed at the beginning."[7] Walltown led to similar work in other Durham neighborhoods and the creation of a land bank to hedge against speculation. One large tract under development, called South Side, lay just beyond the ballpark and American Tobacco.

Self-Help experimented with a lease-to-purchase housing option in Charlotte, North Carolina, one similar to the attempt in Chicago, where it purchased twenty-five properties in foreclosure in the Peachtree Hills neighborhood. Repairs of the homes were made, when necessary, and they were then offered for lease, but with no success. The homes eventually were sold using traditional lending.

Many of these initiatives escaped broad public attention, as did another important area of lending—construction and facilities loans for nonprofit charter schools. This was an outgrowth of Self-Help's work in the early 1990s with child care facilities that provided jobs and expanded opportunities for working parents, especially in rural areas. Charter schools were authorized in North Carolina in 1996 after Republicans, with their first majority in the N.C. House of Representatives in nearly a hundred years, attempted to leverage their position in favor of school vouchers. Democrats, with only a two-vote advantage in the state senate, accepted charter schools, capped at no more than one hundred statewide, instead of forcing a vote on vouchers. Durham senator Wib Gulley, Eakes's former law partner, handled the bill in the senate, with Eakes's urging, and the final vote had the approval of other leading liberal and progressive Democrats.

North Carolina's charter schools were bound by the legislation to meet the needs of at-risk students, provide parents and students with expanded choices of learning, encourage the use of innovation, and improve student learning. Thirty-four schools opened the first year (eighteen of these were still in operation in 2016[8]). Self-Help's Laura Benedict, who had developed the child care lending program, served on a state Department of Public Instruction panel that reviewed charter applications.

Charter school lending created internal tension at Self-Help. Steadfast supporters of traditional public schools saw charters as a way for conservatives to undermine public education and even as a step back from years of racial integration. Opponents feared charters would become a state-funded option to the "Rebel Yell schools," private academies for white students that cropped up in the 1970s in response to court-ordered school desegregation. Others said the charters drained resources from public schools already strapped for tax support. Some Self-Help staff on the commercial loan side refused to work on charter schools applications.[9]

Charter school lending stretched Eakes's own political moorings, said Marc Hunt, who ran the loan program for three years, as well as his own. Reality brought both of them up short. "We had a number of failing school systems in North Carolina," said Hunt, "that were concentrated in areas of poverty and had high concentrations of African Americans, the same geographic places that Self-Help was so interested [in]. Education is fundamental to social and economic vitality and justice. [Charter school lending] was about an educational outcome that reinforces a social mission."[10]

Self-Help limited its lending to nonprofit organizations that could demonstrate that education offered in their schools would be first-rate and that the schools would serve students at risk, mostly children from low-wealth families who were dropping out before graduation or finishing with inadequate preparation for jobs or further study. About one-third of the one hundred new charters in North Carolina received some help, and Self-Help's lending eventually extended beyond North Carolina to clients running inner-city projects in Washington, D.C., Atlanta, Detroit, and Columbus,

Ohio. Hunt was working with nonprofit charters in seven states when he left in 2004. In 2015, Self-Help loaned about $19 million to charter schools across the nation. One $4 million loan was to assist a Nashville, Tennessee, school with a diverse student body to expand from 150 to 1,000 students.[11]

Bonnie Wright was the driving force behind one of the early charter school applications in North Carolina. She was inspired in part by what she had learned after leaving Self-Help in 1992 and working as a diversity trainer in public schools. She helped open Maureen Joy Charter in 1997 with fifty students in kindergarten through fifth grade. All qualified for free or reduced lunch, and the racial makeup was mixed, about fifty-fifty. During the first few years, before a more suitable location was found, classes were held in modular structures that were wired for computers by her geeky husband. Despite Eakes's support for his wife's work, he told her that her participation made Maureen Joy ineligible for a loan, despite her credentials as Self-Help's co-founder. "There was no staff person at Self-Help who could do the loan approval without knowing that this is my wife," he said.

After Wright severed her connection with Maureen Joy Charter, Self-Help and Maureen Joy collaborated on the purchase and renovation of a Durham school building built in 1910 and vacant since 1967. It sat with windows and doors boarded up, its interior deteriorating, in the heart of the city's poorest census tract. The renovation restored the classic features—high ceilings, tall windows, beaded-wood wainscoting—and turned the building into a model of restoration. Maureen Joy Charter relocated there in 2013, offering free lunch and transportation. In 2016, 99 percent of its 615 students in kindergarten through eighth grade were African Americans or Latinos. Ninety percent qualified for free or reduced-priced lunches. The academic record of its students surpassed those of other schools with a comparable demography. The $10 million investment was the largest in East Durham in decades.

"I got a lot of flak from people in the community that I was used to having support from," Wright said.

I was surprised. I had done my research and knew that what happens in communities like this, urban communities. When charter schools start, they tend to serve underserved populations. We thought we would have a more diverse population, but over time we had heavily African American schools, primarily kids who had suffered in traditional schools.

[Opponents] were operating out of fear that [charters] would undercut public or traditional schools, that it would be a white-flight school, or undercut public or traditional schools. I never had that fear.[12]

For-profit charter operations and those servicing students with online coursework did bother Eakes. There were some of both among the more than 150 charter schools operating in 2016 after a Republican-dominated legislature eliminated the cap on charter operations. The legislature then doubled down by shifting money and emphasis from traditional public schools to alternative models, including a voucher program for students attending private schools.

Many of the newer charter schools would not qualify for Self-Help loans, and the challenges for local elected school boards created by the legislature was deeply troubling. The racial imbalance of charters, however, still a problem for traditional schools, was less of a concern for Eakes, despite the howl of many of his friends and erstwhile political allies with whom he and Self-Help had stood together on so many other issues.

Eakes's answer to critics of Self-Help's lending program was a charter school deep in eastern North Carolina called KIPP-Gaston. Self-Help helped it expand over a period of ten years. Students come from disadvantaged African American families whose alternatives were public schools where 40 percent of students leave before graduation. At KIPP-Gaston, students were told on the day they enrolled that if they finished KIPP-Gaston they will go to college. In seven years of graduations, all were accepted. "Anybody [who] expects me to be apologetic for better outcomes [for] children of low-wealth families," Eakes said, "[is] going to have a debate on their hands."

It was a nuanced position for the difficult and intransigent issue of racial segregation that does not satisfy Self-Help's critics. When a loan to a charter school in Los Angeles was highlighted in 2012 in a Self-Help newsletter, Benedict received a call from a longtime depositor. "It was not that we had been hiding that," she said. "It does push some hot buttons with people."

Ventures Fund President Robert Schall said, "We believe charter schools ought to serve a public purpose. They ought to be providing high-quality education to folks who have poor access to high-quality education. If they don't do that, then there is no need for charter schools. That is what we lobby for in state government, and that is what we lend for."[13]

The Self-Help Credit Union celebrated its thirtieth birthday in November 2014. About a hundred people gathered for a modest celebration tacked on to the credit union's annual meeting in the Temple Building on Main Street in Durham. The speeches were short and unrehearsed. On hand were the first recipients of a Self-Help mortgage, a gay couple who had asked forthrightly thirty years earlier, "Do you lend to lesbians?" Katherine Stern Weaver completed the loan application on their kitchen table. The party was a cozy affair, and woefully understated. Bonnie Wright was traveling out of state and absent. Neither she nor her husband care much for ceremony.

The evening's celebration belied the depth and breadth of Self-Help's reach. What had begun with donations from a handful of supporters on a college campus in the summer of 1983, along with the proceeds of that legendary bake sale, was in 2016 part of an enterprise with $1.8 billion in assets, a nationwide footprint, and six hundred employees, most of whom worked in financial institutions.

Over the years, Self-Help held fast to one mission: social-change lending to advance the economic opportunities of women, minorities, and the poor. It was the work that earned national recognition for Self-Help and for its founders. In May 2011, the Ford Foundation selected Eakes as one of twelve social innovators in its first class of Visionaries Awards. "Standing in direct contrast to the predatory financial products that played a central role in the financial crisis," the Foundation said, "Self-Help's work demonstrates the importance of responsible and affordable products in helping low-income people achieve economic security."[14] Four months later, the Foundation elected Eakes to its board of trustees.

In 2013, the Leadership Conference, a coalition of the nation's leading civil rights groups, presented Eakes and the CRL with the Hubert H. Humphrey Award, its highest honor. Conference president Julian Bond introduced Eakes as "courageous and a little quirky," and someone who "doesn't look like or live like a financial power." Eakes dedicated the award to the late Marion Sandler, who had died less than a year before.

Early in 2015, Princeton University honored Eakes with its James Madison Medal, the top award for alumni of its graduate school. In his acceptance speech, Eakes called homeownership "the single best tool for breaking the cycle of poverty."[15] Four years earlier, he had received the John W. Kuykendall Award for Community Service from Davidson College.

By many measures, Self-Help should never have survived those early days. Eakes himself admits as much. But, he and the staff tempered their dedication to a strategic mission with the flexibility to pivot on tactics and be open to opportunities. They left a program that was not working to find something that did. Steve Zuckerman was part of those debates about the future before leaving to pursue other things, returning three decades later. "In the end, the leadership said we do live in a capitalist economy," recalled Zuckerman, "that is the structure of the United States, and we should help everyone, particularly the most disadvantaged, to benefit in that structure."[16]

Out of that debate arose the framework for Self-Help's future, something Eakes called "development banking" in a 1992 speech. He said it was made up of three parts: a regulated financial institution to serve the economically disadvantaged; a nonprofit development entity to take on experimental, even risky, ventures; and incremental, even chaotic, growth, learning by doing and casting off things that do not work.

Self-Help was never about building an institution, said Schall, the founding president of the Ventures Fund. "While we have built quite an institution and have a lot of experience in running a credit union, I would say that if something changed in the way credit unions worked, and we couldn't continue to do the work we do, we would change the institution. We wouldn't change our mission to become what credit unions would require us to do. We would change that institution we use to get our work done. We still have that."

In many ways, Self-Help remains, as Eakes says, a home for misfits: those who hate bureaucracy and can't work in government very easily, along with those whose skills are best suited for the private sector but don't care about making money. For such people, said Marc Hunt, "there is an affinity for a truly mission-driven organization.

"Martin made us reflect Self-Help's mission in a very real way," said Hunt. Eakes would interrupt discussions about new initiatives, even those that came with much-needed underwriting support, giving notice that "this is about our mission. It is not chasing some variation . . . that might be financially productive that might meet some goal that would broaden our mission. It is about a narrow mission of economic justice and wealth building. Trust me, we can get a lot done there. It was that unyielding commitment to mission that makes Self-Help very real."

Self-Help's comfort with seeking creative solutions led people to try new things, explore extraordinary options, and gather experience as they went along. The stops and starts, even the failures, were all preparation that allowed Self-Help to seize opportunities when they arose. The partnership with the Ford Foundation that created a secondary market for nontraditional loans—which put more than 46,000 families in homes they could afford and in which they would build equity, despite the Great Recession—

was both transformational and unexpected. So was the purchase of Second Federal in Chicago. Self-Help's long relationship with the MacArthur Foundation as well as its record with regulators and capacity to turn on a dime helped save nearly a thousand homeowners from foreclosure and a community from losing its financial institution. "It was just a random happening that was creative and opportunistic," said Eakes. "I would never have been able to get that through MacArthur if I had had to go through the normal yearlong vetting process."

It happened again in 2015 as Eakes was seeking a financial partner to help Community Trust Federal Credit Union in Apopka, Florida, a farm community outside Orlando in central Florida. Members of the Sisters of Notre Dame de Namur and a coalition of organizations supporting farmworkers had formed Community Trust in 1982, two years before Self-Help Credit Union was established. Eakes knew Sister Ann Kendrick, one of the founders, and could guess what she wanted as she tried to reach him time and again. Small credit unions like Community Trust were struggling all across the country, their size and limited offerings crippling their effectiveness, viability, and mission. Kendrick told Eakes that Community Trust wanted to be part of Self-Help Federal.

Kendrick and the others had worked heroically for three decades on behalf of African Americans and seasonal workers tied to vast farming operations in central Florida.[17] Eakes told Kendrick that Self-Help could not take on another credit union but volunteered to assist a community development financial institution in Orlando, one similar to the Ventures Fund, to create a version of Self-Help's corporate arrangement with Community Trust as the CDFI's regulated institution. That option collapsed, and so did Eakes's resolve to stay out of Florida. Community Trust became part of Self-Help Federal in January 2016.

In the 1980s, Catholic orders had pumped nearly a million dollars into Self-Help Credit Union, helping it grow and gain strength when there were no guarantees of success. That support gave Self-Help the opportunity and freedom to refine its mission and build a future. Eakes had not forgotten. "Clearly, I was raised a Baptist," he told Kendrick, "but I seem to be subject to Catholic guilt at the same time."[18]

"When I took it to the board, I told them this credit union makes utterly no financial sense for us," Eakes said. "But they have literally been doing the Lord's work. The mission of what they are doing is remarkable, and we have the financial resources to do it." He convinced his staff that

Self-Help's newest opportunities lay between its base in North Carolina and central Florida, in communities along the Interstate 95 corridor through South Carolina and Georgia and into the major markets in Florida. There, Self-Help would shore up its commitment to underserved and unbanked African Americans whose membership in Self-Help institutions had been overtaken by Latinos. "That is where we started," Eakes said. "Our primary connection was to the African American community."

A financial institution's assets are measured by its balance sheet, which in Self-Help's case showed a net income of $21 million in 2015. The Community Trust merger illustrated, and perhaps even quantified, the value of Self-Help's other resources—independence and self-sufficiency, including the confidence to meet difficult challenges. These founding principles allowed Self-Help to make strategic moves and also to pick its political battles without regard to past associations or partisan arrangements, as with charter schools and Eakes's public opposition to an amendment to the North Carolina constitution prohibiting single-sex marriages.

Self-Help supplied talent and expertise in the organization of the Consumer Financial Products Bureau. At the same time, Eakes was tangling with the Obama administration and leading Democrats on Capitol Hill to preserve Fannie Mae and Freddie Mac against attacks from the Left that threatened to close the agencies or, at best, limit their lending capacity in the future.

"I used to joke before the financial crisis," said Eakes, "that in order to make a bad home loan it had to be fraudulent. People cared so much about their home that if they ever got a chance to own something, they would never default." Eakes spent a decade or more defending that premise and pushing banks to include low-wealth borrowers. "Now I am back here where I was 25 years ago. The lending market has contracted and over-reacted [such] that we spend much of our time with administrative agencies making sure they do not overreact, but find the right balance. Real life is always about finding balanced outcomes."

In 2012, Self-Help's critics from the Right alleged that Eakes and the Sandlers were to blame for the Great Recession and were undermining government. The charges were laid out in *Infiltrated: How to Stop the Insiders and Activists Who Are Exploiting the Financial Crisis to Control Our Lives and Our Fortunes*, a 200-page polemic promoted by conservative think tanks such as the American Enterprise Institute. It was not the greed and a host of bad actors in the financial industry that brought the economy down but it was activists like Eakes who coerced government agencies and global financial institutions into lowering home-lending standards. Thus, the crisis was caused by loans extended to low- and moderate-income borrowers, not by the bad behavior and risky financial instruments of Wall Street, as the bipartisan Financial Crisis Inquiry Commission (FCIC) concluded.

Infiltrated also took aim at the CFPB, a product of the Dodd-Frank legislation. Since its creation, the CFPB bedeviled payday lenders, debt collection agencies, and auto lenders, Self-Help's foes for more than a decade. For Eakes, the CFPB was what he called a "game changer." *Infiltrated* called it egregious government overreach that would keep consumers from short-term "small-dollar loans" where the high interest rates—400-plus percent when calculated on an annual rate—are simply a fact of doing business. Supporters of these small-dollar lenders ascribe ulterior, self-serving motives to Self-Help. If these sources of money are closed, then borrowers will have to use credit unions, which were characterized as tax-subsidized institutions using their nonprofit status to thrive at the public's expense.

In September 2016, the Republican majority in the U.S. House passed yet another bill to cripple the CFPB, just days after the CFPB levied penalties amounting to $185 million against Wells Fargo. A CFPB investigation found that bank employees, eager to make internal sales quotas, had opened millions of companion accounts without the knowledge of their customers. The Wells Fargo action followed on other enforcement action that had produced nearly $12 billion in relief and restitution to twenty-seven million customers wronged in cases involving mortgages, credit cards, debit cards, student loans, payday loans, debt collections, and other transactions.

"The financial crisis taught Americans hard lessons about the dangers of a poorly supervised financial system. Without a robust consumer protection bureau, they would be in danger of similar abusive practices in the future," said a *New York Times* editorial.[19] Nonetheless, one of the first targets of Republicans after they strengthened their position in Congress and elected a president of the United States was to pledge to weaken the powers of the CFPB.

The book was right about one thing. Self-Help's alumni "infiltrated" the government. Eric Stein, Self-Help's chief operating officer, helped put the CFPB into place as a deputy secretary in the U.S. Department of the Treasury. Later, he became chief of staff for former congressman Mel Watt after Watt was appointed to oversee the restructuring of Fannie Mae and Freddie Mac. Mark Pearce, the second president of the CRL, became the director of the FDIC's division of depositor and consumer protection after serving a stint as the chief deputy of banks in North Carolina. Keith Ernst left his job as director of research for the CRL in 2011 to become associate director of consumer research and examination analytics at the FDIC. Eric Halperin, an early staff member at the CRL, left for the U.S. Department of Justice, where he helped define fair lending enforcement in the office of civil rights.

Other Self-Help alumni can be found in business and throughout a range of nonprofits. Bill Bynum was fresh out of college and hired by Eakes at the bagel shop in Durham. Thirty years later, he was running the Hope Enterprise Corporation with its community development arm, a regional credit union, and a policy center that serves economically distressed parts of Arkansas, Louisiana, Mississippi, and Tennessee. Bynum was using tools and lessons he learned at Self-Help. "Self-Help has been the starting point for many of us who do work in this space," he said.

The legislation to neuter the CFPB and the publication of *Infiltrated* was a reminder that Self-Help and Eakes's opponents are far from gone. Chief among them are the payday lenders who had once pledged to use $10 million to destroy him personally. That led some of Eakes's friends to believe that a mugging Eakes suffered in late fall 2008 was politically motivated. There was no evidence that was the case, however. He just happened to be in the wrong place at the wrong time in a downtown Durham parking garage after he left his office one evening. Four men left him battered, bruised, and requiring surgery to restore torn tendons in his left arm. Wiry and scrappy, even in his fifties, Eakes had lost little of the grit that characterized his years as a high school wrestler. He drove himself home, called Bonnie, who was out of town, and then phoned his longtime associate Thad Moore, who took him to the hospital. Eakes was at work the next day, albeit a bit groggy. Conspiracy theories surrounding the incident persisted long after. North Carolina remains one of eighteen states where payday lenders are not welcome.

Moore had been with Eakes since there was barely a Self-Help and was one of fewer than a dozen or so associates, out of six hundred, who, in 2016, had spent their careers at what was known as "Self-Help Classic," the home and commercial lending and real estate development side of the organization. The Self-Help that Moore knew so well is more difficult to find. There are staff members at the CRL who never helped a family apply for a home loan or talked to hopeful entrepreneur eager to start a business. At times, policy clashes with practice. Today, retail dominates the business, and a sizable number of employees follow a dress code. Self-Help's human resources department—there wasn't one until the twenty-first century—balances prevailing wages across a broad spectrum, from the going rates in rural Scotland County, North Carolina, to the Bay Area in California.

The core culture remains. Steve Zuckerman introduced within Self-Help Federal a worker-member council like the one that has operated for decades in North Carolina. The new challenge, he said, was maintaining the Self-Help culture that worked and adapting it to new conditions and environments.

Throughout the financial crisis, Self-Help had never stopped lending, although the volume of business dropped precipitously in 2009. It increased from year to year and was rebounding in 2014 when one of its new borrowers in North Carolina was a woman who worked at Opportunity Threads, a small custom cut-and-sew plant in Morganton in the mountain foothills. She was part of a worker-owned business not unlike those that Moore, Eakes, and Wright had struggled to midwife thirty years earlier. Opportunity Threads was organized in 2008, in the throes of the financial crisis. It survived and provides jobs to about two dozen workers who are first- and second-generation immigrants from Guatemala.

Self-Help's secondary market, perhaps the organization's creation with the most stunning impact, was revived in February 2016, when Self-Help, the Federal Home Loan Mortgage Corporation, and Bank of America announced a mortgage program for low- and moderate-income borrowers that read like a revival of the secondary lending effort launched in 1998 with support from the Ford Foundation. The "Affordable Loan Solution" mortgages would be available through 4,700 Bank of America branches. Self-Help's own lending was growing, both in assisting small businesses and in mortgage lending. Internally, it was called Secondary Market 2.0.

"We were asking the right question in 1980 and again in 1990," said Eakes, "that this disparity of wealth between blacks and whites is clearly not the challenge of the next decade but the challenge of the next generation. I used to think that I was being forward-looking by saying that anything worth working on would take a decade or two to accomplish. I read a Reinhold Niebuhr quote in which he basically said nothing worthwhile can be accomplished in a single lifetime:

> There is part of me that is angry and discouraged that here we are now with charts showing disparity of black and white wealth, which was one

of my primary focus points, that under certain measures is worse now than when we started in 1983. I can tell myself, "Well, it would be worse if we weren't fighting the fight we were fighting," but this is where you just can't have self-pity and say, "I carried the baton, and we fought as hard as we could fight." Martin Luther King didn't get to see all of his victories in his lifetime, and some of what Gandhi was fighting for is still being fought out in India. You have your place, you have a lifetime, and you do the best you can with it.

Final Notes

I first heard of Martin Eakes and Self-Help in 2002 during a protracted tangle with Blue Cross and Blue Shield of North Carolina that ended with the insurance company forsaking plans to convert to a for-profit corporation. Some said Eakes's stubborn insistence of conditions of the proposed conversion under consideration by the state insurance department cost North Carolina a health care endowment that could have been worth billions of dollars. Others believed he was right to insist on the particulars of a deal to make sure citizens weren't cheated out of the tax breaks the nonprofit had enjoyed for nearly seventy years.

That's the way it is with Eakes. He puts everything on the line when he goes into battle. I began to see that more clearly nearly five years later, when my daughter, Evan, who had gone to work at Self-Help in 2003, invited me to hear him speak one evening in Chapel Hill. For Eakes, there was nothing special about what he had to say that night; it was a speech he had given many times before. But Eakes has a way of turning the ordinary into the compelling. Hearing, for the first time, his account of Self-Help's improbable rise from assisting worker-owned businesses to becoming the nation's leading lender for low- and moderate-income homeowners was inspiring, particularly for a writer who saw the Self-Help story as the basis for a book. The following day, I wrote Eakes and asked for his cooperation in such an endeavor. He said no.

I later learned that a pair of deep thinkers in the world of philanthropy and nonprofits had taken an interest in Self-Help and they were writing a book. *Forces for Good*, published in 2008, highlighted Self-Help, as it did eleven other high-impact organizations as examples of excellence for those managing and investing in nonprofits. The writers talked about the essential qualities of advocacy, sustainability, mission focus, cooperation, and adaptation, all of which Self-Help shared in abundance with the likes of the conservative Heritage Foundation, Teach for America, and Habitat for Humanity. That treatment was not the story of Self-Help that I had in mind, but I let the matter rest.

Nearly four years later, I made another run at Eakes. By this time, Self-Help was the last financial institution of its kind standing amid the ruins of the Great Recession. I had followed Self-Help's passage through the most difficult days that the nation's financial institutions had seen since the 1930s. Over the years, before my daughter left Self-Help in 2013, she passed along nuggets about Self-Help's creativity and resilience, especially in areas of community and residential development, which was her area of responsibility. I especially admired the work that she and her colleagues in residential real estate development were able to accomplish in Durham, Charlotte, Chapel Hill, and elsewhere. The work was creative, sensitive to the integrity of the community, and produced lasting change for good as neighbors worked together to restore their neighborhoods to health and vitality.

The more I learned about Self-Help, Eakes, and those around him, the more I became convinced that my earlier instincts about a book were right. I made my pitch again. This time, Eakes was reluctant, but he agreed to cooperate. His one condition was that the book not be a Martin Eakes biography.

This is not a biography, but there is no way to write about Self-Help without a large dose of Eakes. He was its co-founder, along with his wife, Bonnie Wright, in 1980, and for nearly forty years he has been at its core, serving as the fissile material in a continuing evolution of a nonprofit that remains faithful to its early mission of extending the civil rights movement to those who have not enjoyed full access to economic opportunities.

Eakes's condition was not some burst of false modesty. Even at the most important occasions in Self-Help's history, he is the one most often standing alone at the back of the room with a sly smile on his face, not at the front bowing to the applause. It is true, as he contends, there would be no Self-Help without the investment of an impressive corps of talented people who could easily have been doing something else with their lives (and making a lot more money). But those folks would not have been at Self-Help if Martin Eakes had not created a place where he could extend them an invite to work together, even if they had to raise their own salaries to remain employed.

Eakes made good on his word to me. Over the course of five years, we talked on ten or more occasions, usually in long sessions that ran on into the evening. He was candid and open to any question, ducking nothing. His participation spilled over to interviews with about ninety others, mostly former and current Self-Help staff members, but with those outside the organization as well. Some were cautious about the interest of a stranger. There had been enough political shots taken at Eakes and Self-Help over the years that some were wary of my motives. There remain a few on my list who never consented to an interview. Not all of those I spoke with were complimentary. A few filtered their antagonism through clinched teeth. Eakes draws that kind of reaction. It's either allegiance or opposition. I did find a few with grudging admiration who could go either way, depending on the issue, but not many.

This book is driven largely by what I learned during these interviews. *Forces for Good* put Self-Help into an institutional context. This book is more about the people and the occasions that make Self-Help unique.

It took some digging to discover a paper trail of Self-Help's work. Many organizations, particularly those in a hurry growing up, seldom take the time to build an archive, often disdaining archives as vanity until it is too late. Self-Help is no different. On one of my early visits with Eakes, he showed me a photograph of Self-Help's early staff that was on its way to a trash bin before someone realized its significance. Just as I was wrapping up my work, Eakes finally got around to organizing bulging files that filled side-by-side cabinets in his office.

Robert Schall, the first and only president of the Self-Help Ventures Fund, performed invaluable service on the policy side. Thad Moore, Eakes's first hire, helped guide me through the early years of the worker-owned experience and the development of the credit union. As the two employees with the longest tenure, they backstopped the memories of so many others who made time for my calls. Mike Calhoun, whose connections date to the mid-1980s, and Steve Zuckerman, Self-Help Federal Credit Union's president, allowed repeat visits and helped me understand the evolutionary path of the organization. Mary Mountcastle's perspective, as an insider and an outsider at Self-Help, was also valuable. Many others gave me their attention, and I am grateful.

Sandra Mikush, deputy director at the Mary Reynolds Babcock Foundation, provided early support on the project as well as access to the foundation's grant files. The Babcock microfiches were an invaluable archive containing early grant requests and periodic reports on progress written by Eakes or others. Without them, I probably would never have found the early analysis recorded by Eakes and others of Self-Help's early steps.

This book took considerably longer to complete than I had anticipated. That's the world of a freelance writer. It was necessary to squeeze my work on Self-Help into a schedule that included assignments that actually provided an income. I am grateful for the support and encouragement of a few benefactors including Jim Goodmon at the Capitol Broadcasting Corporation, the Weaver Foundation, the Mary Reynolds Babcock Foundation, and my good friend Katherine Stern Weaver of Greensboro. Together, they provided $13,000 in underwriting that was indeed welcome when it arrived.

I also thank my daughter, Evan, for that early invitation to hear Martin Eakes speak and for the warm legacy she herself left behind at Self-Help— "Oh, you're Evan's dad, the one writing the book." That put many at ease. My wife, Gloria, was my sounding board, proofreader, and grammar maven. My son, Owen, an accomplished writer and talented journalist, gave the manuscript a very thoughtful read, for which I am grateful, as did a select number of others whose judgment I value.

I am grateful to Duke University Press for accepting an outsider into the world of academic publishing. Director Stephen A. Cohn and editor Gisela Fosado were worthy champions of this book, as well as readers with valuable insight.

Notes

CHAPTER ONE • *Self-Help Who?*

1. Gideon J. Tucker, Final Accounting in the Estate of A.B., 1 Tucker 248 (N.Y. Surr. 1866)
2. Adam Searing, interview with author, May 21, 2013.
3. Jay Richards, *Infiltrated: How to Stop the Insiders and Activists Who Are Exploiting the Financial Crisis to Control Our Lives and Our Fortunes* (New York: McGraw-Hill Education, 2013).
4. Martin Eakes, interview with author, November 28, 2011.
5. Eric Stein, "Principles for GSE Reform," Center for Responsible Lending, October 14, 2012.
6. Martin Eakes's testimony before the U.S. Senate Committee on Banking, Housing and Urban Affairs, Washington, D.C., February 7, 2007.
7. Ellen Schloemer, Wei Li, Keith Ernst, and Kathleen Keest, "Losing Ground: Foreclosures in the Subprime Market and Their Cost to Homeowners," Center for Responsible Lending, Washington, D.C., 2006.
8. Leslie R. Crutchfield and Health McLeod Grant, *Forces for Good: The Six Practices of High-Impact Nonprofits* (San Francisco: Jossey-Bass, 2008).

CHAPTER TWO • *A First Step*

1. Martin D. Eakes, interview with author, November 28, 2011.
2. "Employee-Ownership—Textiles Project," proposal to the Z. Smith Reynolds Foundation by Center for Community Self-Help, March 1980.
3. Frank Adams, interview with author, January 13, 2012.
4. Wes Hare, interview with author, December 27, 2011, and Robert Schall, interview with author, January 31, 2012.
5. Martin Eakes, "Future for Development Banking," speech delivered at the National Association of Community Development Funds, November 7, 1992.
6. Tim Bazemore, interview with author, April 28, 2012.
7. William Bondurant, interview with author, February 13, 2014.

8. Thad Day Moore, interview with author, October 10, 2011.

9. *A Report on the Second Worker Ownership Conference in North Carolina*, July 9–11, 1982, Guilford College, Greensboro, N.C.

10. Susan Fowler, interview with author, February 25, 2014.

CHAPTER THREE • *A Financial Institution*

1. Roy D. High, interview with author, March 4, 2014.

2. The figure of $77 from the bake sale is the one that appears in a later telling of the story. The $65 figure was recorded in a brochure published at the close of the conference. In a 1992 presentation to the National Association of Community Development Loan Funds, Eakes noted White's donation to the credit union. See Martin Eakes, "The Future of Development Banking," November 7, 1992, Self-Help archives.

3. "News Release," Self-Help Credit Union, March 31, 1984, Babcock archives.

4. Wib Gulley, interview with author, December 2, 2011.

5. Steve Schewel, interview with author, June 5, 2012.

6. *1985 Annual Report*, State of North Carolina Credit Union Division, N.C. Department of Commerce, May 5, 1986.

7. June Blotnick, interview with author, February 23, 2012.

8. Jim Brady, "Mill Workers Put Experience to Work—For Themselves," *Greensboro News and Record*, June 24, 1984.

9. Steve Zuckerman, interview with author, February 18, 2014.

10. Martin Eakes, interview with Jeff Cowie and Bill Bamberger, October 19, 1994, Southern Oral History Program, in the Southern Historical Collection Manuscripts Department, Wilson Library, University of North Carolina at Chapel Hill.

11. Thad Moore to Bill Bondurant, May 6, 1983, Babcock archives.

12. Martin Eakes, interview with author, December 20, 2011.

13. Martin Eakes, "Reflections on the Center's First Five Years," Mary Reynolds Babcock Foundation, 1988.

14. Katherine Stern Weaver, interview with author, June 18, 2012.

15. Carol Coston, interview with author, February 24, 2014.

16. Thad Moore, interview with author, October 10, 2011.

17. Larry Johnson, interview with author, April 20, 2012.

CHAPTER FOUR • *Turning Point*

1. Barry Yeoman, "1988 Independent Citizen Award Winner," *N.C. Independent*, December 16, 1988.

2. Marc Hunt, interview with author, May 30, 2012.

3. CCSH to Mary Reynolds Babcock Foundation, March 14, 1985, archives of Mary Reynolds Babcock Foundation.

4. Martin Eakes to Key Supporters, April 8, 1985, archives of Mary Reynolds Babcock Foundation.

5. Jim Blaine, interview with author, May 8, 2012.

6. June Blotnick, interview with author, February 23, 2012.

7. Dana Smith, interview with author, June 11, 2012.

8. Robert Schall, interview with author, January 31, 2012.

9. David McGrady, interviews with author, April 20, 2012, and March 27, 2014.

10. Marc Hunt, interview with author, May 30, 2012.

11. "Assessment of the Center for Community Self-Help, November 1988," study conducted for the Ford Foundation by MDC, Durham, N.C., 1988, 7.

12. "Assessment of the Center for Community Self-Help, November 1988," 27.

13. Katharine McKee, interview with author, February 24, 2012.

14. Martin Eakes, interview with author, April 28, 2014.

15. Frank Adams, "The Workers' Owned Sewing Company: Making the Eagle Fly Friday," ICA Group case study, 1993.

16. Carol Coston, interview with author, February 24, 2014.

CHAPTER FIVE • Innovation

1. "Assessment of the Center for Community Self-Help, November 1988," study conducted for the Ford Foundation, Manpower Development Corporation, November 1988, 41.

2. Martin Eakes, interview with author, May 7, 2013, and Bonnie Wright, interview with author, March 26, 2014.

3. Ron Grzywinski, "The New Old-Fashioned Banking," Harvard Business Review, May–June 1991, p. 89.

4. "CCSH Development 'Bank' Concept Paper," February 18, 1988, Self-Help archives.

5. Martin Eakes, interview with author, April 2014.

6. Katharine McKee, interview with author, February 24, 2012.

7. Martin Eakes, interview with author, May 7, 2013.

8. Lenwood Long, interview with author, May 21, 2012.

9. Andrea Harris, interview with author, December 14, 2011.

10. Dana Smith, interview with author, June 11, 2012.

11. Crawford Crenshaw, interview with author, March 18, 2014.

12. Bill Bynum, interview with author, January 13, 2012.

13. Beth Maczka, interview with author, May 30, 2012.

14. David McGrady, interview with author, April 10, 2012.

CHAPTER SIX • An "Aha" Moment

1. Todd Cohen, "Givers: Abdul Rasheed, Servant Leader," Walter: Raleigh's Life and Soul, February 28, 2013, http://www.waltermagazine.com/givers /givers-abdul-rasheed-servant-leader/.

2. Andrea Harris, interview with author, December 14, 2011.

3. Bill Bynum, interview with author, January 13, 2012.

4. Mae Israel, "Program Helps Low-Level Families Buy Homes," Charlotte Observer, May 20, 1987.

5. "Proposal for Mortgage Payment Guarantee Fund for Low-Income Housing in North Carolina," submitted to Mary Reynolds Babcock Foundation, December 9, 1986, Babcock Foundation archives.
6. Robert Schall, interview with author, January 31, 2012.
7. Bill Dedman, "Atlanta Blacks Losing in Home Loans Scramble," *Atlanta Journal-Constitution*, May 1, 1988, and James A. Johnson, *Showing America a New Way Home* (San Francisco: Jossey-Bass Publishers, 1996).
8. Mechele Dickerson, *Homeownership and America's Financial Underclass* (New York: Cambridge University Press, 2014), 147.
9. Alicia H. Munnell, Lynn E. Browne, James McEneaney, and Geoffrey M. B. Tootell, "Mortgage Lending in Boston: Interpreting HMDA Data," Federal Reserve Bank of Boston, October 7, 1992.
10. Lori Jones-Gibbs, interview with author, May 5, 2014.
11. Robert Schall interview, January 31, 2012.
12. *Report to Joint Legislative Commission on Governmental Operations*, NC-HOME Quarterly Report, Fourth Quarter, 1996, Self-Help archives.
13. Bob Williams, interview with author, March 19, 2012.
14. Melvin L. Oliver and Thomas M. Shapiro, *Black Wealth/White Wealth* (New York: Routledge, 1995).

CHAPTER SEVEN • *"We Did Not Have to Be Geniuses"*

1. Hugh McColl, interview with author, March 13, 2014.
2. *Self-Help Biennial Report, 1993/1994*.
3. *Self-Help Report to Joint Legislative Commission on Governmental Operations*, Self-Help archives, 1996.
4. Michael Calhoun, interview with author, April 20, 2012.
5. Michael Calhoun, interview.
6. Martin Eakes, "Statewide Base and Impact for the Self-Help Development Bank," application to Mary Reynolds Babcock Foundation, 1990, Mary Reynolds Babcock Foundation.
7. Mary Mountcastle, interview with author, January 30, 2012.
8. "Frequently Asked Questions, Self-Help Salary Policy (Revised 6/95)," Self-Help policy files.
9. Bryan Hassell, interview with author, April 16, 2012, and Michael Calhoun, interview.
10. Laura Benedict, interview with author, May 21, 2012.
11. Martin Eakes, "The Future of Development Banking," presentation to the National Association of Community Development Loan Funds, November 7, 1992, Self-Help archives.
12. Melvin L. Oliver and Thomas M. Shapiro, *Black Wealth/White Wealth* (New York: Routledge, 1995), 146.
13. Howard E. Covington Jr. and Marion A. Ellis, *The Story of NationsBank: Changing the Face of American Banking* (Chapel Hill: University of North Carolina Press, 1993).

14. Dennis Rash, interview with author, March 14, 2014.
15. Martin Eakes, interview with author, May 7, 2013.
16. L. M. "Bud" Baker Jr., interview with author, January 31, 2013.
17. Martin Eakes, interview with author, December 20, 2012.
18. Kathleen C. Engel and Patricia A. McCoy, "A Tale of Three Markets: The Law and Economics of Predatory Lending," Cleveland-Marshall College of Law, Cleveland State University, September 1, 2001.
19. Martin Eakes to Ellen Arrick, August 11, 1988, CCSH archives.
20. David McGrady, interview with author, April 12, 2012.
21. Robert E. Litan, Nicolas P. Retsinas, Eric S. Belsky, and Susan White Haag, *The Community Reinvestment Act after Financial Modernization: A Baseline Report*, U.S. Department of the Treasury, April 2000.
22. Eric Stein, interview with author, January 15, 2013.
23. James A. Johnson, *Showing America a New Way Home* (San Francisco: Jossey-Bass, 1996).
24. Frank DiGiovanni, interview with author, May 2, 2012.
25. "Expanding the Secondary Market for Minority and Low-Wealth Home Loans," concept paper, Ford Foundation, December 1997.
26. Robert Schall to Dennis White, March 31, 2005, Self-Help archives.
27. "Ford Foundation Grant of $50 Million Will Generate $2 Billion in Affordable Mortgages for 35,000 Low-Wealth Home Buyers," press release, July 23, 1998, Ford Foundation.
28. Eric Stein, "Principles for GSE Reform," Center for Responsible Lending, October 14, 2012.
29. "Community Advantage Panel Study: Sustainable Approaches to Affordable Homeownership," UNC Center for Community Capital, April 2014, and Roberto G. Quercia, Allison Freeman, and Janneke Ratcliffe, *Regaining the Dream: How to Renew the Promise of Homeownership for America's Working Families*, UNC Center for Community Capital, August 2012.
30. Martin Eakes, interview with author, April 28, 2014.

CHAPTER EIGHT • Cy Pres

1. Timothy Curry and Lynn Shibut, "The Cost of the Savings and Loan Crisis: Truth and Consequences," *FDIC Review*, fall 2000.
2. "Assessing the Economic Development Potential of North Carolina's Savings and Loans," grant application from Self-Help to Mary Reynolds Babcock Foundation, 1988.
3. Tom Byers, interview with author, April 8, 2014.
4. James Grieff, "Proposed Buyout of Thrift Roils Town," *Charlotte Observer*, October 16, 1993.
5. Jane Kendall, interview with author, May 22, 2013.
6. Peter Kolbe, interview with author, June 4, 2013.
7. Catherine Clabby and Joel B. Obermayer, "BCBS Raises Its Defenses," *News and Observer*, June 22, 1977.

8. Adam Searing, interview with author, May 21, 2013.
9. Jena Heath, "Blue Cross Measure Derailed," *News and Observer*, July 24, 1997.
10. Clabby and Obermayer, "BCBS Raises Its Defenses."
11. Martin Eakes, interview with author, May 7, 2013.
12. Editorial, "Fast, Slippery Track," *News and Observer*, June 6, 1977, and editorial, "Too Quick, Too Slick," *News and Observer*, June 21, 1997.
13. Jay Silver, interview with author, March 13, 2014.
14. George Teague, interview with author, undated.
15. Jane Kendall to Tom Lambeth, December 11, 1997, Tom Lambeth files.
16. Barbara Solow, "Blue Notes," *N.C. Independent*, October 9, 2002.
17. Mary Mountcastle, interview with author, May 7, 2014.

CHAPTER NINE • *"Shit Disturbers"*

1. Martin Eakes, interview with author, May 7, 2013.
2. "Mike Easley Targets Lender Accused of Predatory Practices," *News and Observer*, July 23, 1999.
3. "Curbing Predatory Home Mortgage Lending," U.S. Department of Housing and Urban Development and U.S. Treasury Department, Washington, D.C., U.S. Department of Housing and Urban Development, 2000.
4. Paul Stock, interview with author, April 26, 2013.
5. George Teague, interview with author, undated.
6. Roberto Quercia, Michael A. Stegman, and Walter R. Davis, "Assessing the Impact of North Carolina's Predatory Lending Law," University of North Carolina Center for Community Capital, Chapel Hill, N.C., 2004.
7. James Creekman, interview with author, September 5, 2014.
8. Rah Bickley, "Lending Practices Face Checks," *News and Observer*, April 6, 1999.
9. Roy Cooper, interview with author, May 16, 2013.
10. Alan Hirsch, interview with author, April 25, 2013.
11. Mike Easley, interview with author, May 17, 2013.
12. Quercia, Stegman, and Davis, "Assessing the Impact of North Carolina's Predatory Lending Law."
13. William Brennan, interview with author, August 12, 2014.
14. Richard A. Oppel Jr. and Patrick McGeehan, "Along with a Lender, Is Citigroup Buying Trouble," *New York Times*, October 22, 2000.
15. Chris Serres, "Lender to Give Customers Refunds," *News and Observer*, September 7, 2001.
16. "Citigroup Settles FTC Charges against the Associates, Record-Setting $215 Million for Subprime Lending Victims," news release, Federal Trade Commission, September 19, 2002.
17. Amber Veverka and Mark Johnson, "N.C. Treasurer: Ban Payday Lending, Calls Practice Economic Bondage," *Charlotte Observer*, May 2, 2001.
18. Amber Veverka, "Payday Lending Persists in NC," *Charlotte Observer*, December 28, 2001.

19. Deborah Goldstein, interview with author, July 9, 2014.
20. Herb Sandler, interview with author, February 1, 2013.

CHAPTER TEN • *A Box of Rattlesnakes*

1. Angelo R. Mozilo, "The American Dream of Homeownership: From Cliché to Mission," John T. Dunlop lecture, Joint Center for Housing Studies of Harvard University, February 4, 2003.
2. *The Financial Crisis Inquiry Report: Final Report of the National Commission on the Causes of the Financial and Economic Crisis in the United States*, Financial Crisis Inquiry Commission, ch. 7, p. 105, January 2011.
3. *Financial Crisis Inquiry Report*, ch. 7, p. 117.
4. Michael E. Staten and Gregory Elliehausen, "The Impact of the Federal Reserve Board's Proposed Revisions to HOEPA on the Number and Characteristics of HOEPA Loans," Credit Research Center, Georgetown University, July 24, 2001.
5. Roberto G. Quercia, Michael A. Stegman, and Walter R. Davis, "Assessing the Impact of North Carolina's Predatory Lending Law," *Housing Policy Debate*, 2004.
6. Eric Stein, "The Economic Cost of Predatory Lending 2001," Coalition for Responsible Lending, Durham, N.C., July 25, 2001.
7. "HUD, Treasury Release Joint Report Recommending Actions to Curb Predatory Lending," U.S. Department of the Treasury, Washington, D.C., June 20, 2000.
8. Mary Mountcastle, interview with author, May 7, 2013.
9. Mark Pearce, interview with author, September 19, 2014.
10. Deborah Goldstein, "Understanding Predatory Lending: Moving Towards a Common Definition and Workable Solutions," Joint Center for Housing Studies of Harvard University, September 30, 1999.
11. Deborah Goldstein, interview with author, July 9, 2014.
12. "Protecting the Wealth of Minority and Poor Families," Responsible Lending Law and Policy Center, February 6, 2002.
13. Randy Chambers, interview with author, May 20, 2014.
14. William J. Brennan, interview with author, August 12 and 18, 2014.
15. "Lenders Are Gearing up for a 'War' on State Laws," *Inside B&C Lending*, April 14, 2003, p. 9.
16. Chris Kukla, interview with author, October 17, 2014.
17. Don Kidd, interview with author, October 6, 2014.

CHAPTER ELEVEN • *The Emperor's Naked*

1. Ellen Schloemer, Wei Li, Keith Ernst, and Kathleen Keest, *Losing Ground: Foreclosures in the Subprime Market and Their Cost to Homeowners*, Center for Responsible Lending, December 2006.
2. David Wiley, interview with author, October 2, 2014.

3. Victoria McGrane, "Subprime Guru Drives Debate," *Politico*, January 16, 2008.

4. George Brown, interview with author, November 14, 2014.

5. Howard E. Covington Jr., *Favored by Fortune: George W. Watts and the Hills of Durham* (Chapel Hill: University of North Carolina at Chapel Hill Library, 2004).

6. Kelly K. Spors, "Subprime Bill Aims to Mute State Laws," *Wall Street Journal*, February 14, 2003.

7. Claudia Coulton and Kathy Hexter, "Facing the Foreclosure Crisis in Greater Cleveland: What Happened and How Communities Are Responding," Federal Reserve Bank of Cleveland, June 2010, and *The Financial Crisis Inquiry Report: Final Report of the National Commission on the Causes of the Financial and Economic Crisis in the United States,* Financial Crisis Inquiry Commission, January 2011, p. 10.

8. Community Reinvestment Association of North Carolina, *Too Much Month at the End of the Paycheck*, Center for Community Capitalism, University of North Carolina at Chapel Hill, January 2001.

9. Peter Skillern, interview with author, April 21, 2014.

10. George Brown testimony, fall 2003.

11. U.S. Representative Maxine Waters, hearing, U.S. House Financial Services Committee, May 24, 2000.

12. John Taylor, interview with author, October 5, 2014.

13. John Farris, interview with author, October 7, 2014.

14. "A Review of Wells Fargo's Subprime Lending," Center for Responsible Lending issue paper, April 2004.

15. "Lenders Are Gearing Up for a 'War' on State Laws," *Inside B&C Lending*, April 14, 2003.

16. Martin Eakes, interview with author, April 28, 2014.

17. Josh Nassar, interview with author, October 6, 2014.

18. *Financial Crisis Inquiry Commission Final Report*, 103.

19. *Financial Crisis Inquiry Commission Final Report*, 16.

20. Keith Ernst, interview with author, October 6, 2014.

21. Michael Calhoun, interview with author, April 10, 2014.

22. Debbie Goldstein, interview with author, July 9, 2014.

23. Michael Lewis, *The Big Short: Inside the Doomsday Machine* (New York: W. W. Norton, 2010), 197.

24. Gregory Zuckerman, *The Greatest Trade Ever* (New York: Broadway Books, 2009).

25. "Helping Americans Keep Their Homes," press release, Center for Responsible Lending, October 12, 2007.

26. *Financial Crisis Inquiry Commission Final Report*, 11.

27. *Financial Crisis Inquiry Commission Final Report*, 157.

CHAPTER TWELVE • *"We're Here Forever"*

1. Patrick McHenry, "Beware Mortgage 'Reforms'—Increased Regulation Would Hurt Borrowers Who Most Need Help," *Charlotte Observer*, October 27, 2005,

and Martin Eakes, "McHenry Misses the Point—N.C. Law for Protecting Borrowers While Encouraging Loans," *Charlotte Observer*, November 10, 2005.
2. Martin Eakes testimony, May 24, 2005, U.S. House Financial Services Committee.
3. David Hogberg, "Self-Help Helps Itself," *Organization Trends*, Capital Research Center, October 2005.
4. Jim Nesbitt, "Martin Eakes," *News and Observer*, December 18, 2005.
5. Gary Rivlin, *Broke, USA: From Pawnshops to Poverty, Inc.: How the Working Poor Became Big Business* (New York: Harper, 2010), 221.
6. Rivlin, *Broke, USA*, 235.
7. Brad Miller, interview with author, March 6, 2013.
8. Randy Chambers, interview with author, May 20, 2014.
9. Martin Eakes, interview with author, April 28, 2014.
10. Kathleen E. Keest, "The Subprime Housing Crisis," paper presented at the Subprime Symposium, University of Iowa, December 9, 2008.
11. Rakesh Kochar and Richard Fry, "Wealth Inequality Has Widened along Racial, Ethnic Lines since End of Great Recession," Pew Research Center, December 12, 2014.
12. Allison Freeman and Janneke Ratcliffe, "Setting the Record Straight on Affordable Homeownership," working paper, Center for Community Capital, May 2012.
13. Martin Eakes, interview with author, October 5, 2015.

CHAPTER THIRTEEN • *Self-Help Federal—A National Institution*

1. Steve Zuckerman, interview with author, June 5, 2014.
2. Martin Eakes, interview with author, April 28, 2014.
3. Laura Choi, "From Cashing Checks to Building Assets: A Case Study of the Check Cashing/Credit Union Hybrid Service Model," working paper 2013-01, Federal Reserve Bank of San Francisco, January 2013, p. 3.
4. Joe Duran, interview with author, July 29, 2015.
5. "Safety and Soundness: Failed Bank Review of Second Federal Savings and Loan Association of Chicago," Audit Report, OIG-13-028, December 20, 2012, Office of Inspector General, Department of the Treasury.
6. Raul Raymundo, interview with author, August 25, 2015.
7. Randy Chambers, interview with author, May 20, 2014.
8. Steve Daniels, "Congressman, Community Leaders Slam FDIC for Handling of Second Federal's Failure," *Crain's Chicago Business*, August 14, 2012.
9. Martin Eakes, interview with author, October 5, 2015.
10. Steve Daniels, "A Surprise Ending for Second Federal," *Crain's Chicago Business*, November 28, 2012.
11. Alexia Fernández Campbell, "The Heroes Who Saved Chicago's Immigrant Homeowners," *National Journal*, June 12, 2014.
12. Self-Help 2015 Diversity Profile, Self-Help internal document.
13. Martin Eakes, interview with author, April 28, 2014.

1. Tucker Bartlett, interview with author, May 6, 2014.
2. Charles Lunan, "Wachovia Qualifies for Tax Credits," *Charlotte Observer*, April 24, 2003.
3. Josh Shaffer, "Durham Celebrates 10 Years since Opening of American Tobacco Campus," *News and Observer*, September 7, 2014.
4. Michael Goodmon, interview with author, October 5, 2015.
5. Catherine Carlock, "Work Starts on Massive Revolution Mill Redevelopment," *Triad Business Journal*, March 6, 2013.
6. Eddie Belk, interview with author, August 1, 2013.
7. Heather Christine Deutsch, "Walltown: The History of a Neighborhood and a Housing Renovation Program," master's project, University of North Carolina, Department of City and Regional Planning, 2004, p. 47.
8. Mebane Rash, "Charter School Legislation Filed 20 Years Ago in North Carolina," EdNC, April 8, 2015, https://www.ednc.org/2015/04/08/charter-school-legislation -filed-20-years-ago-in-north-carolina/.
9. Laura Benedict, interview with author, May 21, 2012.
10. Marc Hunt, interview with author, May 30, 2012.
11. *2015 Annual Report*, Self-Help.
12. Bonnie Wright, interview with author, March 26, 2014.
13. Robert Schall, interview with author, January 31, 2012.
14. "Twelve Social Change Visionaries Are Honored by the Ford Foundation," press release, Ford Foundation, May 3, 2011.
15. Emily Aronson, "Princeton Celebrates 100th Anniversary of Alumni Day with Festivities, Honors," press release, Princeton University Office of Communications, February 2015.
16. Steve Zuckerman, interview with author, February 18, 2014.
17. Mark Masse, *Inspired to Serve: Today's Faith Activists* (Bloomington: Indiana University Press, 2004), 22.
18. Martin Eakes, interview with author, June 3, 2016.
19. "Bashing the Hero in Wells Fargo Case," *New York Times*, September 18, 2016.

Index